NICHOLAS HARPSFIELD

*For Alice, Thomas, Joshua, Samuel,
Theo, Luca and Brecon*

Nicholas Harpsfield

AND ENGLISH REFORMATION CATHOLICISM

The Charity of Unity

Jonathan Dean

GRACEWING

First published in England in 2023
by
Gracewing
2 Southern Avenue
Leominster
Herefordshire HR6 0QF
United Kingdom
www.gracewing.co.uk

All rights reserved.
No part of this publication may be reproduced, stored in a retrieval system, or transmitted in any form or by any means, electronic, mechanical, photocopying, recording or otherwise, without the written permission of the publisher.

The right of Jonathan Dean to be identified
as the author of this work has been asserted in accordance
with the Copyright, Designs and Patents Act 1988.

© 2023 Jonathan Dean

ISBN 978 085244 973 8

The publishers have no responsibility for the persistence or accuracy of URLs for websites referred to in this publication, and do not guarantee that any content on such websites is, or will remain, accurate or appropriate.

Cover design by Bernardita Peña Hurtado
Typeset by Word and Page, Chester, UK

CONTENTS

Preface and Acknowledgements — vii
Abbreviations — ix
Introduction: On Not Choosing Ignorance — 1

PART I: THE VIEW FROM 1553

1. Waking from Sleep:
   The English Reformation through Marian Eyes — 9

PART II: THE MARIAN REVOLUTION

2. 'Nourished with hope … and confirmed with antiquity':
   Mary's religious revolution — 33
3. 'Profound judgement and deep foresight':
   Harpsfield and the Legacy of Thomas More — 69
4. 'Furthering God's Service': the Canterbury Visitations — 109

PART III: FORGING AN ENGLISH CATHOLIC COMMUNITY

5. 'Holy, Venerable and Sacred':
   The *Dialogi Sex* and Early Elizabethan Catholicism — 129
6. 'Against Charity': The Attack on Foxe — 163
7. Afterlives: Harpsfield, More and English Catholic Identity — 203

Appendix 1. Harpsfield's *Life of Christ* — 239
Appendix 2. The *Dialogi Sex*, outline of chapters and content — 243
Bibliography — 249

Nescire autem quid ante quam natus sis accident, id est semper esse puerum. Quid enim est aetas hominis, nisi ea memoria rerum veterum cum superiorum aetate contexitur?

To be ignorant of what occurred before you were born is to remain always a child. For what is the worth of human life, unless it is woven into the life of our ancestors by the records of history?

Marcus Tullius Cicero, *Orator*, 34 (46 BCE)

PREFACE AND ACKNOWLEDGEMENTS

This is a book long in gestation. It began life as a Ph.D. dissertation within the University of Cambridge, where it, and I, were helped and nurtured in our growth by an array of splendid, wise and generous mentors and scholars. I'm especially grateful to the late Ivor Jones, and to Stephen Burgess, Martin Forward, Leslie Griffiths, Morna Hooker-Stacey, and Fraser Watts, among others, for their kindness and encouragement. My two examiners, Peter Marshall and Richard Rex, were acute, insightful and supportive. I treasure the memory of a conversation with the late Marcus Borg, too, for the impetus it gave towards this project. Above all, I owe a debt of enormous magnitude to Eamon Duffy, my beloved doctoral supervisor, to whose humanity, scholarship, hospitality and faithful commitment I still aspire. He coached me through difficult days, and guided me gently towards the fulfilment of this project, and also the flourishing of my own gifts, at the time and after completion. I am beyond grateful to him and for him.

My debts to other scholars are noted along the way, for conversations and the insight which they brought to me. Friendships of many kinds have also continued to sustain me, and I'm particularly grateful for the time I spent as a member of the British Roman Catholic-Methodist Dialogue, of which I was latterly the Co-Secretary. My friends there assisted me in placing Nicholas Harpsfield's story within the wider narrative of English Catholic experience and identity, and enabled me better to grasp the import of what he lived and died to defend. I'm very grateful also to Tom Longford at Gracewing for his advice and encouragement.

In my current life overseeing theological education and ministerial formation within the Methodist Church, I'm similarly gifted with mentors, scholars, wise guides and friends, for whose encouragement and assistance I'm daily grateful, especially in attempting to maintain any kind of research amid demanding vocational duties. Among many others, I wish to offer deep thanks to Eunice Attwood, Shannon Conklin-Miller, Clive Marsh, Andrea Russell, Nicola Slee, Andrew Stobart and Janet Unsworth for good advice and cheerful encouragement along the way. The Ministries Team at Methodist Church House is a collection of the best, wisest, and kindest souls there are, and I daily count it an inestimable privilege to work with and alongside them. Claire Potter, Nicola Price-Tebbutt, and Paul Wood are rocks of faithful, unstinting support and I am profoundly thankful for their friendship and practical Christian love.

Finally, of course, I must thank my family for their constant love and care, not least in urging me on in the endeavour of committing this project to a published text. Trey Hall is a tower of patience, generous kindness and love, who makes so many things possible. The book is offered to my godchildren, who are far too young, or too sensible, or too focused on more relevant matters to their lives, to need to read this cover to cover: but I hope that they can draw comfort from knowing something of the inheritance of faith in which we all share as Christians, and from the knowledge that they are surrounded by prayers: my own, and that of the saints, of all types and kinds, who have gone before us, and leave us such a rich legacy of faithfulness and witness. In that true Christian love, as Nicholas Harpsfield taught, we are all one.

London
Feast of St Julian of Norwich, 2023

ABBREVIATIONS

CW   The Yale Edition of the *Complete Works of St Thomas More*, Yale University Press, 1963–97
RSTC   Revised Short Title Catalogue
ZL   Zürich Letters (see under primary sources)

INTRODUCTION

On Not Choosing Ignorance
Nicholas Harpsfield and English Reformation Catholicism

Nicholas Harpsfield's remarkable career spanned almost the whole course of the Reformation in England.[1] Born in 1519, Harpsfield grew up during the momentous years of Henry VIII's supremacy, and was educated at Winchester and New College, Oxford, where he received a fellowship and continued his studies in the Law. Little is known of him until 1550, when he migrated to Louvain, eager to escape the increasingly ardent Protestantism of Edward's reign. During this time, Harpsfield was associated with the circle of family and friends of Sir Thomas More: he stayed with More's old friend, the merchant Antonio Bonvisi, upon whose reminiscences, along with those of More's son-in-law William Roper, he would later draw in his *Life of More*.[2] Returning to England at the accession of Queen Mary, Harpsfield was launched on a career in the English church which was meteoric in its progress. In 1554, he was made Archdeacon of Canterbury and appointed a prebend of St Paul's Cathedral, in addition to other livings. As Vicar-General of London, he was well-known for his thorough and searching visitation of the capital, and his vigorous style and passion for conformity and orthodoxy made him a notorious figure in Protestant eyes, notably those of the martyrologist John Foxe, as we will discover, who rated him among the worst of Mary's lieutenants for cruelty and ferocity.[3]

---

[1] For summaries of his life, see for example Chambers's introduction to the Early English Text Society edition of Harpsfield's *Life of More*, or the *Dictionary of National Biography*, and especially the entry for the new edition by Dr Thomas Freeman, to which this sketch is much indebted.

[2] Bonvisi was the recipient of More's last published letter, written with a coal from the Tower, in which More speaks warmly of their close friendship, and calls him 'most trusty, apple of mine eye'; Rogers in More 1947, p. 563.

[3] Foxe 1563, p. 1546; Brigden 1989, p. 625; Duffy 2009, p. 153.

Nicholas Harpsfield

Part I of this book is devoted to a better understanding of the deepest convictions of those, like Harpsfield, who led Queen Mary's religious restoration. The records of Harpsfield's visitation of the diocese of Canterbury in 1557 offer an insight into his, and their, priorities and methods, which in turn reflected those of the Marian restoration of religion itself. Harpsfield was zealous in the cause of restoring the altars and the apparatus of traditional devotion in the churches, but also to ensure the adequate housing of priests and the effective catechesis and care of the people. He set about the better provision of preaching, by ordering priests to provide more sermons, or by instructing local congregations without a priest.[4] The returns also offer numerous glimpses of life in the Kent parishes, and of Harpsfield's pastoral concerns: attention is given to financial matters, cohabitation, Sunday trading, witchcraft, drunkenness and marital difficulties among other, more liturgical, questions. Above all, he sought to re-instil in the congregations of Kent the fundamental beliefs and practice of the old faith, and to supplant both the ideas and material changes of the Protestant Reformation.

Harpsfield's rise continued almost until the moment of Mary's death. In October 1558, he became Dean of the Court of Arches, and the foremost defender of orthodoxy (and thus fighter of heresy) in the land. Mary's death the following month, however, cut short his rise; like most of the senior Marian clergy, Harpsfield could not accept the accession of Elizabeth and the restoration of the royal supremacy. As prolocutor of the Lower House of Convocation, Harpsfield in fact led the clerical opposition to Elizabeth's early efforts to restore royal supremacy in religion and rescind the reunion with Rome. He was also in the vanguard of the resistance to the desire of the Elizabethan regime to undo the significant efforts made under Mary toward the restoration of Catholic devotion and doctrine. The ultimate moment of reckoning soon came when he was asked to participate in the confirmation of Matthew Parker's appointment as the new Archbishop, and to subscribe to the government's religious policy. He was able with a safe conscience to do neither. Along with other unrepentant Marian leaders, he was imprisoned in 1559, and remained in incarceration almost until his death in December 1575. Held in the Fleet prison, Harpsfield and his brother John became symbols of the persecution of Catholics and figures of inspiration for the exiled Catholic community in mainland Europe.[5]

---

4 See Whatmore (ed.) 1950–1; for a discussion of the Marian restoration, see below, Part I. A fuller discussion of the Canterbury visitation is the focus of Chapter 3. There is a helpful summary and analysis of them also in Duffy 1992, pp. 555–64.

5 R. W. Chambers, in his biographical essay in the *Life of More*, pp. clxxxv–clxxxix; see also Duffy 2009, p. 195.

Nicholas Harpsfield and English Reformation Catholicism

During his years fighting heresy and implementing the Marian religious programme in diocese and parish, Harpsfield had also begun a literary career. His Marian writings revolved around the martyr Sir Thomas More, and a careful examination of the Henrician schism against which More gave his life, and its consequences. He was thus at the centre of a Marian project to 'rediscover' More as the figure whose life and death gave meaning to the restoration of Catholicism. Throughout his writings, Harpsfield returns repeatedly to More. Harpsfield was sixteen years old at the time of More's death, and, though he keeps autobiographical detail to a minimum, there is good reason to suppose that it was an event which left a mark on his young mind. Certainly, More's increasing importance in Harpsfield's life, as an icon of the struggle for unity and the resistance to heresy and schism, is evident. Harpsfield believed above all that More's great insight, the essence of his genius, was to have foreseen correctly to what a royal supremacy would lead, and to have had the courage to give his life accordingly. Throughout his career, therefore, Harpsfield rooted himself in what he saw as the vital guiding principle which More had enunciated. It enlightened and informed all his own reactions to the century's religious changes.

These insights, and Harpsfield's commitment to them, emerge again and in their most developed form in the great work of Harpsfield's imprisonment, the *Dialogi Sex* of 1566, published in Antwerp under the name of the exile Alan Cope. Over a thousand pages of often complex Latin, Harpsfield marshalled his extraordinary knowledge and understanding of the Church's history and deployed them against a number of protestant apologists, including John Jewel, John Foxe, and the Centuriators of Magdeburg. The book was reprinted in 1573. Harpsfield's identity as the true author was an ill-kept secret, and in subsequent editions of the *Acts and Monuments*, John Foxe, while altering his material in the light of Harpsfield's criticisms, referred to his opponent by his real name. To the years of Harpsfield's imprisonment belongs also his equally mighty *Historia Anglicana Ecclesiastica*, a huge survey of the Church in England, diocese by diocese, up to the Reformation. It concluded with a history of the heresy of Wycliffe, and a further attack on Foxe. The work remained unpublished until 1622. It is the earlier work, however, which is by far the more important, and which forms the focus of much of Part II of this volume.

Primarily, then, Harpsfield wrote as a historian, convinced like More of the need to establish ecclesial custom and historical precedent as the means to establishing authority within the Church. In one form or another, all Harpsfield's works were historical *tours de force*, intending to crush Protestant innovation and heresy beneath the weight of Catholic practice, enforced over centuries of consistent observation. Harpsfield was a humanist, like his hero, immersed not only in the works of the Church Fathers but also in the great literary works of the Classical world. It was this outlook, this sense of the continuity of thought and faith, which underpinned his whole endeavour. He was also a synthesist, determined not to place humanistic methods and approaches in opposition to the scholasticism of the medieval period, but to point rather to a Catholic orthodoxy which made use of both.

In this same spirit, Harpsfield vigorously defended the traditional practices of the Catholic Church, deliberately and even self-consciously espousing a return to pre-Reformation modes of worship and devotion. He did so, not through some impossible nostalgia which could not deal with change, but because of a fundamental and unswerving conviction that only a return to authentic and established expressions of Christianity could re-train hearts and minds which had wandered towards heresy, and been influenced by it. Harpsfield, in presenting the Mass, images and relics, devotion to the saints and monasticism as institutions which offered direct contact with a living God, was arguing for his own time the conviction that participation in liturgy and devotional practice, more than a thousand sermons, possessed the ability to convert and nurture Christians in true faith. In so doing, he employed, like More before him, the language of the miraculous, fiercely resistant to any Protestant attempts to deny what he saw as signs of divine immanence and consistency in a turbulent and troubled world.

In all of this, and across a long and varied life, Harpsfield was a vitally important figure, both as an embodiment of the Marian Catholic mindset, and as one of the principal transmitters of Marian emphases to a subsequent age. It is to Harpsfield's consistency that we must look, as well as to his influence on later generations, if we are to assess this importance. Seen through the lens of Nicholas Harpsfield, English Reformation Catholicism assumes greater internal coherence and consistency than many of its recent commentators have allowed. The works of English Catholics of the 1560s did not emerge *ex nihilo*, but adopted and developed the themes and arguments of Marian writings; the later recusants are shown to have adapted the work of the generation before them in fashioning their own response to their times. A fuller examination of the works of Nicholas Harpsfield is therefore overdue; his unifying role at the centre of Catholic life and thought in Reformation England helps to reveal some of its contours a little better.

This book proceeds in chronological order, examining the works of Harpsfield in the order they were written. Before this is attempted, however, Part I seeks to establish more clearly the fundamental convictions of Mary's religious leaders, and then deals with 'official' religious publications of the Marian period generally, arguing for the coherence and rigour of the regime's publishing programme, and attempting to re-draw it and thus challenge the common charge that Marian religious writing lacked colour or calibre. With this necessary background in place, the book examines Harpsfield's Marian works, his *Life of More*, the *Treatise of the Pretended Divorce*, and *Cranmer's Recantacyons* in their proper context. Part II moves onto his major Elizabethan work, the *Dialogi Sex*, dealing first with the major themes of the first five dialogues and then, in Chapter 6, specifically with the attack on Foxe's martyrology. Chapter 7 attempts to sketch Harpsfield's importance to the generation which followed him, and draws out the scope and purpose of his *Historia Anglicana Ecclesiastica*, published posthumously. There thus emerges a sense, both of the foundational principles upon which Harpsfield's life and work were based, and of the directions in which they developed over his turbulent and eventful career. Such a perspective also makes possible a judgement about Harpsfield's influence on others, and particularly about how Marian Catholicism shaped its Elizabethan recusant successor, and provided resources for English Catholics struggling to hold to their faith in a time of extraordinary challenge and change.

Why, though, is such a project necessary or desirable? Primarily, perhaps, because John Foxe's version of events has been allowed for so long to determine our understanding of the times, our verdict on Marian Catholicism, and our opinions about Catholicism itself. The anti-Catholic sentiment which made its way unchecked into the seventeenth century and far beyond was deeply influenced by Foxe's polemic. His portrait of a brutal, inflexible, unimaginative, and above all treacherous faith, though brilliantly crafted for a particular moment and an Elizabethan readership, had a longevity which might have surprised him. He was not, of course, by any means solely responsible, but the fact that a candidate for the US presidency as late as 1960 was having to justify his Roman Catholic faith on the grounds that it asked a loyalty of him to an untrustworthy foreign power speaks volumes about the potency of the characterisation, indeed the caricature, which modernity has received from the polarised moment of the Reformation struggle. The neglect of the Catholic view, the marginalisation of the Marian project and the vilification of its leaders and shapers, has rarely allowed the prevailing opinion to be challenged. Even prominent, celebrated historians, as we will see, have too often simply amplified the casual stereotypes they have inherited, and failed to allow proper examination of the evidence to enable an alternative perspective to emerge.

In recent years, too, we have been learning much about the dangers of neglecting the stories, experiences and perspectives of marginalised populations of all kinds. Twenty-first-century prejudices of many sorts are themselves shaped and given fuel by too easily imbibing unchallenged worldviews from and about the past. Privilege, in all the forms it comes, is both disguised and reinforced by the casual assumption of negative views about those outside of its easy superiority. It may seem a little exaggerated to claim that a biography of the work of a sixteenth-century Catholic archdeacon and polemicist makes any contribution to urgent contemporary questions of justice, equality and reconciliation: but Nicholas Harpsfield's story matters precisely because of the ways in which it, and he, teaches us, once again, about the casual reinforcing of a dominant view, or the careless wielding of power. Recovering something of the truth of the Catholic experience in Reformation England, and allowing that to help us, both to understand better and to question afresh much that followed, is in and of itself a contribution, however small, to a wider project of human dignity. We do not allow those who oppose a group of people, or who resist their beliefs, or who despise their commitments, single-handedly to shape our views of the group. Rather, we let that group speak for themselves. We hear their stories. We give them the dignity of speech. We seek to understand the world, and its affairs, from their own perspective.

Quoting Cicero, Nicholas Harpsfield once remarked that a failure to approach the record of the past with openness, humility and proper curiosity, not to mention a willingness to find that we have been wrong, is deliberately to choose ignorance. It is to embrace for ourselves a perpetual infancy, of unformed (and uninformed) opinions, petty, unexamined and selfish desires, immature judgements and narrow horizons. Such a perpetual infancy itself undergirds the contemporary experiences of prejudice and privilege just mentioned. Overcoming it, realising where we have chosen it and need, bluntly, to grow up, is a lifetime's task, and an urgent one. In what follows, I hope to continue the good work begun in recent historical scholarship, of rediscovering and re-imagining one brief period of our shared past, the reign of Mary Tudor, and to suggest that there is a respect and honour due to its leading figures and to their most cherished convictions which redraws our appreciation for their life's work. It is also sheds a new light on much of which followed, and teaches us again about the ways in which prejudice finds a root, and flourishes across whole centuries. In this, we discover something also, an insight which is profoundly contemporary and compellingly urgent, about the nature of the idea of proper Christian charity and human unity for which Nicholas Harpsfield, like his historical hero Thomas More, gave his life.

A note on the text. English translations of Harpsfield's Latin are given in the main body of the text, with the original in the endnotes. Spelling in the sixteenth-century English texts has been updated for quotation in the main body of the text, as an aid to contemporary readers.

PART I

The View from 1553

✢ 1 ✢

Waking from Sleep
The English Reformation through Marian Eyes

On Advent Sunday, 2 December 1554, Bishop Stephen Gardiner of Winchester, Lord Chancellor of the realm, stepped into the public pulpit at St Paul's Cross. In his large congregation were King Philip, Mary Tudor's husband, and Cardinal Reginald Pole, the Queen's cousin and papal legate to England, later Archbishop of Canterbury. Pole had recently arrived in England in order to effect and pronounce the formal absolution of the country for its schism and heresy, and its reconciliation to Rome and to the Pope and his headship of the Church. It was a key moment, and Gardiner made the most, both of the set reading for the liturgical season and of the magnitude of the moment. Preaching from Romans chapter 13, on the text 'it is now the moment for you to wake from sleep, for salvation is nearer to us now', Gardiner spared nothing in the emotion and vigour of his appeal:

> as in sleep men dream, some time of killing, some time of maiming, sometime of drowning or burning, sometime of such beastliness as I will not name, but will spare your ears: so have we, in this our sleep not only dreamed of beastliness, but we have done it indeed: for in this our sleep, hath not one brother destroyed another? Hath not half our money be wiped away at one time? And again those that would defend their conscience were slain: and others also otherwise troubled, besides infinite other things, which you all know as well as I: whereof I report me to your own consciences. Farther, in a man's sleep all his senses are stopped, so that he came neither see, smell, nor hear: even so where as the ceremonies of the Church were instituted to move and stir up our senses, they being taken away, was not our senses (as ye would say) stopped and we fast asleep?

The occasion was resonant with powerful symbolism and pregnant with expectation, and the preacher himself embodied the message he sought to convey. For here was one of the major defenders of King Henry VIII's self-declared supremacy in religious matters and headship of the English Church, now repudiating his earlier views, his prior career, and his exercise of former powers, in a *mea culpa* of extraordinary scope. Driving the point home, Gardiner made sure his listeners understood the depth of his – and thus of their own, and the nation's – error, sin and folly:

> And that we may be the more meet to receive [the Pope's] benediction, I shall desire you, that we may all acknowledge ourselves offenders against His Holiness. I do not exclude myself forth of the number. I will ... weep with them that weep, and rejoice with them which rejoice. And I shall desire you, that we may defer the matter no longer, for now *hora est*: the hour is come.[1]

Nor was this an empty show. Gardiner's change of conviction had been hard-won, and honed in the prisons of Edward VI's government and the desolation of his own guilt. When he addressed the citizenry in London, ahead of Pole's formal ceremony of reconciliation in parliament, it was in the real and confident hope that the trials and disasters of the last twenty years were finally past, and that the future, under Mary Tudor, England's first regnant Queen, would be blessed and secure.

If we are to understand the Marian project, the restoration of religion which took place in her reign, and the beliefs and convictions of those, like Nicholas Harpsfield, who were central to that renewal, this is a critical moment, and a vital message, to grasp. So much of our perception of Mary and her rule is shaped, ironically, by the very man who has preserved this sermon for us: John Foxe. Foxe and his Elizabethan colleagues sought to offer a very particular view of the Marian period to posterity. They have been largely successful in that endeavour, but have also fostered a profoundly skewed and even ahistorical way of thinking about these years in succeeding generations. It is thus crucial to orient ourselves more clearly in those early months of Mary's reign, in the popular understanding of what had gone before, and in the very personal, spiritually agonising and emotionally harrowing experience of people like Stephen Gardiner. We must appreciate that he and a generation of those like him had come to see their previous defence of royal supremacy as an error of insight and judgement of colossal proportions and devastating consequences.

---

1 John Foxe, *The Unabridged Acts and Monuments Online* or *TAMO* (1563 edition, Book 5, pp. 1086–7) (The Digital Humanities Institute, Sheffield, 2011). Available from: http//www.dhi.ac.uk/foxe [Accessed: 28.05.21].

For all his gifts as an administrator, statesman and politician (not to mention the darker arts he frequently exercised in pursuing his goals and purposes, which often make him a deeply unsympathetic actor in Tudor dramas), Stephen Gardiner was not merely accidentally the chosen proponent of the Advent Sunday sermon. His presence in the pulpit was symbolic, and even ironic. He had been a favourite of Mary's father, Henry VIII, and had risen through the ranks at court enjoying the patronage of his royal master, who trusted him with both domestic policy and foreign diplomacy. When the King's 'Great Matter' of his intended divorce from Queen Katherine became the issue the pursuing of which dominated the whole energy of the regime, Gardiner had been persuaded of its necessity and justice, and had sought to offer his gifts to its prosecution. When that project ultimately proved impossible within the bounds of papal obedience, it was Stephen Gardiner who wrote a vigorous, extensive and full-throated defence of the religious revolution in English affairs to which it gave rise and which it demanded: the royal supremacy.

Gardiner was very far from being a lone voice in these matters, but gladly lent his significant talents and his exalted position to the efforts to persuade the English of the necessity of the changes. It was, nevertheless, a profound and even shocking shift for many. The central argument made for the introduction of the royal supremacy was simple, and rested on a professed outrage that a foreign ruler, the Bishop of Rome, had or might claim any sort of jurisdiction over any aspect of English life and affairs. Just as the King could command the bodies of his people, just as he might direct the nation's army or treasury, or direct the work of its judiciary, so, Gardiner and his allies claimed, he also might command his people's souls; so, they said, he was head, and ought to direct the life, of the English Church. Gardiner's 1535 treatise defending the royal supremacy, his *De Vera Obedientia* ('On True Obedience'), asserted that to say otherwise, as had been the case for centuries, was 'absurd', because it implied that the moment the English people turned their hearts and minds to the practice to true religion, they ceased to be the King's subjects, and he was forced to defer to a higher authority: the papacy. King Henry was not the sort of man to defer to anyone, of course. Through his mouthpiece, Bishop Gardiner, he expressed his view that to believe otherwise, and to limit his authority by subjecting it to the Pope, was an act of 'ignorance' at best, and of 'malice' at worst. Ignorance, through works like Gardiner's, could be instructed and redeemed. Malice, being treason, could not. In other words, on this 'Great Matter' as much as on any other for this King, Henry's wrath meant death.

There was, as it turned out, a flaw in the view of the royal supremacy as Gardiner and others defended it. Traditionalists in religion and religious observance, they were persuaded that transferring the headship of the English Church from the Pope to the King (or, as they believed, asserting that it properly belonged to the King, and always had) would do nothing to endanger the basic essence of that Church's faith and practice. A few thought they were dangerously misguided in this conviction, especially as the influences of Martin Luther and other challengers of aspects of Catholic faith exerted their own influence. We will hear more of them, and the precise nature of their beliefs concerning the papacy, later: but the two principal spokesmen for this view were Bishop John Fisher of Rochester and Sir Thomas More, Speaker of the House of Commons and then Lord Chancellor. Their opposition received considerable attention, but did little to halt the direction of policy. In essentials, however, their judgement was absolutely correct and their prediction of how the new policy would work in practice was entirely prescient. The coalition of those advocating the royal supremacy were a diverse group in religious terms, including Gardiner but also more Evangelically minded[2] leaders like Thomas Cromwell and Thomas Cranmer. All hoped that they might use the royal supremacy to persuade the King to lean towards their own preferences in religion. All of them were to a degree successful in that ambition, creating a situation of constant flux, and an unceasing pendulum-swing of change in the English Church for the rest of the King's reign. For this was the major, and fatal, flaw with the Henrician royal supremacy: it relied on the insight, wisdom and constancy of a King who often lacked all three, and governed in his own, very narrow, interests.

As they looked back in 1553, then, bishops such as Gardiner, Edmund Bonner of London, Cuthbert Tunstall of Durham and many other leaders, lay and ordained, in Queen Mary's Church felt they had ample evidence of the folly of their previous position. Almost as soon as the ink was dry on the *De Vera Obedientia*, the influence of Cromwell and Cranmer over the King and the life of the English Church had become ominously apparent. Many of those whose religious preferences were more traditionalist, including Thomas More, had not in principle been opposed to an English translation of the Bible; what did horrify them was the extent to which a new translation could give succour to heresy, as had been evident when William Tyndale had begun to issue his own translation. Thomas More had committed much time and ink to fighting

---

2 I am using the more historically correct term 'Evangelical' for those who embraced the views of Luther and other early reformers, and not 'Protestant', which is of a rather later formation. They were protesting: but in essence simply believed that they were offering a vision of reform based on a fresh encounter with the Scriptures and to be carried out within the Roman Catholic Church.

what he saw as Tyndale's dangerous inaccuracies in his treatment of the text of Scripture; after his death, Miles Coverdale's edition, which incorporated much of Tyndale's work and perspective, became the basis of the official 'Great' Bible of 1540. It was issued with the authority of both Cromwell and Cranmer; the latter supplied an effusive Preface to it, extolling King Henry's enlightened wisdom in giving his subjects access to the scriptures in this way. The title page, lavishly illustrated, depicted the two Thomases, under the patronage of the King as Head of the Church, disseminating this new gift to English Christians, both priests and people alike. Neither man made any secret of seeing the Great Bible as an advance for the Evangelical cause in English religion. Nor was its significance lost on the traditionalists, who had no recourse to any appeal against the King's edict for its publication.

At the same time, Thomas Cromwell began his campaign against the English monastic institutions, a project with roots in reforming ideas held by people of varied convictions, but one which aimed very directly at the enrichment of the Crown and the destruction of any source of resistance to Henry's policies. The monasteries, with their accumulation of land, wealth and power, were ripe for targeting. While the rhetoric about their liquidation, therefore, was often persuasive and even compelling, the end result of the Dissolution was often in stark contrast to it. What began as a great campaign against wealth concentrated too narrowly in too few hands, against a sort of self-indulgent religious practice which did not benefit any but the cloistered themselves, and in favour of a great and just redistribution of English goods for the English ended up with even more wealth in the hands of even fewer noblemen: and especially the King. More than that, the good done by the monasteries, in medicine, welfare, education, scholarship, agriculture and in holding together the regional social fabric was swept away at a stroke. The crumbling ruins of once great religious houses seemed to the Marian generation to reflect the way in which the royal supremacy had led to the erosion of very social contract of Tudor England.

Even before Henry died, such changes in religious life were also apparent in the worship of parish churches, even if such changes were constant, and moved backwards and forwards between both Evangelical and traditional emphases and directions. The slightly more reforming Ten Articles of 1536 were themselves overturned by the more conservative Six Articles of 1539, which re-stated the truth of material presence of Christ's body and blood in the Eucharist. They also reinstated a firm rule against clerical marriage, by which clergy including Archbishop Cranmer were forced to drive their wives into exile, something concerning which Nicholas Harpsfield would later make mischief. Struggles about the language of worship were also at times intense, as Cranmer began to issue English forms, for instance of the Litany, and his opponents fiercely resisted anything but the Latin of Christendom.³ After Cromwell's fall and execution in 1540, traditionalists like Gardiner sought to use their influence to pull the Church in England even further back towards its recent, Catholic, past, asserting and reminding their contemporaries that Henry's supremacy in religion was always meant to *guarantee* the integrity of faith and worship, and not to promote innovation or isolation.

The fundamental problem with this, from Gardiner's perspective, was that, as long as Henry was King, the royal supremacy was essentially tethered to nothing more than the King's own wishes, whims and will. As one recent writer has expressed it, there was no 'mild theological ecumenism' undergirding the Supremacy, as was often claimed, but rather 'an assertion of [Henry's] right to discipline anything he chose to define as dissent'. The destination of English religion under Henry was indeed 'bafflingly uncertain': the content of royal decrees and legislation was contradictory, erratic, subjective and theologically both incomprehensible and arbitrary.⁴ The French Ambassador, Charles de Marillac, writing home, commented that, under the royal supremacy, justice existed 'only if it pleases the King'. He had just witnessed the bizarre and fearful day, on 30 July 1540, on which three Catholic opponents of the divorce were dragged on hurdles from their long and brutal confinement to be hanged, drawn and quartered as some sort of parallel side-show to the burnings of three Evangelicals, including Robert Barnes. It was just three days after Thomas Cromwell's execution; the King's fourth marriage had just been annulled by Cranmer and his fifth, disastrous, marital adventure with Katherine Howard had immediately been begun. Horrified, Marillac reported home that no firm sense of any religious commitment now existed in England: Evangelical ideas were not allowed, and yet the papacy was spurned; the Pope himself was a figure of public hatred, and yet Lutheranism was strictly forbidden and punished with fire. It was, he said, simply a matter of the people doing what they were told, and yet what they were told 'is so often altered that it is difficult to understand what it is'. Henry, he reflected, now possessed an authority over doctrine in the English Church which even the Apostles never had. He went on:

> everything he says must be held as the law of God or the oracle of his prophets, and they not only want to attribute to him the proper obedience for a king to whom all honour, obedience

---

3 For more on Cranmer's earlier English forms of prayer, including the Litany of 1544, see Dean 2012, chapter 2.

4 Marshall 2017, p. 295.

and worldly service is due, but they also make him into a true statue for idolaters.⁵

As we will see, this was exactly the dire prognostication which opponents of the Supremacy had originally articulated throughout the long progress of the King's 'Great Matter' and the evolution of its claims. Gardiner, Bonner and others thus had More and Fisher in their rearview mirror as they sought to defend the outcome of that process, and claim that the English Church still possessed integrity, authenticity and indeed was even more genuinely connected to the life of God since its separation from Rome. In the years after Henry's death, that became an even more difficult enterprise. Indeed, their attempts to defend the royal supremacy on conservative, traditionalist lines, fell apart entirely within months of the King's death, in 1547.

This is not the place for a full account of the brief but eventful reign of Edward VI.⁶ It is necessary, however, to note that these six and a half years (January 1547 – July 1553) became for the leaders of the Marian regime a crucible of shame, repentance and often also personal suffering. They led to a radical re-ordering of their previous views, and the crossing of a Rubicon from which there was no possibility of retreat in their later careers. Those in favour among King Henry's circle at the time of his death, including Edward's uncles the Seymour brothers, assumed places of great influence on the Council which ruled in his name during his minority. These were also individuals of known and relatively explicit commitments to religious reform and Evangelical faith. The new King's godfather, Archbishop Cranmer, was also given a more expansive opportunity to instigate and oversee religious change in the English Church as part of this new Council, and, at this stage of his life, wasted no time and squandered no opportunity.⁷ From the beginning of the new reign, he and his companions set their sights on nothing less than a revolution in English religion, freed from the shackles of Henry's iron control and unpredictable but absolute convictions.

Mary Tudor herself always viewed the religious changes made after 1547 as illegitimate, given that her young half-brother was still a boy and therefore in her view unable to exercise the powers of the royal supremacy himself (even assuming such powers were themselves not heretical,

---

5 Quoted by Marshall 2017, p. 281, and Shagan 2011, pp. 108–9.

6 Several excellent accounts exist, among them MacCulloch, *Tudor Church Militant* (1999), and the relevant sections of Duffy's *The Stripping of the Altars* (1992), MacCulloch's *Thomas Cranmer* (1992) and Marshall's *Heretics and Believers* (2017).

7 Cranmer's own views had been in development, especially on the Eucharist. The course of that development is both fascinating and somewhat difficult to chart, but by far the best account remains that of MacCulloch 1996.

as she believed), nor legally to delegate them to others around him.[8] Nevertheless, the use made of them by the Council certainly provoked enormous distress among those who shared her beliefs and her perspective. It soon became clear that the Mass would be a highly symbolic example of the kinds of ecclesiology and practice which Cranmer had in mind for England; and that his ambitions for this new Evangelical England, under its boy King, were lofty. Even so, the Mass was very far from being the only focus for such reforming zeal. In a relatively short space of time, the whole fabric of religious life and devotion changed. If Gardiner and his allies had thought the dissolution of monastic life to have been dramatic and violent, they could perhaps not have imagined the iconoclasm that was before them in early 1547.

The two successive editions of the *Book of Common Prayer*, in their liturgies, directions for worship and attendant rubrics and elaborations, represented a complete overhaul of the worship of the English people. In 1549 and then even more so in 1552, Cranmer acted as architect of a whole new structure of devotion. In the process, he simultaneously also oversaw real changes in the fabric and structure of English parish churches which represented an absolute repudiation of the medieval Catholic past. New prayers and forms in the English language and mandated for use in every congregation across the land now resonated around buildings sometimes scarcely recognisable from the decorated, colourful, vibrant spaces they had recently been. A commitment to a universal sense of one's access to God led to the demolition of the rood screens which separated the altar and its priests from the people. Evangelical concern about the dangers of idolatry splashed liberal quantities of whitewash onto walls decorated with images and murals of saints and biblical scenes and asserted a renewed focus on the Bible itself, placed centrally on its lectern. In the process, many stained glass windows were also sacrificed to catechetical correctness. And, when a loved one died, mourners by 1552 were left in no doubt at all by the liturgy itself that purgatory and the ongoing intercession of the saints were fictions of Catholic devising, and that the departed was now simply at rest, awaiting the general resurrection and the outcome of God's preordained election.[9] In his preface to the new books, Cranmer had sought to defend the changes, asserting the need for structure and ceremony, whilst also decrying the 'dark excessive multitude' of such things by the time of Henry's death, and the 'vanity and superstition' which they represented in English religious life. The 'superstitious blindness of the rude and unlearned', he maintained, now needed to be tutored by the

---

8 Richards 2011, pp. 216–17.
9 See Dean 2012, pp. 106–9.

pure Word of Scripture, and by churches and ceremonies whose clarity, simplicity refinement and focus were an aid to the inculcation of what he viewed as true Christianity.[10]

For traditionalists, though, Cranmer's words and appeal were horrifying apologies for heresy and sacrilege. The actions of Edward's regime profaned at a stroke the rich imagery, devotional art and Eucharistic practice of centuries. It was in this last area, the changes to the Mass, that they felt most keenly the violent severance of the English from the life-blood of Christendom, and the realm's consequent and absolute isolation from the wellsprings of a shared faith. As such, they felt, England had committed a most grievous act of apostasy, leaving itself outside of divine favour and utterly bereft of the comfort, connection and aid which the proper celebration of the Mass, under papal supremacy, had brought. Even as the rubrics in the Prayer Book insisted that what remained on the table after the Communion was still merely bread and wine, and that 'the Curate shall have it to his own use', the architecture of churches was again altered to reflect this insistence: medieval stone altars were demolished and plain wooden tables set lengthwise down the church. There was no sacrifice here, then; Christ was no longer known in the 'Real Presence' of his body and blood at the altar; the priest offered no invocation to the Holy Spirit to bless, inhabit and transform the elements. Like worshippers in Reformed Zurich or Strasbourg, English communicants were simply instructed to eat and drink as 'a perpetual memory' of Christ's death.[11] The Forty Three Articles, prepared for publication just as Edward died in 1553 and never officially promulgated, went on to drive these points home: the sacrament of Holy Communion was a memorial only; it involved no sacrifice, Christ having died once for all; it entailed no physical presence, Christ having ascended fully and bodily into heaven; and it therefore was wrong to use the consecrated host for any kind of devotion, procession or further subsequent elevation.

Reflecting the views of fellow Catholics under Edward a few years later, Nicholas Harpsfield offered a vivid portrayal of the effects of all this, and an interpretation of what it meant in striking biblical terms:

> Then should you have seen in the place where Christ's precious body was reposed over the altar, and instead of Christ his crucifix, the arms of a mortal King set up on high with a dog and a lion, which a man might well call the abomination of desolation standing in the Temple that Daniel speaketh of.

---

10 'Of Ceremonies, why some be abolished and some retained', prefacing the 1552 *Book of Common Prayer* (and also at the end of the 1549 edition).

11 On the changes of and between the books of Common Prayer, see Dean 2012, pp. 94–103.

He went on to offer an inverted version of a popular Evangelical idea that Edward was England's 'Josiah': the boy king in the Hebrew Scriptures who oversaw a radical reform of religious life in ancient Israel. Whereas the biblical King reformed, corrected and abolished idolatry, Edward had 'increased and amplified the errors and abuses that his father began', such that Antichrist was foreshadowed and Catholic religion 'quite overthrown'.[12]

Bishop Stephen Gardiner had tried to express the criticisms outlined above at the time, and articulate his profound anxiety about the spiritual jeopardy into which English people had walked, led in their sleep by those whose motivations he now believed to be wicked and whose grasp on theological and ecclesiological truth he thought heretical and dangerous. He had resisted the Edwardian Council and Protector Edward Seymour, Duke of Somerset, almost from the very beginning. He found himself imprisoned at various times, and ultimately deprived of the bishopric of Winchester as he opposed what he now saw as the monstrous intrusion of an apostate regime on the affairs of his diocese. From the Tower, he penned a mighty response to Cranmer's first major theological treatise, the *Defence* of 1550. This *Explication and Assertion*[13] was published in 1551 and reflected his now open and outright hostility and implacable opposition towards the religious policy of the Edwardian Council. Cranmer replied in the *Answer* the following year; the two engaged in a detailed, sometimes bitter and often tedious debate about biblical texts, patristic authorities and the traditions of the Church.[14] Both men clearly had past records to defend, as well as present axes to grind: if the difficulty for Cranmer was that he had indeed changed his mind about the Eucharist over the years, Gardiner's was that, although fairly consistent in his theological approach, he had himself been a vocal proponent of the royal supremacy, by whose very logic and provisions

---

12 N. Harpsfield (ed. Pocock) 1878, pp. 282–3; the Josiah trope was a popular one amongst Edwardian Evangelicals, even if the attribution of it to Thomas Cranmer in Edward's Coronation sermon is now proved to have been false.

13 *Explication and Assertion of the true Catholic faith, touching the most blessed sacrament of the altar with confutation of a book written against the same* (R. Caly, Rouen, 1551).

14 Cranmer's two texts were: *A Defence of the True and Catholic doctrine of the sacrament of the body and blood of our saviour Christ, with a confutation of sundry errors concerning the same, grounded and stablished upon God's holy word, & approved by [the] consent of the most ancient doctors of the Church* (London: Reynold Wolfe, 1550) and *An Answer of the Most Reverend Father in God Thomas Archbishop of Canterbury, Primate of all England and Metropolitan unto a crafty and sophistical cavillation devised by Stephen Gardiner doctor of law, late bishop of Winchester, against the true and godly doctrine of the most holy sacrament of the body and blood of our saviour Jesus Christ* (Reynold Wolfe, London, 1552).

the changes he so despised had now been introduced. The depth and ferocity of his repentance about this is felt in the 1554 sermon with which we began. The convictions expressed in the *Explication* would undergird the rest of his life and career.

For those leaders of the Marian religious revolution, such as Bishop Gardiner, the early resistance to the royal supremacy, and the detail of its appeal, thus came to exercise an enormous hold over their consciences, imaginations and convictions. As they surveyed the ruins of the monastic institutions, recalled the endless religious changes and innovations of the 1540s and early 1550s, and assessed the recent history of England, the essential percipience of More and Fisher and their allies seemed to them ever more remarkable, and worthy of attention and emulation. There was, however, another strand to their response to the state of affairs, and to affairs of State, by 1553, which was entwined with their horror about religious change in a way which it is often difficult for modern minds to grasp. It was an argument possessed of no less a sense of devastation, anger and heartbreak than their resistance to changes in religion, because it was in their minds so closely related to them and their effects. This second strand, which we must grasp in order to understand not only the Marian period, but also the work of Nicholas Harpsfield and subsequent Catholic recusancy and writing, concerned England's descent, not only into heresy, but also into what Gardiner and others perceived as social destruction and incipient anarchy.

Writing in his *Treatise on the Pretended Divorce* during Mary's reign, Nicholas Harpsfield described how, in his view, the 'enormities' of Henry's reign led to even greater calamities under Edward, a son sent as a sort of punishment for the crimes of his father's policy. At the top of his list, if not the worst features of it – that was reserved for the sacrilege we noted above – Harpsfield described the 'dangerous events as chanced to the realm in civil and politic matters', including the 'abasing of the coin', the 'great tumults and bloodshedding' of various acts of sedition, and the internecine battle fought between the King's uncles, which culminated in the execution of one and a effort to subvert the very line of succession itself.[15] Such observations about civil unrest and political upheaval are vitally important in understanding the Marian view of things. Cardinal Pole and his circle have sometimes been criticised for looking back with rose-coloured spectacles to what they saw as the peaceful, eirenic days of the 1520s as they dealt with the restoration of religion in the 1550s: but in fact, from their perspective the royal supremacy had indeed brought with it a constant and turbulent series of risings and rebellions, of an unprecedented severity. When in August

---

15 Nicholas Harpsfield (ed. Pocock) 1878, pp. 276, 281.

1553 Mary's new regime pleaded for the people to live together 'in quiet sort and Christian charity', it was no merely routine request. They felt that the religious errors of the previous twenty years had directly produced alarming unrest, by striking at the very foundations of what enabled harmonious communities and an ordered, peaceful society. A few months later, Mary and Philip were still speaking of their 'disgust' at the 'divers stirs and rebellions' which had engulfed the nation before their reign.[16]

Some of the uprising since the royal supremacy was seen as a necessary resistance to it. King Henry had found his authority seriously challenged only once, during the 'Pilgrimage of Grace' of 1536. It had its roots in two synchronous movements, one among Lincolnshire men and the other, more widespread, among gentry and their followers in and around Yorkshire. Central to the rebels' demands were a number of related issues: an end to the dissolution of monastic houses, a return to settled forms of devotion, especially concerning the Mass, and a more consensual, less intrusive and tyrannical, approach to government. Their claims, intriguingly, were thus both religious and political and, in their minds as well, the two were inextricably entwined. In the course of its march south, carrying banners emblazoned with images of the five wounds of Christ surrounded by a chalice and paten, the Pilgrimage gained force and numbers. There was a moment of real danger for the regime, averted only through some diplomatic engagement and a subsequent deception, perpetrated on the pilgrims by a furious monarch. Even if Henry was able to break the promises he had made to them, including one to hold a parliament in York, he was left in no doubt about the strength of feeling the Pilgrimage represented, and of the dangers of simply relying on his royal authority to do whatever he wished.[17] It also illustrated that religious change precipitated social unrest.

The other acts of sedition and rebellion which would have been in the minds of Mary and her lieutenants as they reviewed the Henrician and Edwardian years would have been far more troubling. They saw in them the kind of destabilisation of the nation itself which we noted above, and which would lead to more and worse rebellions until the restoration of religion provided the stable structures needed to renew civil society itself. The introduction of the new Prayer Book in 1549 had been resisted by some traditionalists, especially in the South West;

---

16 On the criticisms of Pole, see for instance Loades 1991b, p. 124. The decree is quoted by Richards 2011, p. 219. Mary's and Philip's decree to a local commission on sedition is quoted in Loades 1991a, p. 225.

17 For an account of the Pilgrimage, see Marshall 2017, pp. 244–53, or, more fully, Moorhouse 2002.

but that same year also saw Kett's Rebellion in Norfolk, a much more Evangelically minded affair. The protestors were demanding an eclectic array of measures, including further reform in religion as well as the addressing of economic and agrarian concerns. In the end they were suppressed forcefully, but not before celebrity Evangelical preachers like Matthew Parker, later Archbishop of Canterbury, had tried to sway them to a more agreeable frame of mind. With disturbances and threats all across the south of England, over a variety of questions, issues and concerns, this so-called 'commotion time' of 1549 was a moment of genuine threat. It also revealed, as Peter Marshall comments, how 'fragmented and fractious' was both the faith of the people and their opinion about the realm itself, just over fifteen years into the royal supremacy.[18]

In Marian eyes, the worst acts of sedition were to come, and were led by the Council itself. The effort to deprive Mary of her right of succession as the young King's life ebbed away, an effort which he himself, of course, led and approved of, seemed to them a particular and egregious violation of sacred obligations. Harpsfield later described Edward's betrayal of his sisters in this matter 'strange and unnatural'. After Edward's death, of course, his Council had attempted to subvert Henry's will and the natural succession by the effort to place Jane Grey on the throne; the armed resistance to Mary's accession was led by the Duke of Northumberland, John Dudley, who was also Jane's father-in-law, and the *de facto* Protector after the execution of Seymour. Just months after Mary had triumphed over Northumberland and the plot against her, too, she had had to summon all her courage, resilience and shrewdness of judgement to resist another rebellion. This was led by Sir Thomas Wyatt, ostensibly in opposition to her plans to marry Philip of Spain but in reality, as Mary discerned, a far more dangerous effort to oust her from her recently acquired throne.

Looking back early in Mary's reign, the leading figures in her administration all detected an alarming pattern in all this which confirmed for them a basic conviction: heresy leads to treachery. Illegitimate changes in religious life lead to social decay, anarchy, unbridled upheaval among the people, economic ruin, and seditious activity. They believed, simply, that when England under Henry severed its ties with the rest of Christendom and cut itself loose from the Catholic faith of the rest of the world, it had fatally undermined the very foundations of national life and political health. This may seem a rather strange view now, but it was central to their whole understanding, and to the direction of the Marian restoration. Furthermore, they believed it was a view now supported with ample and disturbing evidence from the foregoing twenty years. In

---

18 Marshall 2017, pp. 331–2.

the wider scheme of history, it was not a very long time: merely a 'little season', as Harpsfield observed, but one horrifyingly full of 'plagues' of every kind: heresy; economic crisis and the devaluation of currency; excessive taxation; the decline of prayer, fasting and alms-giving; familial breakdown; an increase of fraud and of lawlessness; and the catastrophic effects on agriculture, charity, education, piety and local economies of the dissolution of monastic houses. Harpsfield himself felt it would require 'a long time and an excellent orator' adequately to describe the 'profound depth and greatness of these ... calamities'.[19] Thomas Martin, prosecuting Thomas Cranmer at his trial in 1555, expressed the scope and scale of the disaster of the royal supremacy most succinctly and vividly of all:

> Whether these be not the fruits of your Gospel, I refer me to this worshipful audience: whether the said Gospel began not with perjury, proceeded with adultery, was maintained with heresy, and ended in conspiracy.[20]

Finally, in relation to this, it is vital for what follows to remember that *it had all been predicted* at the time of the divorce in the 1530s. Gardiner and Harpsfield and their associates, looking back across those twenty years from their vantage point of 1553, thought they were seeing the absolute proof of the dire prognostications which Fisher, More and others had then made as the royal supremacy was first floated. Thomas More had had plenty to say against the innovations (as he saw them) of Martin Luther, when he had stepped in to respond to Luther's attack on the King's *Assertio* of 1521. His *Responsio ad Lutherum* of 1523, written when Henry was still pursuing his policy of studied and dogged defence of papal primacy, had predicted that monarchs who dabbled in Luther's dangerous ideas for the increasing of their own power would soon rue the day. Their subjects, he warned,

> drunk with the blood of princes and revelling in the gore of nobles, enduring not even common rule, with the laws trampled underfoot according to Luther's doctrine, rulerless, without restraint, wanton beyond reason, they will finally turn their hands against themselves, and like those earthborn brethren, will run each other through.

Views such as these, too, were soon apparently borne out in the Peasants' Revolt in Germany in 1525, from whose fallout Luther was quick to distance himself, despite the peasants themselves citing him as an inspiration. More in all likelihood also saw the Sack of Rome in 1527,

---

19 Harpsfield (ed. Pocock) 1878, pp. 283, 298–301.
20 Quoted by Duffy 2009, p. 108.

which he mentions in his *Dialogue Concerning Heresies* of 1529, as further proof that heresy inevitably leads to instability and violence. By 1533, when he was fast falling out of favour with royal policy, he repeated in his *Apology* this central plank of his belief: heresy is inseparable from the social decay and lawlessness to which it inevitably leads, a claim which may have felt a little remote to English people with no knowledge or experience of recent Continental history.[21] It is all of a piece, too, with More's now controversial attitude towards the treatment of heretics, also echoed in the life and career of Nicholas Harpsfield, to which we shall return.

This, then, was the view from 1554, so stirringly articulated by Stephen Gardiner, now restored to the bishopric of Winchester, and elevated to the role of Lord Chancellor. Mary's preservation from the vicissitudes of the foregoing two decades, from the cruelty done to her by her father and the monstrous injustice which her brother had attempted, seemed miraculous to many. Her accession was wildly popular among the majority of the population. Yet, even more than her own salvation, the rescuing of the nation itself under her reign seemed to them both the most extraordinary divine intervention, and the most urgent task for the coming years. As we strive to understand that project in the next three chapters, the groundwork laid here is vital to keep in mind. The heresy of the royal supremacy led inevitably to violence, suffering and social decay, as well as to a multi-headed Hydra of sedition and treachery. A faithful few, and in particular Sir Thomas More, had been possessed of the insight and foresight accurately to predict all this, even as they formulated their response to the royal divorce and the supremacy: their witness and legacy were therefore of paramount importance in moving forward wisely. Finally, the cure would have to mirror the infection itself: only by returning to the *status quo ante* of the papal supremacy and shared Catholic faith and practice with the rest of Christendom could Mary and her Council hope to rectify the wrongs which had occurred, and once again lay the firm foundation of a flourishing, peaceful Commonwealth. It was hoped that thus the 'little season' of the royal supremacy would soon become a fleeting moment of national madness, and a moral tale from which future generations might learn and be warned.

---

21 The *Responsio* is quoted by Richard Marius 1999, p. 303; see pp. 437–8 on the *Apology*. On the sack of Rome, see Curtis 2011, p. 80.

Nicholas Harpsfield

The context and conditions for the restoration

So much for the vital perspective and consequent commitment of the leaders of Mary's Church as they looked backwards at the start of the reign. A proper understanding of how they actually addressed the task this set of convictions framed for them depends first upon a grasp of the priorities and achievements of the Marian religious restoration itself. This may seem a simple enough task, but in fact the prevailing view among those who have studied the reign of Mary Tudor was, until comparatively recently, an almost wholly negative one. In considering the main achievements of those years, therefore, it is helpful to keep that shifting and largely unfavorable opinion about the direction, content and efficacy of her reign and of its key influencers, especially in religious terms, in mind. Before moving onto the vital contribution of Harpsfield and his work, firstly in parish reform 'on the ground' and secondly in terms of his published output, a sense of his own context and position is best gained from the course of Mary's reign itself, and the methods by which her renewal of Catholicism in England was enterprised. Harpsfield both shaped, and was shaped by, the work of his peers and colleagues and must be seen as an integral part of the way the Marian authorities approached the task, and made their case.

Mary's reign began positively enough, and with a sense that in fact Catholics and Protestants alike rejoiced that the rightful, Tudor, heir had inherited the throne. The efforts to supplant Henry's daughter with the young, obscure and obviously manipulated Jane Grey vanished with the Suffolk morning mist as the new Queen made her triumphant progress from her base at Framlingham to London. Indeed, one more recent appraisal describes a 'wave of popular counter-revolution' which the government was able to ride in the general rejoicing.[22] Nor was there any doubt about Mary's intentions in religious policy, which at no point had she hidden. Some clearly felt strongly enough to flee for the safety of Reformed cities in Europe; most, however stayed, either resigned to losing the gains they felt had been made under a woman who was nevertheless God's rightful and duly anointed sovereign, or genuinely ecstatic at the reversal of fortunes. Some began to celebrate the Mass again even before it was legally re-introduced, an act of lawlessness hardly likely to be censured or punished by the regime.

We should not underestimate nor disregard the huge challenges Mary faced, coming to inherit her father's throne. She was, in the first place, a woman: and the first to reign as monarch in her own right. She was attempting something unprecedented in the history of English

---

22 Marshall 2017, p. 363.

monarchy. Then, by nature of those very religious laws just mentioned, she was still legally Head of the Church in England, even if she and her closest advisers felt such a thing was not only heretical but actually impossible. Nonetheless, she was forced to issue legislation for changes in the Church and its life by the powers of the royal supremacy until papal authority could be restored, something which was deeply uncomfortable. She knew, further, that her commitment to the restoration of Catholic religion presented an enormous challenges after the political shifts and changes of the previous twenty years, now firmly embedded in the national *zeitgeist*, and the liturgical revolution of the previous six, which had utterly and swiftly transformed English churches and their worship. She faced a parliament by no means amenable to her wishes or her will, and a political chess-game for which she would need patience, persuasive powers, and depth of insight.

There were, among the plethora of difficult questions which beset Mary and her Council in 1553, two particularly thorny problems. The first was the fate of the formerly monastic lands now in the hands of private gentry, many of whom were the very members of Parliament whose votes the Queen needed to make any progress. Clearly, she could not rely on any altruistic *largesse* from those whose wealth had been increased in this way; and thus she found herself forced into a much more conciliatory, compromise position than the one she might have wished for in the glacial negotiations of the early months of her reign. Both cause and consequence of all this was the time it took, simply to wind up the machinery of government in a more effective way, and to begin to legislate for the kind of change the regime envisaged. Mary had no choice but to 'make haste slowly', picking her way carefully between vested interests, powerful politicians, intransigent opinions (including her own!) and committed devotees of the previous reign who were not prepared to give way without resistance.

Secondly, there was the question of the royal marriage. After some wide and deliberative consultation, Mary came to a very determined desire to marry her cousin Philip of Spain, and was prepared to weather the inevitable resistance that such a proposed match brought. Facing down her critics, Mary married Philip in 1554, but at a cost to her public persona and popularity, and with considerable dissent from some of those around her and in parliament. The terms of the marriage had to be very carefully negotiated and drawn up; although Philip took the title of King of England, his powers were significantly circumscribed, and the rights and privileges of any children to be born to the couple were similarly thoroughly delineated. The innate xenophobia of many English men and women was often in full view as Philip made his way to the marriage in Winchester and then to London with the Queen; he seems to have tried to affect English manners and preferences, even trying the beer, but he was facing an uphill struggle. Nor was he able to respond to Mary's obvious affection for him with quite the same degree of attachment. After the honeymoon period, he was rarely to be seen in England again, only adding to her sense of loneliness and isolation.

These sorts of troubles were augmented by difficulties in personnel. Mary's principal ally in the project of the re-introduction of Catholic faith and practice was to be her cousin, Reginald Pole. Pole had for a time in his youth been something of a protégé of King Henry, nine years his senior, who had subsidised his European education and enjoyed his scholarly relative's brilliance and support. The divorce had driven a wedge between the two men, however, and Pole had sought exile amid the humanist intelligentsia of the Catholic Church on the continent. Appointed a cardinal, Pole became a leading figure among the reforming wing of the Catholic Church, and a leading framer of the early stages of the Council of Trent. As one of the so-called *Spirituali*, he sought reconciliation with some Lutheran ideas and impulses, and represented a conciliatory voice in the debates of the day, convinced of the need for the reform of the Catholic Church, whilst still firmly seeing the papacy as the guarantor of authenticity, unity and integrity. However, in his grief about affairs back home, Pole had also published fierce denunciations of the royal supremacy, railed against the outrage done to Queen Katherine, and, as papal legate, supported those, including the participants of the Pilgrimage of Grace, resisting the King's religious policy. Henry, with his characteristic and pathological inability to be crossed or disagreed with, had retaliated in grotesque and brutal fashion. Not only was Pole himself condemned as a traitor, but his English family, including his sainted mother Margaret, Countess of Salisbury, had been butchered in 1541, in an act of appalling savagery and injustice. The consequences of this very personal family history were to have enormous influence on the regime's portrayal of Henry, including Harpsfield's account of events, which was heavily influenced by Pole, his mentor, leader, and close associate.

The difficulty with having Pole as her right hand man was that Mary was forced to wait a long time for his arrival back in England. In addition, he took a hard-line and intractable view on some of the key issues which faced her in 1553, and which had to be resolved. Appointed as papal legate again by Pope Julius III in 1553, Pole languished in Brussels for months while back home Mary and her ministers fought with a reluctant parliament over the issues of monastic property and the Spanish marriage: Pole was conservative on the former and was apparently dubious about the latter. In the end, he reluctantly agreed to a dispensation to allow former monastic lands to remain in the hands of their current owners, so that religious reform could proceed. During 1554, some progress was slowly made, after these concessions: a few Evangelical bishops were finally deprived and replaced with those committed to a Catholic revival; and members of parliament became a little more pliant, reassured that their own fortunes were not under threat. It was not until the very end of 1554, though, that Pole was able finally to cross the English Channel, and commence what he viewed as his sacred task, of the full reconciliation of England with Rome, papal obedience and union with Christ himself through His Holy Church.

In the meantime, the cardinal legate lobbied his royal cousin determinedly and somewhat sanctimoniously from afar, attempting to frame her own understanding of the recent past, and their family history, to fit her for the task ahead. Pole was clear that Mary needed to prioritise her own commitment to God and Christ's Church, over any filial devotion she might feel to her late father. Criticising the regime's early gentle tone towards Henry, he castigated such leniency, when the King himself had been the whole source of the chaos and error which had engulfed the realm. 'If you will not now not speak ill of him', he thundered, 'let him alone, speak no good of him'. Citing already the martyrdom of More and Fisher, he asserted that both they and Henry could not be 'of blessed memory': Mary, and all her subjects, had to make a simple and irrevocable choice between the two, even if that meant disowning and disavowing her own family.[23] The task of religious rebuilding and renewal which lay ahead was going to make very exacting demands on everyone: and on no one more than the Queen herself.

There were also, we should remember, going to be difficulties at the end of the reign. These would have a double impact: on the government's own capacity to continue the restoration of religion, and on the verdict of subsequent generations of historians about the efficacy of the whole project. Finally appointed to the now-vacant See of Canterbury after Thomas Cranmer's eventual execution in Spring 1556, Pole was already mired in the morass of his deteriorating relationship with the new Pope, Paul IV (Gian Pietro Carafa), who been elected the previous summer. Carafa was a man whose instincts, principles, morals and theological convictions were a world apart from Pole. A stern, unyielding reformer, anti-Jewish, persecuting, stubborn and fundamentalist about his own narrow understanding of orthodoxy, he detested the spirituality of Pole and his circle, whose approach to the Evangelicals he thought heretical in and of itself. He made it his own, ferocious and draconian, personal vendetta to bring Pole and his associates to justice. One such, Cardinal Giovanni Morone, was thrown into prison: he had to wait until Carafa's death to

---

23 Duffy 2009, pp. 39–40; see also Mayer 2000b, p. 210.

be exonerated and released. The Pope similarly demanded Pole's return to Rome, with similar intentions; protected by Mary, the Archbishop resisted making a journey whose consequences he could foresee all too clearly. In the meantime, though, the breakdown of relations severely impeded his ability to exercise his prerogatives as a papal legate. As the stalemate continued, England was also gripped with plague, economic downturn, poor harvests and a devastating war in France. The authorities thus necessarily spent the last year of Mary's reign simply trying to help a populace through extraordinarily trying circumstances: it was not a moment in which continued and serious reform efforts were as easy to accomplish. And then, on the same day in November 1558, the premature deaths of both the Queen and her Cardinal Archbishop of Canterbury brought the whole project crashing to the ground.

All that was unforeseeable, however, when Stephen Gardiner offered his listeners a vision of a re-awakened nation. Just days earlier, the speech with which Reginald Pole prepared England for the reconciliation with Rome and to papal supremacy in late November 1554 had also been a masterpiece of rhetoric. As Eamon Duffy remarks, it has been somewhat neglected in our efforts to understand the Marian religious policy, but a familiarity with its themes enables us to see very clearly the foundations of all that was to come, including and especially the work of Nicholas Harpsfield. Pole sought to describe the enormity and providential character of what he thought was happening in lofty prose and heightened imagery: the Queen was likened to her namesake, the mother of Jesus, and his own restoration to England made to mirror the realm's restoration to proper relationship with the rest of Christendom and ancient religious identity. He dwelt on the themes we have examined before, of the capricious and unpredictable character of justice under Henry after the schism, the breakdown of law and order, the uprooting and denigrating of true religion, and the catastrophic consequences for every area of national life of the 'willful defection and schismatical revolting' which the royal supremacy, and the changes brought in under it, represented. And he focused on some themes which will occupy us considerably in assessing Harpsfield's subsequent work and influence, of the particular grace of the Henrician martyrs like Thomas More, whose 'honour, pre-eminence and dignity' were a clarion call to the English to give themselves again, like those brave witnesses, to the cause of the Church's unity and a radical realignment in their identity and priorities. Two days later, on St Andrew's Day, the formal absolution and reconciliation took place, in extraordinary scenes, without precedent or subsequent repetition in English history.[24]

24 Duffy 2009, pp. 43–6, and Mayer 2000, pp. 221–3.

Finally, after long delay, and almost a year and a half of preparation, the real work could begin. There was much to do: in the parishes, the medieval fabric of the churches was gone. Rood screens had been torn down, altars demolished and imagery obliterated. The paraphernalia of the liturgy survived in a few places, under floorboards or secreted in people's homes; in most places it had long since been destroyed. Chantries had been re-purposed, and monastic institutions closed down and their property sold. For some of this, there was now no solution, especially after the negotiated compromises of 1554. The rebuilding of such material elements as could be restored would not happen overnight. Even more serious, though, was the way Evangelical teaching had taken root in English hearts and minds. The reconciliation with Rome had to be effected, not just with parliamentary legislation but also with dynamic, appealing tools for the re-instilling of Catholicism. The re-introduction of the Mass had to be supported with parish churches able to be once again the focus of devotion and the centre of communal worship, suitable settings for such a holy rite, and the coming of God in physical form once again into the heart of every local community. That also required an effective priesthood, able alongside the authorities to oversee the kind of renewal in both private conviction and public piety which was Mary's vision and Pole's intent.

Nicholas Harpsfield, at the heart of that project and its implementation, especially in the dioceses of London and Canterbury, has much to show us about how it was done, with what resources and following what theological priorities. In a subsequent chapter, we will follow in some detail his efforts at parish level, drawing on the significant records he left behind. Before that, through the published and printed material of the period, we may gain a better understanding of the kind of efforts which were made, and the tactics and appeals employed to the readers of Marian England. In approaching this body of material, though, it is important to note its neglect and misinterpretation over many years of scholarship on the period of Mary's reign and the character of her government. A careful analysis and a proper accounting for the work of Nicholas Harpsfield is a crucial part in the necessary and overdue re-examination of Marian religious policy, and the restoration of Catholicism, which for too long was dismissed as inadequate, misdirected and a colossal failure. It is worth taking a moment to assess that criticism, and thus to understand why such a reassessment, and with it an understanding of Harpsfield's contribution, is sorely needed.

PART II

The Marian Revolution

☩ 2 ☩

'Nourished with hope ... and confirmed with antiquity'
Mary's Religious Revolution

Even if some have felt the evidence exists, as we will shortly discover, to question the efficacy of Mary's religious policy, no one can seriously doubt its sincerity, as a project flowing directly from her own deepest convictions. Having observed the Queen tending to poor and diseased subjects in Holy Week of 1556, participating in renewed ceremonies which had had no place in Cranmer's prayer books, Pole's secretary Marc Antonio Faitta expressed himself a fan. Describing Mary as 'a great and rare example of goodness', possessed of humility and a love for the faith which could not have been more touching in this very public display of compassion, Faitta stressed that her piety, the 'devotion and affection' with which she prayed, were striking and unusual. Waxing hyperbolic, he went on to suggest that 'there was never a Queen in Christendom of greater goodness than this one', a verdict which may seem a little overstated, but also offers an interesting eye-witness account of her public piety and private interactions with some of her most disadvantaged subjects. The time she gave to their care, and the genuine kindness with which she dealt with them clearly made a forceful impression.[1]

Flowing from this deep-rooted piety and commitment, Mary felt a concomitant passion about the need to restore Catholic faith in England as she reunited the realm with the rest of Christendom and the community of Christian nations through papal obedience and reconciliation. This meant re-erecting the physical and material infrastructure required for authentic devotion in the parishes; and it meant rooting right belief, proper conviction, true devotion and authentic practice once more in the lives of the English. The two were obviously related tasks, and dependent upon one another. As we have seen, they were also large

---

1 Quoted by Whitelock 2009, p. 276.

and challenging projects, given the swift revolution of the Edwardian period, the destruction of medieval parish church interiors, and the years in which the royal supremacy had been taking root. Not only that, but circumstances beyond the Queen's control, and especially her early death, left the window of opportunity for the bulk of this work very narrow indeed. In both aspects of the project, parish conformity and printed instruction, Nicholas Harpsfield played a key role, as we will see. First, it is necessary to situate his contribution in the wider scene of the work and success, contested as it is, of the authorities' work.

Even before that, however, it is helpful to offer a brief survey of previous scholarly views of Mary's restoration of religion. Until very recently, the prevailing view has been of its moribund, ineffective, tone-deaf and out-of-touch character. The retrospective judgements of John Foxe, a prevailing and long-lived anti-Catholic sentiment which permeated even the supposedly dispassionate and empirical work of historians, and above all a modern distaste for the horrors of the burning of heretics have cloaked the actual achievements of the reign in a sort of smoke-screen of their own. We will deal head-on later with the burnings; but it has proved difficult to appreciate the real achievements and contributions of people like Nicholas Harpsfield because of the way this negative assessment has so often led to a failure to examine the period afresh, and with new evidence. In what follows, therefore, after a reminder of the scholarly consensus about Mary, her reign, and her leading lieutenants, we will examine more closely the printed literature of the reign, both as a corrective to much of these verdicts, and as a foundation upon which to build an examination of Harpsfield's own writings of the reign itself.

Re-assessing the reign

It is necessary to begin with A. G. Dickens, whose treatment of the Marian period in particular crystallised the prevailing English retrospective of it[2]: Dickens's own preoccupations and judgements both reflected and entrenched a negative view of the reign. In his definitive study, *The English Reformation*, he devoted a chapter to what he termed 'Queen Mary's Contribution'. It takes up just thirty pages of over 460, and deals sketchily with the events of Mary's reign, but predominantly with the

---

2 Dickens's work was, admittedly, published after the account of Philip Hughes, published in 1942, but Hughes's favourable assessment of Mary's reign made little use of printed material, except briefly to praise the *Profitable and necessarye doctryne*. Ironically, he nevertheless dealt at length with Foxe's account of the death of Rowland Taylor, as does Dickens.

burnings of the Protestants, their views, lives, deaths and martyrdom. Though he barely mentions Marian religious writing, he assesses the contribution of the queen quickly and negatively. She was, he claims, only really concerned with 'the medieval past rather than with the seminarist future', introduced with Reginald Pole the Cardinal Legate only an 'arid legalism', and with him 'displayed the tragedy of the doctrinaire called to practical leadership', fatally lacking a sense of the practical, the possible, and even the moral. Far from the loss of Calais, Dickens contends, Mary should have died with her heart engraved with the damning criticism that she failed to discover the Counter-Reformation.[3]

The verdict of Dickens moulded subsequent approaches to Mary and her efforts to reintroduce Catholicism to England. Indeed, his interpretation of the five years from 1553 perhaps still reflects the popular view of them, that they strove only to destructive and ill-intentioned ends. This is undoubtedly as much a tribute to the indefatigable pen of John Foxe, as to any contemporary historian. Foxe's vivid descriptions of the heroic deaths of the Protestants, and his lurid accusations about the proclivities of the main persecutors, men like Edmund Bonner, Nicholas Harpsfield and Stephen Gardiner, have buried themselves deep in the collective subconscious. By initiating such a persecution, which was so easily able to be used for polemical ends, the Marian authorities handed their opponents an easy and open goal, whatever else might be said about the justice and rectitude of their actions. Beneath the easy headlines of that, however, more recent research has begun to show that in the project in the parishes, buttressed by the production of printed devotional and other material, the authorities had actually had the run of play.

The most thorough historian of the Marian period is David Loades, whose evolving judgements have been in many respects a useful corrective to the views of Dickens. Though he found much to be said in praise of Mary and her ministers in many areas, Loades criticised their efforts at printed propaganda. He detected a lack of order and purpose in the appearance of what was published, and he made trenchant criticisms of its quality too. By comparison with the contemporary Protestant material, he found the Marian literature tedious and lacking in fire and colour. Consistently, Loades found, the Marian material lagged behind that of its opponents in both quality and quantity, failed to find an appropriate mode or tenor for its discourse, and contributed to what remains the failure of Marian Catholicism.[4] He made exceptions, of course, for works like Bonner's *Profitable and Necessary Doctrine*, which

---

3 Dickens 1967, pp. 382–5.
4 Loades 1991*b*, pp. 281–8.

as examples of their genre seem to work; but the regime emerges from his study as fatally flawed in the area of published propaganda.

Two articles written after the publication of *The Reign of Mary Tudor* modified Loades's position somewhat. Though in broad outline his criticisms of how little was achieved, and what opportunities were lost, remain, he also singled out a couple of areas worthy of greater praise. Most significantly, he drew on Thomas Watson's *Wholesome and Catholic Doctrine*[5] as a work exuding some of the air of continental Catholic renewal conspicuously absent elsewhere. Watson, especially in his work on penance and auricular confession, was, Loades conceded, offering an attractive faith to his readers and hearers (the material is in the form of sermons), by presenting them with a model of 'thoughtful and sensitive spiritual counselling', a model not so very far removed from the successes of the continental Counter-Reformation, the emerging benefits of which Mary's church has been criticised for avoiding.[6] Loades acknowledged Pole's efforts, in bringing eminent continental Catholic scholars to English universities, to inject useful European elements into the English situation, and in attempting to restore clerical education and diocesan rigour, but still concluded that the material of Watson, Bonner et al represented the 'educated, civil piety of Pole's youth' rather than the new 'fighting creed' which Marian Catholicism needed to be to flourish. He also asserted that the Marian authors encouraged an unhelpfully individualistic attitude, in particular towards the sacraments, rather than a notion of communality.[7] There is, of course, some irony in the fact that Loades and Dickens have both criticised Marian Catholicism and its propaganda for its aridity, tedium and 'uninspiring eirenicism',[8] whilst also seeing its greatest failure in its sending of hundreds of heretics to violent and cruel deaths.

The late Jennifer Loach was the first to find much very constructive and positive to say about the printed material of the Marian years, though the article in question represented an unacknowledged climb-

---

5 Thomas Watson had been imprisoned under Edward; a keen supporter of Mary and her policies, he was restored to his post as Master of St John's College, Cambridge, in 1553, played a large role in public disputations, including with Cranmer, Ridley and Latimer, and was subsequently Dean of Durham and then finally Bishop of Lincoln.

6 Loades 1991b, p. 208. The word 'emerging' reflects the fact that Dickens's original criticism was faulty, in assuming a fully fledged Counter-Reformation in 1553, instead of admitting its nascency; cf. Duffy 1992, pp. 525–6.

7 Loades 1996, pp. 14–15, 17; he also criticises the regime for its essentially Erasmian (as opposed to Loyolan) spirituality and outlook.

8 *Ibid.*, p. 6.

down from her previous work.[9] In an article printed in the *English Historical Review*,[10] Loach pointed to the achievements of Pole's legatine synod of 1556 as being an indicator of his, and the authorities', aim during the period. In particular, Loach stressed the central importance placed on the priesthood under Mary, as preachers and purveyors of spiritual guidance and catechetical instruction. Loach observed the vigour of much of Marian writing, even that much was published abroad as an advert for the real achievements of the regime in restoring traditional religion in England. She also saw the deliberate lack of fierce polemical intent in the writings of Marian authors as a strength; flying in the face of previous scholarly opinion, she detected in the very eirenicism which Loades has criticised the seeds of a Catholic renaissance in the parishes of England. As she put it, 'Brooks ... and Proctor ... seem as likely to have appealed to their readers as the ranting and often salacious writings of Bale and Knox'.[11] The weakness of Loach's work is its compact and incomplete nature; the article nevertheless contains the seeds necessary for a fundamental re-evaluation of the material.

That re-evaluation was continued and encouraged by the publication of Eamon Duffy's *The Stripping of the Altars* in 1992. In particular, Duffy's reassessment of the Marian period called for a better understanding of the major works of instruction and propaganda published at the time, and especially the works of Bishops Bonner and Watson, whose reasoned appeals for a return to the 'beauty of holiness' deliberately rejected the 'blustering scurrilities' of their Protestant opponents. Duffy was also the first to draw attention to Nicholas Harpsfield's archidiaconal visitation of the Canterbury diocese as overlooked evidence in the search for Marian Catholicism's priorities. His careful study of the officially produced Primers of the reign challenged the view of Dickens that the Marian authorities lacked the creativity to produce an acceptable or distinctive English Catholicism; rather, Duffy claimed, they were testament to the 'resilience, adaptability and realism of the Marian attempt to restore Catholicism to the people'.[12] The traditional view of a moribund regime failing to inspire the religious behaviour of its subjects was facing serious challenge.

Christopher Haigh, perhaps *par excellence* the defender of some of the many elements of Mary's reign which are normally universally derided,

---

9 Loach 1975; the article examines Protestant work in the Marian period, but prefaces that investigation by describing the works of the regime's critics as 'more numerous and more able' than those of the authorities, which she calls 'pallid and pedantic'.
10 Loach 1986.
11 *Ibid.*, p. 147.
12 Duffy 1992, pp. 529–30, 543.

gave some attention to the issue of printed books in his work on the period. Building on Loach's insights, he stressed that it was always the intention of the writers and their patrons to re-instil Catholic truth in an embattled laity, rather than to attempt to engage with the Protestants in tit-for-tat polemic, and beat them at their own ferocious game. He also drew attention to the enormous constraints placed on Mary, Pole and their collaborators by the events of the period and the accidents of history. As he pointed out, the books published under Mary tell us not so much what the Marian Church was like, but rather what it was becoming.[13] In terms of the Counter-Reformation too, his observation that there was more to it than the Jesuits, famously rejected by Pole,[14] bears much further scrutiny. Other more general elements should not be ignored, and they were present in English Catholicism under Mary and in the content of the books published at the time: discipline, self-examination and penance, spiritual direction and a lively appreciation of the Mass. In short, Haigh claimed that Marian religious works were 'effective: ... well judged, well organized, and well expressed'.[15] The tide of opinion begins to turn more decisively with Loach and Haigh, the results of whose research lack fulfilment only by needing to be extended to more material.

Lucy Wooding attempted to breathe new life into the study of English Catholicism in the Reformation period. In *Rethinking Catholicism in Reformation England*, published in 2000, she sought to trace a thread of continuity, not just through sixteenth-century Catholicism, but through sixteenth-century religion in general. In other words, she sees the reform movement, in both its Catholic and Protestant manifestations, as a more integrated and unified one than had hitherto been allowed. Catholics, she argued, drawing on the same humanist imperatives towards an *ad fontes*, cleaned-up Christianity as their Protestant opponents, ended up with a religion which in its main emphases and tenets bore more resemblance to its great adversary than the polemic or the historiography of the period generally admits. The Marian Church, long misunderstood, is actually neither rooted in the late medieval period nor the Counter-Reformation, but rather grows from Christian humanism and a Henrician outlook which is more 'evangelical and reformist' than reactionary, and from an event, the break with Rome, which gave both

---

13   Haigh 1993, p. 217; Brigden 1989, p. 628 suggests that, in London at least, reconciliation and conformity were successfully managed under Mary.

14   On this, see Duffy 2009, p. 30. Pole was not hostile to the Jesuits, nor to their approach *per se*; but his own plans for England were perhaps more ambitious than their approach would have allowed, and certainly better focused on particular English needs than their universal *modus operandi* would have been.

15   Haigh 1993, p. 216.

humanism, and Catholicism a 'new lease of life'. In the literature of the period, she finds this writ large: an emphasis on scripture which springs from a humanist outlook, a reformist inheritance which dispenses with Catholic paraphernalia such as saints and monasteries and the papacy for very similar reasons to those of the Protestants, an attitude to Henry VIII which looks back on him as a 'godly and reforming prince', a playing-down of the doctrine of transubstantiation, and a rejection of old beliefs about humanity's ability to move towards God of its own volition, in favour of a more 'modern' view of a belief in grace alone for salvation. For Marian Catholicism, Wooding wants us to see Henrician Catholicism minus the royal supremacy.[16]

There is a number of difficulties with Wooding's thesis, aside from the errors she makes about individual works. Perhaps the greatest and most glaring is that, while she argues for a less definite and easy division between Catholicism and Protestantism than is usually described, she does not allow that other movements of thought and schools of belief could have been similarly nuanced and variegated in outlook. The very division on which she rests her revision, that between a new humanist approach to learning and the old scholastic frame of reference, is a strained, overused and doubtful one; indeed, the evidence of even the Marian literature itself is that writers were finding in their medieval inheritance as well as in their humanist education resources for the rediscovery of true and traditional faith. The other unlikely division in Wooding's work is that Henrician Catholicism itself was somehow able to define itself easily in contradistinction to an 'other' in faith or practice. Henry's Church was a maelstrom of claim and counter claim, fierce rivalry and burning ambition, if not for oneself, then for one's own version of catholicity and authenticity of belief: as we have seen and our Marian authorities have already described. It simply does not permit of being boiled down to an irreducible essence, which subsequently transmitted itself to, and is clearly discernible in, both Edwardian Protestants and Marian Catholics. Indeed, at times the only unity possessed by religion under Henry seems to have been Henry himself. If the Marians found any resources for restoration from Henry's church, they were from the very beginning, the 1520s, and the fight against Luther; from the 1530s they appear only to have learned lessons.

It is, of course, undeniable that humanism had profoundly affected and influenced those of all beliefs in England in the early sixteenth century; but Wooding's failure to understand the gulf which still yawned between the world views of Catholic and Protestant at the time is the fatal flaw in her work. Indeed, her theory at times even seems faintly

---

16 Wooding 2000, pp. 10, 80–1, 114–16, 167.

condescending: all but suggesting that Marian Catholicism was worthy and acceptable after all, because it rested on a premise not unlike the contemporary Protestantism of its day. In particular, she wanted to see the Marian Church as at best half-hearted about its restoration of papal oversight, and says that the papacy was, in Marian eyes, 'irrelevant to the Catholic faith in England'. The pope served a merely 'administrative function' in the minds of most Marian bishops and churchmen, and was not regarded as a spiritual head. To this end, she posited some tension between the official policy of Mary and Cardinal Pole and the writers of the published works of the reign.[17] Though Wooding is right to see Marian Catholic writings as worthy of reconsideration, she has missed their explicitly anti-Protestant content, their vivid espousal of a distinctive Catholic sacramental viewpoint, their firm foundation on the papal supremacy and indeed their refusal to offer any common ground in dealing with their Protestant opponent. Seen as such, they emerge as a dynamic and effective response to the exigencies of restoration and to Protestant challenge.

As a corrective to many of these views, the work of W. L. Wizeman offered a very different view of the religious works produced under Mary. Wizeman argued for the 'coherence and uniformity' of the works published under Mary, with more official backing than has sometimes been assumed, and revealed their strong and effective advocacy of traditional Catholic teaching on the sacraments and the papacy. He offered a picture of a church under Mary full of confidence, and finding renewed confidence in its rediscovery of such doctrine, and also questioned the easy delineation posited between humanist and scholastic outlooks. Wizeman further began to trace the importance of the clergy trained in Mary's reign to recusant Elizabethan Catholicism. In 2008, Eamon Duffy continued the work begun in his earlier writing in *Fires of Faith: Catholic England under Mary Tudor*, in which he offered a further elaboration of his claims about the robust, creative and effective nature of Mary's reign in general and religious policy in particular. He re-examined the career of Reginald Pole especially, re-orienting our understanding of the aims of the authorities, and revealing compelling evidence as to their efficacy and vision. It is important to note that Duffy in turn was drawing in part on contemporary developments in scholarship concerning John Foxe, and the construction of martyrdom at the time. In this, the work of the John Foxe Project, and Thomas Freeman as its main inspiration and guide, have been of inestimable value.[18] What follows, then, seeks

---

17 Ibid., p. 128.

18 Wizeman 2006; Armstrong 2003 – see p. 715 for a discussion on the clear division between humanism and scholasticism which Wooding posits, and the articles

to build on these developments in insight, both by continuing to challenge the deficiencies in older but long-trusted readings of the Marian restoration, and by offering further evidence as to the competence and effectiveness of its main architects.

Marian views of Edward VI

The portrait we have sketched of the years preceding Mary's accession, as seen through Marian eyes, is essential to understanding the printed material of her reign. Again and again, it is the backdrop to Marian writers' defence of the main planks of her policy: the return to papal supremacy, the rigorous reintroduction of a sacrificing and absolving priesthood, the renewal of a colourful sacramental theology, and, indeed, the unrelenting persecution of obstinate heretics. Any idea that, for the most part, Catholic authors in the 1550s wanted to see 1547 as the decisive moment of disaster is only half true[19]: most looked back to the decisions of the early 1530s with the revelation of hindsight, seeing in them the seeds of the destruction of orthodoxy. For men like Stephen Gardiner and his peers, the conversion required was at great personal and spiritual cost; but they saw in the situation as it stood at the death of Edward in 1553 no alternative but to repent of their former approval of Henry's supremacy, as we have seen.

At the heart of their sense of loss is the abolition of the Mass, and with it a Catholic sacramentalism. In the changes in the order for communion under Cranmer's liturgical revision, changes which Marian authors universally describe as incessant and extreme, Catholic traditionalists saw the purposeful destruction of the channels which offered heavenly grace and comfort to earthly seekers. If one seeks a major printed target for Catholic anger, it is the books of Common Prayer of 1549 and 1552, their eucharistic theology moving steadily towards Zurich, their instructions for the arrangement and conduct of communion tearing up by the roots practices which had been the very fabric of English religion for centuries, and indeed, of Christian religion everywhere. Thomas

---

by Rex 1989b and Underwood 1989, to which Armstrong refers, especially Rex's view that Fisher, for instance, was a key figure in the development of a synthesised 'independent tradition of theological scholarship' whose successors were figures as varied as Whitgift, Stapleton and the Jesuits (pp. 123–6). See also for example Doran and Freeman (eds.) 2011; Evenden and Freeman (eds.) 2011. Recent surveys of the English Reformation, and notably Peter Marshall's excellent *Heretics and Believers* (2017), have incorporated these newer discoveries and perspectives.

19   See, for example, Wooding 2000, pp. 129, 132–3, in which she cites Pole, Standish and John Harpsfield as men who saw the roots of the troubles in 1533, but were nevertheless in a minority.

Watson, Bishop of Lincoln and one of the regime's ablest writers, in the first of his *Two Notable Sermons* of 1554, expressed incredulity at the intent and extent of the Protestants' eucharistic hooliganism. Like the Turks, they have invented a religion devoid of any real and lively external expression of its faith, only a reliance on the inward feelings of the heart; their individualism and memorialist language has left believers with isolation at the communion table and despair that faith should ever become lived and real. Like others before and at the time, Watson exposes what he sees as the folly of the reformers, after 1500 years of Christian worship, deciding that actually Christ was really saying to his disciples 'this is not my body', and he lays the blame firmly at the door of the 'Zwinglians and our great archbishop his disciple'.[20] The full passion of Watson's fury at this desecration and even abolition of the holy needs to be experienced to be appreciated:

> O what wonderful effects be these, which by this blessed Sacrament be wrought in the worthy receiver, against the devil and his temptations, against the flesh and her illusions, against the vicious affections of our corrupt mind: what conscience had these men, our late teachers and pastors, destroyers of Christ's flock, to rob us of this treasure, which is the cause of so great benefits, and in the place of that, to plant among us a bare ceremony of bread and wine to put us in remembrance of Christ in heaven (as they said) which neither by their own nature nor yet by any institution either of God or man, be able to bring to pass in us these effects I have spoken of.[21]

Watson was not alone in this view, nor in the concomitant intent to rebuild the Mass. He is perhaps the best spokesman, though, for this essential aspect of the Marian project. The other, also frequently expressed, is that same sense, already seen, that the abolition of traditional liturgical and theological expression of Catholic and universal faith has inexorably led also to a breakdown of the charitable and societal structures which have held England together for centuries. In the anarchy of the chancel area of churches is seen in microcosm the chaos into which English society had fallen under Edward, without charity, order or stability. Roger Edgeworth, the star preacher of the West Country, silenced for several years by the Edwardian authorities, reflected sadly in the dying months of the king's reign on the loss of the kiss of peace at the Mass, a practice which from the Church's earliest days had bound believers in 'concord, amity and friendship' and which now lay unused. His sermon was published only in 1557, a potent reminder of the excesses

---

20 Watson 1554, sigs. B iv–v, D iv and O v.
21 *Ibid.*, G iii.

of Protestant religion.[22] Henry Pendleton had reflected in 1554, in a homily among those published with Bonner's *Profitable and Necessary Doctrine*, on Isaiah's parable of the vineyard: his conclusion was that not only was the vineyard itself now desolate and unfruitful, but the heretics had even torn down the enclosing hedge. The chaos, confusion and social decay were ubiquitous: 'I mean all good order, as well in the church, as in the commonwealth'.[23] John Christopherson connected the rise of sedition, witnessed in Wyatt's rebellion, and the breakdown of established social mores, with the legacy of the Edwardian catastrophe, in no uncertain terms:

> after the same sort did children order their parents, wives their husbands, and subjects their magistrates: so that the feet ruled the head, and the cart was set before the horse ... so that the old men's saying was herein verified, that when Antichrist should come, the roots of the trees should grow upward.

John Standish, rewarded with his old job as Archdeacon of Colchester in 1558 after he had proved his renewed papalism, wrote in 1556 that the spirit of the Edwardian years had been the spirit of Babel, of human arrogance and ambition, whereas Mary's reign was a new Pentecost, presided over by God's Spirit, of unity and concord, in which community 'every member be member to all other'.[24]

Here then, are the very convictions already noted about what happens under a royal supremacy: in the loss of the traditional expressions of faith, the Mass, confession, a priestly understanding of the operation of pastoral care and spiritual counsel, and even of the papal supremacy, the carpet had been pulled from beneath the feet of English society to such an extent that confusion of every kind resulted; heresy became indivisible from treason; heterodoxy was the bedfellow of greed and individualism; reformed belief had dealt the fatal blow to social order as well as religious truth. Anyone wishing to assume an easy link and an obvious inheritance between Henrician and Marian Catholics must first understand this. For those who had clung onto traditional religion under Henry, the period of Edward's reign was an unmitigated disaster. John Harpsfield's second *Homily of the Primacy* was quite clear in tracing the root cause of the problem back to Henry and the break with Rome:

---

22 Edgeworth 1557, pp. 367–9.
23 Bonner 1555, fol. 41.
24 Christopherson 1554 (no pagination) and Standish 1556, conclusion (no pagination); see also Duffy 2001, pp. 96–100, on Hogarde and Edgeworth and Marian reflection on the loss of the Mass.

what miseries have been fallen amongst us, since our disobedience against the see of Rome, and since the time, that temporal princes did take upon them, that office, which is spiritual, and not belonging to the regal power ... I need not in words to declare, forasmuch as you have felt the smart thereof in deed.[25]

What the writings of the Marian religious authorities are aiming at, then, is indeed a return to late medieval religion, but in a way which respects its own historical context, and learns the lessons, positive and negative, of the previous thirty years. They begin with the Mass.

Sacraments and the priesthood

To those who were growing accustomed to the 1552 Prayer Book communion service, the re-introduction of the Mass would have seemed like a return to a very different age. To those who cared about the theology which underpinned such praxis, the change was even greater, and more significant. For the Marian writers root their understanding of the Mass in the miraculous, in the immanence of God and grace, and in a sacrament which effects real and discernible change in the faithful communicant. Far from the stark memorialism of the Edwardians, the defenders of the Mass under Mary emphasise the wonder and efficacy of the heavenly medicine the host represents. Bishop Bonner of London, whose definition Pole wanted disseminated throughout the land, describes the Mass as a place of spiritual nourishment, a place where hope and grace are conferred as aids to believers in 'this transitory world'. Writer after writer emphasises this efficacy of the Mass, in language and descriptions full of an apotropaic, miraculous, dynamic Eucharistic understanding from a previous age; the language of transubstantiation is widely and confidently used. John Harpsfield wrote two homilies in Bonner's collection, the first 'declaring that in the Blessed Sacrament of the altar, is the very body and blood of our Saviour Christ', the second simply 'of transubstantiation', arguing that 'impossible' stories in scripture, of what is hidden being revealed, lend support to the belief. Watson, Christopherson, Edgeworth and the anonymous author of the treatise on the Mass contained in the regime's official lay prayer-book, the so-called 'Wayland' primer, all declare their commitment to a belief in

---

25 Bonner 1555, fol. 54; see also Pendleton's sermon (no. 8) in the same collection, against Wooding's claim that the Marians admired Henry's reformism. I am grateful also to Professor Eamon Duffy for an early copy of his article, 'Cardinal Pole preaching' (Duffy 2016), which analyses Reginald Pole's 1557 St Andrew's Day sermon, including his memorable assertion that, under the Henrician schism, the English were denied any grace from the sacraments, even though they maintained them.

the Real Presence in its strongest form. In doing so, they encouraged the nation to 'stay us in the faith of the Catholic Church, that neither carnal reasons, grounded upon the feeble intelligence of man's natural wit, neither the deceitful judgement of our senses, should make us once to doubt of any one truth in Christ's religion, were it never so contrary to the course of nature, never so far above our capacities, and never so absurd to the appearance of our outward senses'.[26]

This re-instilling of the holiness of the sacrament of the altar was central to the reintroduction of the Mass to England. The Wayland Primer, issued with official authority, included in many of its editions *A plain and godly treatise concerning the Mass*, a work which crystallised many of the concerns and preoccupations of the age, especially in seeing the discord and liberty of the early 1550s as flowing from the abolition of the Mass. The unknown writer uses strong biblical imagery also to invest the host with miraculous and salvific power, an idea worlds away from any Protestant's understanding of what happened at communion:

> for if the corporal garment of our Saviour Christ touched with faith had virtue and power to heal the diseased, how much more power and might must needs the very presence of his immaculate holy and divine flesh and blood, have to help and heal the ghostly diseased when it is devoutly touched with constant faith and fervent charity.[27]

Authors such as John Aungell culled patristic sources to demonstrate the pedigree of the belief that reception of the sacrament brought healing, life and increase, and provided access points to the miraculous; the very moment of consecration itself shows the miraculous 'great good will of God towards us', that men's hands hold the Christ who sits in heaven.[28] Thomas Watson, in his sermons from early in Mary's reign, commented that the wonder of the Mass is that it works in the opposite way to all other human food: the consumed host converts human flesh into the 'immortal and lively' divine substance, rather than being subsumed itself into human flesh. The host is not merely a holy thing, Watson asserts, it is very holiness itself, accessible to humanity, the 'substance of all grace', as he later put it, a medicine for souls, a balm for sorrows, a guard against evil and, most of all, the joiner of the communicant into

---

26 Bonner 1555, fols. 57, 59–60; Watson 1554 *passim*, 1558 fols. xxxvi and Sermon Eight *passim*; Christopherson 1554 (unpaginated); Edgeworth (ed. Wilson) 1993, pp. 238–40. Wooding 2000, p. 167 argues that humanist elements in the Marian description of the Mass mean that a full understanding of transubstantiation is played down.

27 Primer 1555, sig. R ii; see also Duffy 1992, pp. 537–43, on the Primer's status.

28 Aungell 1555, fol. xix.

and with the body of Christ himself. With that in mind, Watson for one urged on his readers frequent reception, not as an annual custom or thoughtless ritual, but as a vital expression of faith, effective to work salvation and sanctification in the believer, and essential to unite him with Christ: 'the oftener he cometh the better it is'.[29]

The restored Mass, then, became the place of miracle, of a tangible and powerful holiness, and of the very presence of God, effective in the life of the believer, not just for increasing faith, but for the setting right of every human ill. There is no sense in the writings on the Mass of a gentle or incremental remedying of Edwardian excess. The reduced memorialism of Cranmer's 1552 service is swept away by a vigorously asserted and colourfully described doctrine of a sacrament conveying in full the grace it signifies. This renewed appreciation of the old Mass, described by Watson as the place where the faithful recipient is 'nourished to everlasting life, and made fat with God'[30] must have seemed a stark contrast to the language of the Prayer Book: for those who presented it, it was thought to be an area of major victory over the faith their opponents described.

This was not the only respect in which the Mass was described as dynamic and effective. As a riposte and a corrective to their fundamental critique of Edwardian England, whose social fabric frayed because its religious inheritance was lost, the Marian bishops and writers identified the Mass also as a key focus for community. Yet their idea of the community involved was broad, and drew on another element of traditional Catholic belief, a sense of the immanence of the saints. At the moment of consecration and reception, they contended, the community of saints on earth shares worship and fellowship with those in heaven. So Edmund Bonner emphasised the Mass as a joiner of living communicants with the departed, and saw the twofold purpose of receiving the host was for the recipient 'in this world to be a lively member of Christ, and in the life to come, to be co-inheritor with him in the kingdom of heaven'. Watson too saw the 'fellowship with angels' as a vital part of the profound spiritual experience of the Mass.[31] For it is Christ's body in which all people, living and dead, are brought together and joined in mystical union, reminded through his death of their charitable obligations to one another, and of their indissoluble oneness as members of a redeemed humanity. As with heavenly, so with earthly community: Edgeworth's lament for the loss of the kiss of peace in the Eucharistic liturgy, an act which signified

---

29 Watson 1554, sig. E v, and 1558, fols. xxxvi, liii and lxi.
30 Watson 1558, fol. ii.
31 Bonner 1555, sig. aa.iii; Watson 1554, sig. T iii.

and made this obligation real, has already been noted[32]; Christopherson, urging obedience to the queen on his readers after Wyatt's rebellion, abhorred the individualism of the Protestant ethos, and, talking of the abolition of the distribution of holy bread rather than the Mass itself, makes a strong case for that which 'put us in remembrance, that as those pieces of bread be all of one loaf, so we be all members of one body ... and knit together in one faith and one charity'.[33]

The re-introduction of the Mass and the renewal of a sense of its power and holiness, then, was a central plank in the Marian approach to restoring Catholicism. The language of the writers responsible for its rehabilitation, however, points to much more than the charge of 'legalism' which still haunts their work. Bonner, Watson and the rest were not simply imposing attendance at the Mass upon the English as a sign of their loyalty to queen, pope and true faith. They were not using the Mass purely as a 'central indication of Catholic loyalty',[34] a litmus test of orthodoxy. Rather, they wrote vividly, passionately and persuasively of the Mass as a powerful focus of numinous mystery, a contact point between frail humanity and gracious divinity, a centre of healing, renewal, community building and human regeneration. They made their appeal in the strongest terms, not just to enjoin participation, but to inculcate the beginning of understanding. Loades has noted Pole's belief that insisting on attendance at the Mass was the best way to revive and replant faith in the people's hearts,[35] and certainly parish priests and church wardens were responsible for ensuring attendance: but this is not the basis upon which the writers of the period proceed. Their rediscovery of the old faith, expressed in its most fundamental way, made a direct and powerful appeal to English hearts and minds. Bonner's resolution, expressed in his preface to the *Profitable and Necessary Doctrine*, that attractive expositions of pure faith are now more necessary to the English people than endless attacks on the Protestants, is borne out in this material; the English are invited to find in the Mass their direct connection to God restored.

Given the holiness and importance of the Mass as a place where the distances of space and time between Christ's death and the contemporary believer were collapsed, and his sacrifice made fully available on the altar, Marian writers stressed the need for worthy reception. Part

32 See above, pp. 42–3.
33 Christopherson 1554 (no pagination).
34 Wooding 2000, p. 116.
35 Loades 1991b, p. 272, where he contrasts Pole's view with Mary's commitment to preaching: there is no need to posit such a sharp difference of opinion, however: see Duffy 2016, and in particular his reassessment of Pole's views as expressed to Carranza in 1558.

of their strategy for that was a determined effort for the reintroduction and reinvigoration of the sacrament of penance. It was, nevertheless, only a part of the reason for their defence of what to the Protestants had been the unnecessary and unholy introduction of a middle man into the process of forgiveness and restitution. It certainly helped the communicant to receive worthily if he had confessed and been restored to divine favour, but there was deeper and greater purpose in encouraging penance too. For it was in the whole sacrament, of self-examination, discussion with a priest, absolution and the performance of satisfactory acts that the Marians vested spiritual healing for the individual and the reordering of society. As with the Mass, they began to encourage more frequent use of this sacramental channel of grace offered by the Church, that, as the exercising of faith became more than merely a loyalty badge, so the believer grew in grace themselves, and were increasingly held and nurtured within the Church and true faith by the learned habituality of its ceremonies and sacraments, constantly and attractively described as conveying the grace they signified.

This overwhelming, even at times overpowering, emphasis which the Marian writers placed on penance deserves greater notice. Roger Edgeworth, in his sermon *Entreating of Ceremonies and Man's Laws*, delivered in 1548 and rooted in the faith of the 1536 Ten Articles, had, whilst affirming the four sacraments unmentioned in the Articles,[36] spoken of baptism and penance as the only two necessary for salvation, leaving the Eucharist out of the equation. His stress on penance was necessarily greater, it being the antidote throughout life to the danger into which humanity fell through sin after a once-for-all baptism.[37] As Marian writers restored and defended all seven sacraments, they continued to labour the pre-eminence of penance. Of the twenty nine sermons of Thomas Watson's *Wholesome and Catholic Doctrine* dealing with individual sacraments, no fewer than eleven deal with penance and its associated activities, dealing with its general usefulness, encouraging sinners not to despair, warning against assuming God's mercy, outlining approaches to contrition, inward confession, priestly confession, satisfaction to a neighbour and post-confession living. Watson is at pains also in all of this detailed instruction to encourage frequent and serious self-examination as a continual way of life, bolstered and augmented by occasional confession to a priest and the use of absolution and satisfaction as routes into personal renewal. Bonner's section on sacraments treats first of penance, placing it above the Eucharist as the first and prime means of spiritual amendment and growth. Richard

---

36 That is, Confirmation, Matrimony, Orders, Extreme Unction.
37 Edgeworth 1558, p. 186–7.

Smith's *Buckler of the Catholic Faith* deals first with human free will, describing the penitential system as the avenue given for humans to increase in grace by co-operation with God, in fierce contradiction of the Protestants' 'hopeless' anthropology. In understanding the reason for this constant and strongly argued position, there lies a key to seeing the Church which the Marian writers were attempting to build and sustain.

As with some parts of their description of the Mass, the Marian writers consistently use medical imagery of penance and the penitential system. As with the sacrament of the altar, so with penance, they stress its extraordinary power to effect change: the priest is the dispenser of divine remedy to a wounded humanity. John Christopherson, defending Marian religion against the charges of the Protestants who, with Wyatt, had attempted to regain control by force, outlined the intimate connection between penance and the Mass; the former sacrament is a necessary and proper preparation to the latter, without which the believer could not attain to the awesome goal which was the aim of reception, namely participation in Christ's passion, and enjoyment of the healing and salvation it offered.[38] So also the treatise in the Primer asked why, if the Eucharist was a bare memorial, Paul had urged the Corinthians to self-examination before consumption, concluding that penance existed for just such a pre-Mass purpose.[39] Edgeworth too had connected the two, rounding on those who rejected, with a belief in transubstantiation, the Church's claims of the efficacy of confession, 'as though GOD were not able by his officer to deliver them from the prison and bondage of their sins' and criticising that view as much as that which denied the efficacy of a sacrificing priesthood. Penance for him was the 'necessary remedy to save [men's] souls', the 'true *Viaticum* meat to strengthen us in our journey'; priests are the enactors on earth of things ordained and ratified in heaven, and with the greatest power of all, to remit sins and pronounce absolution, by which humans have 'blessed regeneration and true liberty'.[40] Thomas Watson put it even more strongly, describing the effects of penance in a passage of considerable rhetorical and imaginative power:

> what a great power and virtue hath this virtue of penance, which by the mercy of God remitteth sin, openeth paradise, healeth the contrite man, maketh glad the heavy, revoketh a man from destruction, restoreth him to his former good state, reneweth his old honour, repaireth all the decays of virtue, maketh him acceptable and bold with God, and doth purchase of God more

---

38 Christopherson 1554 (no pagination).
39 Primer 1555, sigs. S iii and U i.
40 Edgeworth 1557, pp. 238, 250, 265, 347–8.

plenty of grace then he had before.[41]

Bishop Edmund Bonner too saw penance and satisfaction as the medicine which cured the underlying disease of sin, and not merely the symptoms. It was a system which the Protestants lacked, by which wrongdoers not only found restitution and restored harmony with God and others, but were also enabled to rise above sin altogether, provided they rooted themselves firmly within a frequent use of the penitential system. Quoting Chrysostom, he chided those who thought that mere repentance was enough, without reference to satisfaction or sanctification: 'it is not sufficient for a man that is wounded to pull out the dart out of his body, but he must also get medicines to heal the wound'. For Bonner, penance not only provides assurance of heavenly forgiveness, but, used properly, changes character and fosters holiness. So it did for Watson, whose eleven sermons cover every possible angle. As a riposte, rather than a concession, to the Protestants, he allows for private, inward, confession in cases of venial sins or scarcity of priests, showing that this has always been Catholic practice, coupled with daily prayer or repetition of the Pater Noster. Like a doctor seeing a sick man who is too poor to buy his medicine, and so provides for it himself, God sees the repentant sinner who alone cannot help himself, and meets him with an outpouring of healthful grace.[42] Indeed, the grace is prevenient, demonstrated to Catholics in the gifts of conscience, remorse, the desire to abandon sin, and the provision of the means to do so, even before the act of penance is begun. And, for those who are sick of heart or mind and do not feel this divine imperative to strive for spiritual health, God has cast down a 'chain' from heaven in the penitential system onto which they can cling. Using the same allusion as Bonner, Watson follows his imagery through, citing satisfaction as the medicine applied to the wound once the dart has been removed.[43]

In this vivid sacramentalism, vital elements of traditional faith are recovered and presented, not as approximations, but as a vibrant alternative to the comparatively bare formulae which were the product of Edwardian innovation. Alongside it, and part of it, were emphases also which belonged to the Catholicism from before the Reformation, but which were finding new currency and importance in the renewal of the old faith across Europe. The Counter-Reformation which Mary 'failed to discover' in fact expresses itself rather distinctly in some elements of these writings, and nowhere more than in those on penance. For, in the encouragement to believers to be more assiduous in self-examination,

---

41 Watson 1558, fol. lxxxii.
42 Watson 1558, fol. cix.
43 Bonner 1555, sig. Siiii; Watson 1558, fols. cxxvi ff. and cxliiii.

more committed to auricular confession to a priest, and more careful in restoring harmony through satisfaction, the Marian Catholics tapped directly into the Counter-Reformation at one of its deepest wells, and one very well suited to answering what they perceived as England's most pressing needs.

Roger Edgeworth's devotion to penance as he tried to hold the traditionalist line under the early depradations of Edward's ministers has already been seen; noting a connection between those who would abolish it, and the followers of the heretic Novatius, who similarly were taught to 'despise the second table or raft after shipwreck, that is penance', he frequently and consistently spoke of 'soul health', and the unavoidable necessity of penance and restitution. Rooting his argument in the need for a sacramental priesthood, Edgeworth argued from the first letter of Peter that the presbyter was the one invested with the divine grace which healed humanity, that grace which 'maketh the administration of the Sacraments effectuous and able to perform that they signify'. The spiritual fatherhood of priests is thus more to be honoured than that of earthly, carnal fathers, on the ground that they are the 'doers of that birth, which we have of God, and of that blessed regeneration and true liberty, by which we be made the children of God'. Jewish priests had the power only to discern whether the leprosy of their people had gone or not, not the power actually to cure it; Christian priests have both.[44]

In such a renewed priesthood, the agents of divine health for their flock, was placed great confidence and optimism, as those who would revive true faith and those truly faithful. Edgeworth had seen a traditional form of priesthood as a *sine qua non* for the enabling of his 'soul health', a focus of confession, from whom the words of absolution could be heard and believed as words of God, an arbiter of judgement and wisdom through whom the broken 'chain' between earth and heaven, and the fractured bonds of society, could be restored. More than that, the priest was for the individual a provider of comfort, strength, discernment, wholeness and an assurer of grace. The rediscovery of the priesthood had a profoundly pastoral motive and intention. So John Aungell, providing what in essence was a compendium of patristic proof texts for a sacramental Catholicism, for the benefit of parish priests, drew on early church notions of the pastoral nature of confession to a priest, and quoted Augustine, who described the priest to whom the believer regularly confesses as 'the partner of thy conscience'.[45]

We will examine later the centrality of parish visitation in the Marian restoration. An early pioneer in this regard, Bishop Bonner's 1554 articles

44 Edgeworth 1557, pp. 141, 339ff., 347–8.
45 Aungell 1555 (?), fol. lxxxviii.

for the visitation of his diocese of London had seen the resumption of the Mass and the reintroduction of penance as the two key aspects of his task. In them he had urged his clergy to exhort people to participate in both and then examine 'whether any person have refused or contemned ... to be confessed and receive at the priest's hands the benefit of absolution'.[46] Beneath the legalism lies a real pastoral intent, conveyed in the language of 'benefit', that only in the mode of guided confession established by tradition and antiquity does real peace and reassurance come. Bishop Watson also thought it important to understand how great a power was given to priests, in pronouncing absolution, that, in turn, their people might understand that such authority was given to priests not for their own sake, but for the sinner's, that 'his conscience may be quieted and he fully reconciled to almighty God'. In the sermon *Of confession to a man's neighbour, whom he hath offended*, Watson reminds his readers again of the need to believe that the priest absolves not on his own account but by God's authority, that the sacrament works in the believer the grace it signifies, that the words of absolution are words of God.[47]

The subject matter and genre of this material on the sacraments in general, and the twin pillars of the Mass and penance in particular, reveal important elements, of course, about the internal structure of the Marian restoration. It is an obvious statement, but a neglected insight, to observe that it was a priestly restoration, dependent upon a learned and lucid priesthood and disseminated through priestly channels. The Marian religious authorities were unashamedly and unapologetically sacerdotal, relying on a renewed priesthood for the renewal of traditional faith, and seeing the inculcation of their programme as 'top down', flowing from bishops to priests to people in preaching, catechesis, spiritual direction and sacramental observance. Thus, naturally, much of the printed material of the reign takes the form of sermons, by which the priests educated themselves and through which they would pass on the party line to their local congregations, unsullied by any passage through their individual interpretations or glosses. In addition, compendia of scriptural or patristic proof texts were produced to bolster the priorities of the regime. Edmund Bonner's dislike of slugging the argument out with his opponents in endless polemic and insult was a generalised one, as was his desire for good, colourful, catechetical material. They resulted in very little Catholic writing being published under Mary which was not predominantly aimed at presenting the old faith, for their own age, in appealing and attractive terms. Both in quality

---

46 Frere and Kennedy (eds.) 1910, vol. II, 335.
47 Watson 1558, fols. cxvii and cxxxii.

and quantity, Bonner's wishes seem to have been fulfilled.[48]

The refurbishment of a sacrificing priesthood under Mary lay naturally at the heart of the whole restoration of faith, and was the subject both of strict articles from the bishops and fierce criticism from Protestant opponents. John Bale, the one-man tabloid press of the reformation period, in 1554 published a *Declaration of Edmund Bonner's articles, concerning the clergy of London diocese whereby that execrable Antichrist is in his right colours revealed*, based on the bishop's first set of visitation articles. Bale's method was to quote each article, and then proceed to pour scorn on the sexual mores of both author and recipients as a tried and tested means to prove the abomination of the whole establishment. The solemn tones of the articles reflect the concerns of the Counter-Reformation, as well as a very Tudor concern for order and uniformity, demanding residence and energetic visitation from his clergy, emphasising the importance of the probity, order and integrity of their own lives, calling for transparency in their dealings in the parish, and ordering them to be particularly scrupulous in the administration of the sacraments, and in particular the Mass and penance. Bale weaves around this a tirade of accusations of sodomy, paedophilia, whoring and debauchery, and caustically questions Bonner's own parentage.[49] Bale's approach is to hope some mud sticks by being thrown in copious amounts; but his work, by including Bonner's articles, actually reveals the real priorities given to the Marian clergy. It also exposes the difference in rhetoric between the regime and its Protestant opposition. From that difference, much of the criticism of the aridity of Marian writing has come, but it rests on a misapprehension. The sermons produced for the growing intake of Marian priests[50] to preach to their congregations offered vibrant metaphors of the sacraments: they were described as being provided like the ring given by a master to a vassal as a sign of covenant and commitment, or as akin to the gifts of a prince to his army, in weapons, nourishment, medicine, encouragement and the provision of reinforcements.[51] They were not detailed allegations of libidinous excess. There is every reason to suppose that Jennifer Loach's assessment of the relative attraction and appeal of these two approaches is correct: Catholic writing under Mary, by self-consciously avoiding tit-for-tat exchanges, emerged the stronger.

Whether or not they worried about ongoing Protestant anticlerical-

---

48 Duffy (2016) notes Cardinal Pole's defence of the priesthood in his 1557 St Andrew's Day sermon.

49 Bale 1554, fol. 12.

50 Haigh 1993, pp. 215–16, notes a boom in the number of ordinations under Mary, after a decrease under Edward.

51 So Bonner and Watson respectively, in their general surveys of the seven sacraments; Bonner 1555, fols. Liv–Mi; Watson 1558, Sermon One *passim*.

ism, the leaders of the Marian Church carried on their programme, of renewing the priesthood in order to renew the faith of the parishes, with energy. Pole's legatine synod of 1556 famously included legislation for the establishment of diocesan seminaries for those 'intended for holy functions', and especially the otherwise uneducated poor, long before they became part of the Tridentine reform package.[52] The need for care in choosing and training priests, reflecting Christ's care in the education of his disciples, and the deference due to those who 'have such power as almighty God would neither give to the angels, not to any of the archangels, or to any other angels of heaven' had been the subject of a passionate sermon by Edgeworth late in Edward's reign, when such things were in disarray.[53] The publication of his work in 1557 demonstrates his ongoing concern for that very subject, and was supported in similar terms by Watson the following year. He devoted a sermon to outlining *In what estimation the Prelates and other ministers in Christ's church ought to be had of the people*, calling parish priests the 'causes of our spiritual life', and declaring that 'by them we are made Christen men, by them we have the true knowledge of God, remission of our sins, participation with Christ in the unity of his mystical body the Church'.[54] Watson's whole belief about the priesthood, in this and the preceding sermon, could be encapsulated in the idea that the sacrament of order was well named, and created and sustained order and unity in church and society by a clear, hierarchical structure of mutual responsibility and respect. It is difficult to know how effective the message was in the parishes; but it was central to the endeavour. It certainly would have had the semblance of greater novelty than the methods used to undermine it by its opponents.

One final word needs to be said of the rediscovery of the sacraments as described by the major Marian authors. That is that, sometimes explicitly, usually implicitly, they are offered as a radical critique of Protestant understanding of the nature and place of faith. Bonner's first concern in the *Profitable and Necessary Doctrine* was to describe real faith, the kind of faith without which it is impossible to please God. He highlights its ability to override the power of a reliance on human reason alone, which leads to blindness. Only an immature faith merely assents to a certain theology; faith which is tried and tested and true asserts itself in action. Bonner sees faith, or knowledge, as both the driving force behind obedience to God's commands, and also the residual force which remains after a falling from obedience. It is faith which drives the believer who

---

52 Dixon 1891, p. 466.
53 Edgeworth 1557, pp. 347–8.
54 Watson 1558, fol. clx.

has fallen away to the sacraments, places where faith meets and receives grace; the sacraments are the framework within which faith may be expressed, and where resources may be found to live faith out in charity and hope. In the constant battle and struggle of the Christian life, Bonner argues, the knowledge of faith is what drives Christians to obedience, and a reliance on the places where, in the Church, God's presence is felt. In all of this, he pours scorn on the notion of 'faith alone', a spurious concept alien to scriptural and patristic witness; it does not know of a faith which does not need the sacramental pattern of the Church to sustain Christians in their journeys, nor of one which by itself assures the believer of perseverance to the end.[55]

These two themes, of the correct nature of faith, as issuing in obedient action and sacramental observance, and of the right and secondary place of human reason, are liberally peppered throughout these works. A faith which, disabled by a Protestant reliance on reason, cannot bring itself to believe in the real presence of Christ at the altar or the power of the priest to absolve sin, is no faith. The cart has been set before the horse. And the 'faith' that offers only certain election or damnation to humanity, about which they can do nothing, is a counsel only of despair, not the gift of a gracious God. The Primer's treatise on the sacrament of the altar professed amazement at the inability of Protestant reason to accept the miraculous, wondering how they interpreted Christ's life, or even the gift of faith itself:

> thus shortly should we have no article or our faith unconverted and un-misconstrued: for all are above reason, yea if we should believe nothing else then that which should seem agreeable unto reason, we should have no faith at all.

'Faith alone' has meant no faith at all; 'scripture alone' has 'subverted all the Scripture'.[56] Richard Smith, more conservative than some, launched in his *Buckler of the Catholic Faith* a withering attack both on a denial of the miraculous, which lies at the heart of faith and sacrament, and also on the faith of the Protestants, which denies humanity's ability to co-operate in its own salvation, leaving it helpless to move towards God. Such faith removes any need for obedience to the sacramental system on the desperate premise that salvation and damnation are fixed, irrevocable and unchangeable.[57] Bishop Paul Bushe of Bristol, writing to Margaret Burgess, the woman whose after-dinner conversation had appalled him

---

55 Bonner 1555, Section One *passim*.
56 Primer 1555, sigs. X i and Y i; Edgeworth had used a similar argument, that if 'natural reasons' precluded a belief in miracle, then all faith was false, since the incarnation could not be allowed either; 1557, pp. 290–1.
57 Smith 1554, Part One *passim*, fols. 59–60; 1555, Part Two *passim*.

by its ignorance and error, reminded her that 'grace is of more force and strength than is nature'.[58] Roger Edgeworth's earlier complaint that people disbelieved the sacraments, because they were 'addict and wedded to their carnal senses',[59] became a commonplace as Catholic writers wove together two fundamental criticisms of Protestantism. The faith they offered and urged on their readers sought holiness by rooting itself in sacramental channels of grace, and understood that it offered the insight to holy and higher things of wonder and mystery that a reliance on mere human reason would destroy.

In the rediscovery and advocacy of the sacraments, and particularly those of penance and the Mass, the architects of the Marian restoration felt they found resources adequate to the several tasks before them. They saw them as correctives to the endless change in religion of the Edwardian period. For some, this was a return to a system rooted in antiquity and tradition, resonant with a proud and nostalgic familiarity; for others, mostly the young, the argument needed to be presented and described in dynamic and appealing terms. For all, the sacraments had to be renewed in a manner which either overrode or subverted Protestant polemic and the Edwardian experience through direct and vibrant appeal. For the sacraments represented not merely an assent to truth, not just a loyalty test, not only a rigid legalism, but a locus of healing, transformation and real human change. John Churchson spoke for the whole group of Marian writers when, in describing the true nature of the Church, he stressed the sacraments as places where there was real 'participation' in the divine truth and grace. Against the 'hopeless' theology of the Edwardian catechism, that man is unable to please God by any means, the Marians rediscovered the principle that *lex orandi* really does mean *lex credendi*; they placed their hopes, and efforts, for the success of the restoration of Catholic faith in the sacraments as channels of real grace in the richness and wonder of whose ceremony, theology and expectancy the English would forget the limits of their reason and the shallowness of the 'late Doctrine'[60] they had endured.

In addition, as has been suggested in connection with the Mass,[61] the sacraments for the Marians were supremely, though not solely, the place for the recreation of community and the renaissance of charity. Often implicitly, they rooted their understanding of the rise of division and the death of unity in the loss of a meaningful catholicity, whose figurehead was the pope, and in the return to an old faith which for

---

58 Bushe 1556, sig. B vii.
59 Edgeworth 1557, p. 240.
60 Churchson 1556, sig. H i.
61 See above, p. 44.

centuries had been largely unaltered, before Henry's advent, they saw their best chance of success. For this was not a project of Henrician Catholic renewal, but purely of Catholic renewal, a Catholicism rooted in centuries of praxis and universal consent. This was a re-formation of an old and stable community, the sacramental community focused on a sacrificing and absolving priesthood and expressed communally, in a united devotion in the presence of God in church and in a continual effort towards a profoundly social holiness in everyday life.

Any assertion that the Marian restoration had an extremely individualistic attitude, especially to the sacraments, seems therefore questionable. The writings of the period consistently claim precisely the reverse. They do so for the simple reason that the sacraments underpin their attempt to return England to an age *less* individualistic and *less* governed by private reason and opinion than that of Edward. Pendleton's and Christopherson's insistence that Edwardian heresy was inevitably responsible for sedition, dissent, rebellion and the loss of fraternal love in England have been outlined; Edgeworth and Gwynneth both saw the multitude of strands of opinion within Protestantism as a sign of its disease and the division in society to which it gave rise. Pendleton and Smith saw in the dissolved monasteries the setting in motion of this terrible train of events; for Smith, the monasteries had been the shapers of social cohesion and charitable provision, educators, employment creators, agricultural patrons, suppliers of soldiers and environmental conservators. The selling of them to the highest bidder was an act of outrage to the common weal, and an abomination to scriptural notions of Christian charity within a community. The remedies to this dislocation and fragmentation were: the Mass, in which the believer was encouraged to sense his union with all other believers, living and dead, in the body of Christ; penance, in which the priest actively reconciled neighbours to God and one another; and generalised acts of community religion, which asserted unity in diversity. In worship, the Latin prayers of the priest acted as 'umbrella' to the individual vernacular prayers of a whole community,[62] and a shared and common framework of belief, nurtured through orthopraxy, was reborn.

Even in this inculcation of communal charity, there was an expectation that the sacraments changed hearts and reformed lives; the spirit, received at confirmation, shaped a deeply charismatic community with its seven gifts and its godly wisdom. So at least urged Roger Edgeworth's early sermons, preached under Henry and published in 1557, on the gifts of the Spirit as ones which bonded and forged community. In a later sermon, the sixteenth on 1 Peter, Edgeworth used the story of the

---

62 The view of Christopherson 1554 (no pagination).

miracle worked by God with the oil and flour of the widow of Zarephath to demonstrate the way in which heavenly miracle and divine provision sustain and encourage those who practise charity, and undergird charity itself. In the twelfth of that series, he had asserted that loving the brotherhood meant not just loving individuals, but loving the whole, continually offering oneself that the unity and peaceable stability of the Christian commonwealth in its local situation might remain.[63] His powerful evocation of the charismatic power vested in the Church to make and maintain unity and charity finds many echoes in the Marian writings, as their authors sought to forge a new community, in which participation in holy things acted as the stimulant for concentric circles of mutual care and respect; so John Churchson wrote of the need for connectedness, reminding his readers of their need to be linked to Christ, the Church's head, and that 'the joints wherewith the body is joined to the head, be faith charity and the sacraments'.[64] Much confidence was placed in the sacraments as catalysts for mending the ills of the recent past and establishing the foundation for the future; taken on its own terms, the literature for communicating and feeding that intention possesses very considerable merits.

Other areas of belief; Philip of Spain and the papacy

There are nevertheless elements of traditional religion of which the Marian literature says little or nothing. Though deeply rooted in late medieval faith in many respects, the corpus often largely ignores much of the external apparatus of traditional Catholicism: the cult of the saints and the sanctity of their shrines, pilgrimage, the sign of the cross, Mary the mother of Jesus, prayers for the dead and monasticism. So too, there is very little discussion of purgatory, and virtually no attempt to revive it as an essential part of belief. The outstanding exception is Richard Smith, whose two part *Buckler of the Catholic Faith* saw a belief in purgatory, and more especially a realisation of the link with the departed which the Mass made possible, as essential, and stressed the efficacy of the sign of the cross in miraculous terms which were pre-Reformation in their Christocentric devotion and vivid concentration on the passion.[65] Smith is something of a lone voice, but that does not necessarily mean that he was a conservative maverick who spoke against the will of the

---

63 Edgeworth 1557, pp. 320–1; 281–2.
64 Churchson 1556, sig. J ii.
65 This feature actually had much in common with Marian writing about the Mass; cf. J. Harpsfield in Bonner 1555, Homilies Two and Three; Smith 1554, fols. 61 ff.; Watson 1554, fol. T iv; Bushe 1556, fol. B iv.

authorities. Mary had restored him to Oxford Regius Chair he had lost under Edward, and Lerinhad appointed him one of her chaplains; he dedicates the book to her. Also important are the returns of Nicholas Harpsfield's own visitation in the Canterbury diocese, which indicate that the traditional apparatus of religion, holy water stoops, the rosary, processions and church decorations, were being vigorously restored.[66] We will return to these in Chapter 4, as they may indicate that in such matters a decidedly 'grassroots', on the ground kind of approach was felt better than polemic writing.

This silence on material aspects of religion is reflected again in the emphases of the devotion of the Wayland Primers, which, in their caution around the miraculous and pre-Reformation Catholic practices like indulgences, have been described as being of 'sparer tone and less perfervid atmosphere' than their predecessors.[67] All this may have been for the same reasons outlined above: the urgent task was the re-imposition of a framework of sacramental behaviour, free from some of the extraneous elements which the Protestants delighted to attack with easy arguments based on a *sola scriptura* approach. The calendar restored by Mary's 1554 Articles had been that from the late Henrician period, trimmed down and shorn of some of its late medieval content.[68] In this, many have seen a wholesale return to Henrician Catholicism: Erasmian, reformist, essentially 'English' and uninterested in much of the late medieval past. Even if this description realistically encapsulates religion under Henry (and it does not), the Marian material seems rather to suggest a more complex picture, of a restoration based on and rooted deeply in the late medieval inheritance, indebted to a humanist reformist approach, but shaped and directed by the exigencies of the restoration. Marian Catholics were unapologetic about defending apparently outdated notions of sacramentalism and holiness, even if they had an instinctive sense of both the priorities and the necessities of a project of restoration.

It would also be wrong to assert that the writings of the period were faultless. Some of the writing, simply in terms of quality, is tedious and repetitive, resting on lists of scriptural or, more often, patristic material, repeated verbatim for its authority. Some, as for instance John Harpsfield's first sermon on the papal primacy, the ninth of those published with the *Profitable and Necessary Doctrine*, are written in a dull didactic style which does not leap off the page and which it is hard to imagine

---

66 See, for example, Whatmore (ed.) 1950–1, pp. 64, 68, 99, 101.
67 Duffy 1992, p. 540; the Marian authorities actually eliminated spurious indulgences and miraculous promises unfounded in tradition or scripture.
68 Frere and Kennedy 1910, ii. 328.

being received with excited approval by its hearers. The second instalment of Richard Smith's *Buckler*, published in 1555, a year after part one, is sketchier, less systematic and less colourfully engaging than the previous volume, even though it contains some points of greater quality. Some books deliberately set out to be compendia of handy texts for the use of priests and educated laity, such as John Aungell's *Agreement of the Holy Fathers*, a work whose provision of patristic witnesses to and authorities for the orthopraxy of the universal Church was designed to help mid-sixteenth-century Englishmen to see the truth of Augustine's old maxim that he would not have believed, but for the compelling nature of the consistency of the Church's practice.[69] To judge Aungell's work as tedious when compared to a Bale or a Knox is fair comment, but it is not to compare like with like: resource manuals are not polemical bedside reading. Bonner and others might even have been pleased to see the extent to which modern scholars have dismissed their work for its lack of polemical fire: in their determined aim of presenting a living faith and not maligning its opponents, they had been successful.

The major area, however, in which the regime itself and thus those who wrote to defend it found themselves under attack was that of national independence and identity; Protestant authors made a direct and strong appeal to Henrician notions of England's independence, distinctiveness and purity as a means to challenge Mary's twin obsessions: her determination to restore papal supremacy, and her passion for the Spanish husband she had married in 1554. In doing so, she had ignored all opposition in her single-minded attempt to draw a man she had come to love into an alliance to keep England Catholic, and rooted in Europe's deep streams of Catholic loyalty. Philip of Spain thus had to be defended; in defending him, the Marian writers were on ground exposed to enemy attack.

They chose several methods of defending the position England found herself in. Most tried to portray Philip as the provider of the continuity with continental faith England had given up, the prince by whose rule Englishmen would rediscover their unity with all of Christendom. So Richard Smith, in the first part of the *Buckler*, begins with a preface to the reader, in which he portrays Wyatt's rebellion as a symptom of the social anarchy under Edward, and obedience to Mary and Philip as its cure. Philip, as a head of state leading people to a new unity with Rome and thus with God himself, is almost a holy figure, rebellion against whom is rebellion against God himself.[70] John Harpsfield's sermon on the anniversary of the reconciliation to Rome tried to point up the ben-

---

69 Aungell 1555(?), sig. C i.
70 Smith 1554, Preface to Reader.

efits of the arrangement, focusing on Mary and Philip, with the help of Pole, as the restorers of the nation.[71]

The approach of John Christopherson was the most concerted and effective, when, writing after Wyatt's rebellion, he tried to redraw the perception of Philip entirely, independently of the normal portrayal of him as the facilitator of England's reunion with the rest of Europe. Tracing Philip's ancestry back to Edward III, and providing a family tree at the back of the book to prove his point, Christopherson contested that Mary's marriage to him was a profoundly unifying event, uniting England not just with her European co-religionists but also with her own history and past commitment to a religious and political catholicity. For, although his foreignness would have been no sufficient grounds for attack, Philip is not foreign at all, and in marrying Mary and assuming a measure of responsibility for England's rule he has been 'called home'. His connections with Mary go back on both sides, to a time when a monarch marrying outside the country was no strange thing, as indeed witnessed by Mary's own father's marriage to Queen Katherine, Mary's mother. Philip becomes the emblem of unity, of all kinds and in every sense.[72]

Christopherson's effort is the most ingenious and energetic, and cleverly exploited the uncertainty and tension after Wyatt's failed rebellion, but one wonders whether it could really have shaped the hearts and minds of the English, hostile to the reign of a foreign king. The power and ferocity of the works of the likes of John Knox and Christopher Goodman by 1558 had reached a peak of intensity, accusing Mary of the 'betrayal' of England into a foreigner's hands and expressing horror at the Spanish match which fed into the uncertainty of the whole situation: Philip had proved an absent husband, and the longed-for child had never come, an embarrassment to those who had written of Mary as Sarah, Hannah, or Elizabeth, the bearers of miraculous and chosen children late in life.[73] It is probably a sign of the effectiveness of the Henrician supremacy and its earliest apologists (including some of Mary's foremost minsters and bishops) that notions of English independent pride could be so appealed to by the Protestants; it is also a sign of the unprecedented situation which England faced with Mary, a queen regnant wanting to marry and provide an heir. The fact remains, however, that Mary's defenders had a hard time defending her marriage, and their attempts to do so remain one of their weaker areas. Many simply avoided the issue altogether;

---

71 J. Harpsfield 1556, sigs. B vi ff.
72 Christopherson 1554 (no pagination).
73 Knox 1558, p. 48; and Goodman 1558, pp. 33–4; on Mary's child, see, for example, Smith 1554, Preface to Reader.

only Christopherson managed an argument which rested on more than the assertion of the benefits of the reunion with Rome for which in any case Philip had not been responsible.

Another fault line, in Protestant eyes, was the subject of the papacy. Certainly, the kind of Protestant language and argument used against the popes and the Church of Rome had, by the 1550s, become firmly embedded in the popular imagination. Perhaps in England more than anywhere else in Europe, the strongly nationalistic tone of the royal supremacy had made a reconciliation with Rome more difficult to defend. The seeds of independence and pride in the distinctiveness of the nation had been planted and watered over more than twenty years; the English church, like the English people, was united by the single rule of a benevolent, godly and pious monarch, free from the contamination of foreign influences or the disruption of an alien church or its corrupt head. Much of the force of this is implied by Protestant writers of the Marian period, drawing on the deep well of opposition to Rome it had created. Henry VIII's removal of the papal supremacy wins him fans, but becomes implicitly assimilated with many other of his achievements, some of them not solely Protestant concerns. So the anonymous author of the 1554 *Dialogue or Familiar Talk* repeatedly praises him for his patronage of an English Bible, as well as his dissolution of the monasteries, and Gracyous Menewe saw his decision to divorce Katherine as crucial, even if the lines become muddied when he cites her successor Anne Boleyn as an example of one who suffered for truth as a minister of the gospel.[74] Protestant historiography saw England as a seed bed of all kinds of heresy too; the exceptionally tedious Anthoni DeAdamo (likely another pseudonym) wrote in 1556 that the extra-scriptural horrors of transubstantiation had been concocted in England by a diabolic conspiracy between Archbishop and Pope: but his historical accuracy is at best sketchy.[75]

The indefatigable John Bale gave the appeal to English anti-papalism its strongest spin, publishing in 1553 his *Vocation of John Bale to the bishopric of Ossory*, a work which rooted Bale's own heroic campaign against popery, with all its customary (for Bale) scatological and libidinous consequences, in the fight of the faithful remnant throughout England's history.[76] There is no end to Bale's pride in his own achieve-

---

74   *Dialogue* 1554, sig. B v; Menewe 1555a, no pagination.
75   DeAdamo 1556, fol. 236.
76   It followed, for example, Bale's earlier tract, *The Image of bothe churches*, which roundly attacked Tunstall, Gardiner and Bonner for their attempts to defend traditional faith, calling them those who 'hold up this glorious whore in her old estate of Romish religion'.

ments, as there is no end to his tirade of accusations of one kind of sexual excess or another against the Catholics and their priesthood. Bale describes his own experiences in Ireland, rejoicing in his afflictions as the papists rejoice in their excessive luxury. The popes, predecessors of the one to whom England is now reconciled, have polluted the pure faith brought to England by Joseph of Arimathea with their own blasphemies; Augustine came from Pope Gregory, the first of a 'swarm of monks' and 'like lazy locusts sprang forth of the pit bottomless' to be libertines, superstitious, and addicted to false ceremonial. Bale lists the most famous Archbishops of Canterbury, all contaminators of English faith, though a few possessing some creditable features. All, of course, were sodomites. He also taps into the image of Henry VIII which the propaganda of the royal supremacy had fostered, the Davidic champion of truth who threw the 'Goliath of Rome' from the land.[77] This kind of tone persists into the end of the reign, and in 1558 John Knox and Christopher Goodman made some use of similar themes and ideas. After pages of fierce denunciation of Mary's right or ability to reign, Knox links her with the 'pestilent and detestable generation of papists' to which she belongs and with which she is attempting to banish orthodoxy and scriptural Christianity. Goodman turns on Pole, the traitor who had fled rather than accept Henry's supremacy, and now returns to link England with a Spanish King and a foreign pope.[78] These were emotive modes of discourse which appealed to English pride, built on English nationalism and thus easily portrayed Mary as a disastrous return to a previous unenlightened age.

The apparent horror and disgust felt towards this English papalism seem to have rooted themselves firmly in all subsequent historiographical treatments of the Marian period. Most authors have assumed that the whole regime was tainted by its association with the renewed papal supremacy, and that what Loades calls Pole's 'wholehearted ultramontanism'[79] dictated the correct literary response of the regime's defenders. Trying to rescue their reputations, Lucy Wooding attempted to exonerate the Marian authors from the charge of actually having believed in the Roman supremacy by denying the importance of it in their work. She found a silence in their work on the subject, and suggested that even those who wrote explicitly in favour of the papal supremacy saw the pope as no more than an 'administrative' necessity, and not a spiritual head. Apart from Pole and handful of conservatives like Standish and John Harpsfield, the subject was mostly one to be 'passed over in

---

77 Bale 1553, fols. 2, 3, 12–13, 14, 15.
78 Knox 1558, fol. 55; Goodman 1558, fols. 33–4.
79 Loades 1991b, p. 368.

silence'.⁸⁰ Wooding detected a profound caution and even opposition to the pope in Marian religion which spread right up as far as many of its stoutest defenders.

It might be correct to imagine some unease at a popular level at the re-introduction of a system so deeply embedded in their subconscious as evil, heretical and perverse. But any assertion of a silence and caution from the authorities on the subject are demonstrably wrong. By any assessment, a good number of key writers assert the importance of the papacy for an English context, in some form or other. John Harpsfield contributed two sermons on the primacy to Bonner's collection, and Bonner's commitment was emphasised by his insistence in the 1554 articles for visitation that the Pope be restored to the missals and breviaries. Richard Smith lauded the reunion with Rome as testament to Mary's greatness, in 1554. John Standish's *Trial of the supremacy wherein is set forth the unity of Christ's Church* of 1556 was entirely devoted to proving his thesis, that any kind of unity depended on papal headship. Roger Edgeworth's 1557 sermons contained an assertion of the papal authority, presumably interpolated into the original Henrician script, in which he claimed that 'there be as well holy Scriptures as ancient writers, which proveth abundantly the said primacy of the pope'. John Churchson, in his *Brief Treatise* on the nature of the church, described the importance of the successors of Peter as the guarantors and producers of spiritual continuity and sacramental authenticity through a continual priesthood.⁸¹ Most of all, the regime tackled the issue head-on and boldly. Public declarations on the papacy were firm in their language, such as John Harpsfield's *Notable and learned Sermon*, delivered in St Paul's on the anniversary of the reconciliation with Rome in 1556. The sermon was intended as a model for use by non-preaching curates throughout the land in the annual national celebration of the reunion which was enforced in every parish; this was legislation which in fact prefigured later Protestant anniversary celebrations. It expressed the regime's commitment to the papacy and its desire to re-educate the people about it in the strongest way.⁸² Cardinal Pole's own 1557 St Andrew's Day sermon made the case for the papacy vigorously and unflinchingly.⁸³

Even those writers who do not explicitly announce their commitment to the papacy can be argued to have seen it as fundamental. Author

---

80 Wooding 2000, pp. 127–35.

81 J. Harpsfield in Bonner 1555, Sermons 9 and 10; Frere and Kennedy 1910, ii: 368–9; Smith 1554, Readers' preface; Edgeworth 1557, pp. 193–4; Churchson 1556, sig. J iv.

82 Duffy 2016: it also indicates Pole's commitment (often questioned) to preaching.

83 Strype 1721, vol. III, no. LXVIII, p. 492; see also below, Chapter 3.

after author cites the so-called Vincentian canon, St Vincent of Lerins's test of catholicity, that it was important to believe that which 'is every where, always, and of all generally received, observed and believed'.[84] The notion of universal historical consent as the foundation of true religion was a commonplace; it seems unlikely that, for these authors, an assent to the necessity of the papacy did not underlie their descriptions of catholicity too. Further, it is not clear what might be meant by an 'administrative' papacy: it is difficult to see how the restored papal supremacy could not have had spiritual connotations for those who championed its re-instigation, seeing in it their only bulwark, both against the kinds of heresy recently witnessed in England, and for the re-establishment of a competent, authorised, apostolic priesthood for the sacrament of the altar, the focus for the forming of Catholic identity. The sea change in English Catholic thinking after Edward was more significant than that.

Finally, there are signs that, by the end of the reign, new work was being produced which saw the need to present a strong case for the papacy by revisiting the disputes of the Henrician era, maybe as the need to settle orthopraxy in the parishes diminished. The difficulties Pole was already in by then, and the general paralysed state into which he and much of the church with him descended, after Carafa's accession to the papacy, are reflected in the decline of published work in 1557 and 1558. Yet Nicholas Harpsfield, by then established as one of the regime's best and most effective champions, had in manuscript two works which aimed to redeploy Henrician events as testimony to the correctness of the Marian course of action. The *Treatise on the pretended divorce* of Henry and Katherine was one, a thorough reinvestigation of all the issues, including the supremacy, and of their historical outcome. The other was connected with what was arguably the most important publishing event of the reign, William Rastell's 1557 folio edition of the complete English works of Sir Thomas More, published in the year of Pole's St Andrew's Day sermon and referred to within it. This, Pole's sermon, and Harpsfield's *Life of More* resurrected More as a figure of supreme importance for English Catholics, the somewhat reluctant papalist who had the prophetic wisdom and insight to see to what misery and decay a royal supremacy would lead, and gave his life accordingly. The next chapter focuses on these works, as crucial to our understanding of the papacy in England, and as further indications of the Marian impulses from which they sprang.

---

84 As translated by John Proctor (sig. D vii), the Marian church's keenest patristic scholar, whose *Way home to Christ and truth* of 1554 was purely a translation of Vincent with a preface by Proctor himself.

Conclusion

The Marian restoration of religion emerges from such a survey in rather better health than many have suggested: clear about its distinct identity, firm in its difference from its opponent, and focused on its priorities. Real, yet somewhat inevitable, weaknesses remain in both the content and some of the style of the works published under Mary, but so does much creativity and rigour, and a clear-sighted ability to focus on essentials. Coupled with the enormous progress made in the parishes towards the renewal of pre-Reformation religion, and the publication of impressive teaching material, Harpsfield's work on More and the divorce would have had potential for the continued shaping of English hearts and minds, especially when read in conjunction with More's own words, published simultaneously by William Rastell. But it came too late, into a church already at odds with Rome again, and to a country whose queen and papal legate were dying, and in despair, and was thus never published. In many senses these were the real failures of the Marian restoration: the advent of Carafa to the papacy and the premature deaths of Mary and Pole. These factors probably outstrip the disastrous public relations exercise that was the persecution of heresy, and any residual resentment about the role of Philip, who was by now absent from England altogether. The fact remains though, that the Marian writers advocated and extolled the foundations of the restoration, its renewed priesthood and sacramental system, before venturing onto some of its more exposed and unstable ground. Far from being embarrassed by those things, however, they launched a clear strategy late in the reign to address them.

When the citizens of Bridgnorth greeted the news of Mary's proclamation with 'great joy, casting up their caps, lauding, thanking, and praising God Almighty with ringing of bells and making of bonfires in every street', they reflected a widespread enthusiasm for her accession.[85] There is every reason to suppose that her unashamed Catholicism was a large part of her appeal for some, and not just her Tudor legitimacy. The rhetoric which her propagandists disseminated, about the horrors of social anarchy and the inherent instability of heretical belief which belonged to Edward's reign, seems to have found an audience ready to be convinced of its truth. It was certainly upon this belief that the whole Marian programme of religious renovation proceeded. That renovation, too, was well advanced, materially, and in the minds of the English people, by the time of Mary's death. Her misfortune was to die

---

85 Quoted from Hartshorne's extracts from the Register of Sir Thomas Butler, Vicar of Much Wenlock, by Haigh 1993, p. 205.

with the burnings of the heretics a strong memory and her ecclesiastical project unfinished. If we allow ourselves that most unhistoric luxury, a 'what if', and enquire what kind of Catholicism a long-lived Mary would have left England, the answer, based on the printed material of her short reign, would be: a dynamic one. It would have been rooted in the past yet responsive to the present, recognisably the old faith yet open to the energy which was revolutionising faith across Europe. It would have been, as John Churchson had hoped in 1556, a faith which drew upon both new and old elements of 'God's treasure'[86] in forming and inspiring English reconnection to the well springs of the rest of Catholic Christendom. It was in this Marian Catholicism, moreover, that Nicholas Harpsfield was rooted. His advocacy of its priorities and practices found first voice late in Mary's reign, as examined in the next chapter, but was to inform and shape every subsequent work as well, and, through him, Elizabethan Catholicism too.

86 Churchson 1556, sig. A ii.

✣ 3 ✣

'Profound judgement and deep foresight'
Harpsfield and the Legacy of Thomas More

Far from being a disaster that was somehow both insipid and persecuting, then, there is compelling evidence to suggest that the Marian restoration proceeded with a clear sense of priority. The literature of 1554–6 presented, attractively and enthusiastically, an essentially practical appeal for a return to orthodoxy. Even though evidence of a regime-directed management of what was published is minimal,[1] the literature demonstrates a basically shared approach, born out of pastoral (usually episcopal) concern and rooted in pragmatism and realism. At the heart of all that was being attempted was the need for the Mass to be restored to English parish life, and for a sacramental framework of faith to be rediscovered and renewed in the English religious consciousness. Edmund Bonner, Thomas Watson, Reginald Pole, John Christopherson and the others clearly thought that the overhaul of parish life and the revival of the Mass were the easiest and most attractive ways in which to argue the case for the return of papal supremacy. So, English parish churches and their liturgy were aglow once more with colour and image and traditional forms of ritual; so altars were restored to their former place and purpose; so the English were encouraged to renew their direct contact with, and access to, God.

Neither do suggestions that the Marian regime was reticent about explaining the theological foundations of its policy hold much water. The leaders of Queen Mary's restoration were perfectly clear about what they were doing, and why they were doing it. Vital to their whole-

---

1 A point made to me by Dr Thomas Freeman at a meeting of the Cambridge University Faculty of Divinity Church History Seminar, May 2002.

hearted re-acceptance of the supremacy of the pope was their own bitter experience of England's recent history. As the reign continued, and the old faith was re-established, English Catholic writers began to be less wary in making the supremacy, and its vital importance, more clear. In particular, their fiercely critical attack on the changes in religion under Henry and Edward became ever more fundamental to their self-understanding. Believing that the Marian restoration marked the welcome end to a period of devastating upheaval and sacrilegious experiment, they sought to write the history of the times through which they had lived. The project was intended to draw the lessons of the Henrician schism as the seedbed of Edwardian heresy; and it was designed to draw from the final faithful spokesmen of the medieval age a testimony vital for the future. Central to the project was Thomas More, and the prime shaper of it was his first biographer, Nicholas Harpsfield.

Harpsfield's *Life of More*, written in 1557 to coincide with Rastell's publication of the folio edition of More's English works, was never published in his lifetime.[2] It may have circulated in manuscript, but certainly never achieved the widespread dissemination surely intended for it. Neither did its companion volume, the *Treatise on the Pretended Divorce between King Henry the Eighth and Queen Katherine*.[3] Some scholarly attention has been paid to the *Life*; very little to the *Treatise*. Yet Harpsfield makes it very clear that he intends them to be read together. Drawing his biographical account of More to a close, he laments that his work 'waxeth long enough' without having properly examined Henry's divorce. He goes on:

> I will spare and forbear that discourse here, and add it afterward in a special and peculiar Treatise all alone by itself.[4]

The *Life* deals with More biographically, and especially with his stand against the royal supremacy. The *Treatise* deals in detail with the issues surrounding the divorce, but all as a form of apology for More's refusal to swear the oath connected with it and the supremacy. The basic thesis of both books, and the predominant feeling of the Marian religious leaders, is spelt out in the opening pages of the *Treatise*, in which Harpsfield observes that 'happy had it been for King Henry and the realm if he had never attempted to break and dissolve the said marriage, and had hearkened to the good, grave, and godly counsel of Sir Thomas Moore'.[5] A prophetic voice from England's recent past, Thomas More

---

2 N. Harpsfield (ed. Hitchcock) 1932, hereafter referred to as *Life*.
3 N. Harpsfield (ed. Pocock) 1878, hereafter referred to as *Treatise*.
4 *Life*, p. 213.
5 *Treatise*, p. 15.

is the mouthpiece through whom Harpsfield constructs his appeal to the English to learn the lesson of their and their leaders' sins, and to be reconciled to Catholic unity.

To these two books a third should almost certainly be added. After the momentous events of Thomas Cranmer's trials and execution, a short tract was written, though again, not in the event ever published, outlining his career and describing his final months. *Bishop Cranmer's Recantacyons*, written in Latin, was clearly intended as a piece of propaganda in support of the Marian regime and religious policy in the wake of the death of the man most responsible for leading England into heresy. Its nineteenth-century editor, while acknowledging its origin amongst Harpsfield's papers, rejected any suggestion that he was the author. Yet Gairdner's repudiation was based on error. He suggested that, since Harpsfield is mentioned in the third person in the text, he cannot be the author. The Harpsfield referred to in the text, however, is Nicholas's brother John, the 'theologiae doctor', and not Nicholas himself, whose own doctorate was in the law, and who played no part, as his brother did, in Cranmer's trial.[6] Other elements, as MacCulloch comments, point more clearly to Harpsfield's authorship, including his characteristically complicated Latin sentences and clauses, and his use in the tract of the work and person of More. While the purpose of the book is obviously partisan and polemic, its history, under closer scrutiny, appears also to be largely reliable.[7] More even than these elements, the words with which the author concludes his work indicate the purpose of Harpsfield, whose mind was already engaged in the More project, and for whom the recounting of the life of his hero More represented a far more agreeable task than the 'unwelcome and unpleasant' one of revisiting of the life and death of his anti-hero, the heretic Thomas Cranmer. He prays that 'may it fall to me after this to celebrate the life and achievements of good men, rather than be necessary to deal in my writing with the wicked crimes of sinners'.[8] There is every indication in all this that his work was taking shape and evolving in his mind, perhaps even as he wrote. The three works form a kind of late Marian triptych: the heresy of Cranmer, the disaster of the divorce and the stance of More, as didactic images, call-

---

6 N.[?] Harpsfield (ed. Houghton), *Bishop Cranmer's Recantacyons*, Philobiblion Society Miscellanies 1877–84, p. 23: hereafter referred to as *Recantacyons*.

7 MacCulloch 1996, pp. 584–5, 596; MacCulloch draws on the book fairly heavily in reconstructing Cranmer's last months, placing it alongside Foxe's equally biased account and other source material.

8 ['bonorum potius vitam atque instituta mihi posthac exornare liceret, quam sceleratorum nefaria crimina literis perstringere necesse sit'] *Recantacyons*, pp. 113–14.

ing on Englishmen to learn from their history and preserve their unity within Christendom.

David Loades saw Rastell's 1557 publication of Thomas More's English works as an essentially private project undertaken without the backing either of Cardinal Reginald Pole or the Queen.[9] When seen in the context of Harpsfield's work, however, which is at pains to commend Rastell's work to a wider readership, and of Cardinal Pole's contemporary oratory, a different interpretation of events begins to emerge. Pole himself claimed a close friendship with Thomas More. More's opposition to Henry's divorce, and the demise to which it led, had been the centrepiece of Pole's *De Unitate* of 1536, a work which made extraordinary claims about the voices of the martyred More and Fisher being stronger even than scripture.[10] Pole's devotion to More, and the closeness of their relationship, must have been intense, even allowing for the exaggerations of Pole's rhetoric.[11] Their shared fundamental convictions about Henry's appalling breach of the unity of Christendom led to execution and exile respectively: and the subsequent events of Edward's reign, witnessed by Pole from the European mainland, did as much to prove to Pole that he (and More) had been right as they did to prove to the 'traditionalists' that they had been wrong.

Harpsfield's own affection for Thomas More, and his growing conviction of the late Lord Chancellor's appeal and attraction for English Catholics after the schism, had been nurtured and fostered in exile with the More circle in Louvain. It may even have been there that his biography first began to take literary shape, nurtured by Harpsfield's close relationship to More's dear friend Antonio Bonvisi, a relationship later mentioned by Nicholas Sander.[12] When combined, however, with the equal commitment of his patron Pole, another friend of Bonvisi, for More the lay martyr, Harpsfield's work most likely assumed even greater importance. Harpsfield's closeness to Pole, and the personal authority the association had brought him by 1557, should not be underestimated or overlooked. As Archdeacon of Canterbury, he largely oversaw the diocese both before and after Pole's return; but his was a post with particular authority, even above other archdeacons. The diocese of Canterbury was unusual in having only one archdeacon, firstly, but the post also gave its holder the right to hear certain confessions, and the

9 Loades 1991*b*, p. 288.
10 Gregory 2000, pp. 265–7.
11 Mayer 2000*a*, p. II:60; 2000*b*, pp. 24–6, 47; Pole referred to More throughout the *De Unitate* as his 'best friend', based on a relationship which Mayer dates back to Oxford in 1518.
12 *Life*, p. clxxx and especially note 3; see pp. 138–9 for Harpsfield on Bonvisi and More.

power to install suffragan bishops throughout the province.[13] Harpsfield, further was on an upward trajectory, acquiring new preferments and appointments from the Cardinal up until the end of the reign, by which time he was, in addition to archidiaconal responsibilities, Dean of Arches and the foremost detector of heresy and enforcer of orthodoxy in the land. As Mayer says, to judge by Harpsfield's career path, he and Pole 'must have been close'.[14]

The timing of Harpsfield's work is thus significant too. The *Life* was completed in 1557; it points towards Rastell's folio edition of More's English works, and its sentiments were echoed by Pole's assessment of More in his St Andrew's Day sermon of that year, which used More as a central figure in its appeal to its hearers. Pole described More, 'for his wit, virtue and learning, most esteemed of any temporal man within the realm, and no less esteemed in other realms, for the fame of his virtues', nevertheless allowed by God 'to be assaulted of the envy of Mankind ... only to make him leave the Unity of the Church, as greater Temptation could not be come to a man: Yet to overcome all, showing such Constancy of Faith, as he might be a Miracle, marvellous Example, to stay all other'.[15] This cannot all have been coincidental. Rather, as was suggested earlier, the Marian religious authorities began to turn their attention in 1556–7 to the need to reinforce the papal supremacy in the minds of the people. They chose Thomas More as the iconic lay martyr through whom to make their appeal. Harpsfield was at the centre of this programme, writing a trilogy concerning the divorce, Cranmer's leading role in it and subsequent punishment, and the prophetic opposition to it of Thomas More.

Harpsfield's patronage of Rastell's 1557 work, similarly, would have been of no small importance. He claimed, indeed, at the end of the *Life* that the papal supremacy was a subject in which people were now 'riper and more fully instructed', perhaps indicating the regime's deliberate strategy of education implied by Pole's sermon.[16] In the light of these clues, and given Harpsfield's closeness to Pole, and his position as a member of Pole's 'inner administrative circle', intriguing questions emerge about the extent to which the writing of the works actually occurred because of 'official' backing and direction. The most conclusive piece of evidence appears at the beginning of the *Recantacyons*, when the writer claims to be working at the request of one 'to whom I ought to refuse nothing', a remark which, whoever he has in mind, implies

---

13 See Whatmore (ed.) 1950, vol. I, p. 4, for a more detailed discussion.
14 Mayer 2000a, pp. XII:206, XIV:432; 2000b, p. 290.
15 Strype 1721, vol. III, p. 243; see also Duffy 2016.
16 *Life*, p. 213.

some sort of official commission by a higher authority.[17] If Harpsfield is assumed to be the author, then the suggestions, both of a lack of any 'central' organisation of religious propaganda, and of the essentially private undertakings of Harpsfield and Rastell, begin to look dubious. It even starts to seem more likely that the More project was undertaken through the direction of Pole himself, and as a new impetus in the ongoing re-education of the laity under Mary. The work on More enshrined many of the basic convictions of the Marian religious authorities and disseminated them to the populace through a figure at once authoritative and attractive, holy and honourable, a figure whose stance was now authenticated by the glow of martyrdom. As with the diocesan visitations in Canterbury, so with official propaganda: Harpsfield's skills were central to the progress of Pole's purposes.[18]

Eamon Duffy has more recently further demonstrated the weight of the case, that Harpsfield's biography of More and the *Treatise* were part of a more concerted and officially sanctioned project, focusing on the martyrs of King Henry's reign, those who resisted the royal supremacy and the royal divorce even unto death, as a counterpoint to the heretics being executed at the time. To suppose otherwise, he claims, is now 'inconceivable'. More, as presented by Harpsfield in the *Life*, offers Marian readers a perfect sense of what true martyrdom looks like, and a reminder of the Augustinian tenet that it is always that cause for which one dies, and not the mere fact of death itself, that makes the martyr. As we will see, the very Marian project of ensuring that the reign of not only Edward VI but also Henry VIII was seen in its true light, as a period of descent into heresy and sedition, would be perfectly served by the story of More. Not only that, but More's life and death would point Harpsfield's readers to the root cause of all the evil the fallout from which they were still attempting to heal: the King's 'Great Matter' of the divorce from Queen Katherine.[19]

History or hagiography?
Harpsfield, More and his contemporary critics

Thomas More is a figure whose reputation has been subject to careful and often critical scrutiny in recent years; because of a failure to understand him in the context of his own times, and in the light of his writings

---

17 *Recantacyons*, p. 1.

18 Wizeman 2002, pp. 68–71, argues for a greater co-ordination and an element of royal authority for what was published under Mary, despite its apparently disparate nature.

19 Duffy 2009, pp. 179–85; see also Houliston 2011, p. 43.

and work against heresy, the saintly picture of him which made its way into the twentieth century has been challenged. At a popular level, this is understandable enough, but aspects of the 'rediscovery' of the real More seem to have made their way into scholarly discussions of him too. In the unearthing of the real More, attention has often focused on his earliest biographer, Harpsfield himself, and at his feet is laid the blame for transmitting to posterity an unbalanced and unreliable picture of the man he came so to admire. Yet it is just as important to understand Harpsfield's own work in its context, and to be wary of jumping to condemn him for unreliability. For his work on More and his times is a vital and neglected window onto the heart of the Marian restoration of religion, and turns out in many essentials to be more reliable than his polemical purpose might suggest.

It is the question of Harpsfield's use of the theological and ecclesiological thought of More himself that most needs to be examined. There is a widespread suspicion of biography written with a polemical intent, criticism which is actually largely unjustified in this case. One of Thomas More's most comprehensive recent interpreters has identified Harpsfield's project as the source of much of the misunderstanding which still surrounds the Lord Chancellor's life and work:

> As the biographies of Roper and Harpsfield testify, the myth-making possibilities in More's life and death were far more important to his followers than the particular intricacies of his thought.[20]

On this view, Harpsfield's assessment of More's work proceeded upon 'deductive' lines, an approach unclouded by any critical engagement or objective perspective, and was therefore profoundly misleading to his own and succeeding generations. Rastell's labours in making More's English works available to an English public was a work undertaken 'not for their actual intrinsic matter, but for the doctrines they could be taken to embody in the minds of the counter-reformers': whatever Fox means by this.[21] Certainly, at the heart of such a purpose lies hagiography, and it is for this, and for the error which it indubitably produces, that Harpsfield stands accused.[22] Yet he was, in fact, a biographer careful to rely on the evidence of the *ipsissima verba* of his subject, as will be seen.

20 Fox 1982, p. 254.
21 *Ibid.*, pp. 1, 3, 114–16.
22 It is worth noting that even attempts to defend 'hagiography' as a valid historiographical technique come unstuck. So Greene (1971), pp. 199–200, says that 'it need not be a pejorative term': but almost immediately concedes that the author is forced, sooner or later, to 'fall into the role of the myth-maker'.

Nicholas Harpsfield

Others have added different, distinctive, elements to such criticisms. Thomas Betteridge's literary study of the historiography of the English reformations devotes a section to the *Life of More*, a book whose blatant purpose is the creation of what he calls a More 'mythos'. It is for the book's apparent lack of a coherent historicity that it is most criticised here; Harpsfield's account of the trial and execution of his subject is described as an 'escape from history'. In other words:

> More, the exemplary virtuous politician, the writer of *Utopia*, the perfect family man, becomes More the martyr.

This is to suggest that Harpsfield is guilty of the 'sidelining of spiritual and religious issues' in his description of the profoundly secular events which initiated the English reformation; for him, it is claimed, the reformation represents a 'largely secular event that produced religious effects almost by chance'. Harpsfield's work fails because it defines the Marian Church's predominant characteristic as a knee-jerk reaction against all that was done under Henry: the events of the 1530s are thus still defining and determining the Church's 'structure and status'. Yet, as will be seen, Harpsfield's main concern is for the spiritual and religious issues which lay at the heart of Henry's schism and its motives. The literary-critical flights of fancy upon which Betteridge's work is based, moreover, seem to miss its main, historical, function and purpose, dwelling on the possibilities of metaphor and allegory implicit in the work rather than its explicitly stated intent. The latter line of enquiry is more fruitful and more reliable.[23]

A number of separate but related criticisms are made in such views which are based on an inadequate understanding of the full scope and the actual content of Harpsfield's work; neither is his Marian writing placed in the context of that time and the work of his colleagues and contemporaries. In the first place, the profoundly polemical nature of *all* published work on religious matters in the first half of the sixteenth century ought to be fully recognised. It is ironic that the same author who lambasts Harpsfield's hagiographical myth-making of More seems to swallow entire the version of him offered by John Foxe, whose own intentions should be clear. Indeed, the main point at issue, More's treatment of heretics, is not an area in which Harpsfield makes the slightest effort to conceal anything; on the contrary, he is proud of his man's credentials.[24] And Harpsfield's polemic is derived, as will be demonstrated,

---

23 Betteridge 1999, pp. 130–6; see, for example, pp. 130–1 on the story of the 'deflowering' of the virgin.

24 Fox 1982, pp. 114–20; he cites Foxe's view of More and asserts that 'as much as one would like to ignore it, one must concede that More did display lack

from the deeply polemical work of More itself, sometimes quoting it directly. Harpsfield's eager expectation of Rastell's publication, and his directing his readers towards it offer a very different construction than a deliberately distorting purpose on his part. Rastell himself had prefaced the book, in dedicating it to the queen, with an expression of his hopes for it: that it might reform true Catholic doctrine in English hearts, and encourage godly habits in them too. His concern is for posterity, in the hope his uncle's writings will play their part in Mary's extermination of heresy which, if her reign lasts, he foresees as being likely to be entirely successful.[25] Rastell had even employed Thomas Paynell to index the large tome, so that individual topics dealt with by More could be easily accessed. These are not the words or actions of men in the business of twisting the theological legacy of a spiritual hero.

The predominant thrust of the criticisms made of Harpsfield's work on More, though, remains the charge of 'hagiography'. The word is used by his critics interchangeably with 'myth-making', to indicate the deliberate falsification by Harpsfield of the truth of More's life, thought, and death, the self-conscious twisting of the facts by which More becomes an empty but holy vessel, ready to be filled with Marian polemic of a kind profoundly at odds with More's actual convictions. As such, it is a criticism which needs to be challenged, as lacking a proper understanding of Marian Catholicism, as well as of the extent of Harpsfield's project, and his fidelity to his subject. An examination of the work reveals that Harpsfield's theology, in fact, is consistently dependent on the very works of More that Rastell was labouring to publish, and that the fundamental convictions which led More to his death were those which underpinned Harpsfield's own writing well beyond the death of Queen Mary.[26] Further, in the themes of martyrdom and the attack on pseudomartyrology which the work on More and Cranmer constituted, Harpsfield was carrying forward earlier Catholic work on the subject, and laying the foundations for his assault on John Foxe ten years later. Scholarship which takes Foxe as the creator of the martyrological genre should pay closer attention to these works. If, then, Harpsfield's purpose was not so much hagiography (as defined by Fox, Betteridge and Greene) as the accurate distillation of More's thought for a Marian readership, what in fact were the main features of such a work?

---

of charity and an almost demoniac violence towards his opponents'. This view fails to understand contemporary attitudes to heresy and interpretations of charity and is too uncritical of Foxe himself. See Chapter 4 below. On Pole's own evocation of the burnings, see Duffy 2016.

25 Rastell 1557, *Letter Dedicatory*; *Life*, p. 100.
26 See below, Part III.

The death of traditionalism: Harpsfield's authorial motive

Central to the inspiration and purpose of these three works was Harpsfield's share in the experience of English Catholics, and especially the so-called 'traditionalists' who had attempted to argue for the retention of the practice of medieval Catholicism whilst accepting (with whatever motives) the royal supremacy. Indeed, the books themselves make no sense unless viewed in this perspective. More, Fisher and Pole represented a minority view in the events surrounding Henry's divorce and eventual assumption of ecclesiastical control, but a minority view which came to be seen by Catholics as indisputably correct. We have already paid close attention to the retrospective view of the effects of the royal supremacy, surveyed by Marian leaders from 1553/4. By the time of Mary's accession, they saw, to a man – and woman – that utter devastation of England's Catholic culture and identity. As can be quickly discerned from the Marian literature, it was the abolition of the Mass which most heartbreakingly brought home to Catholics the true character and effect of what had gone before.[27] The plain communion tables of the early 1550s, set length-wise down the chancel, most graphically represented the abandonment of unity and truth in Edwardian England. Ironically, it was Cranmer who expressed the position of the 'traditionalists' most devastatingly, when he said to Gardiner that, with Henry dead, 'you stand post alone, after the fall of the papistical doctrine, as sometime an old post standeth when the building is overthrown'.[28]

This was the starting point for Harpsfield's work on Thomas More, and his *bete noire*, Thomas Cranmer. This was the basic conviction which underpinned Harpsfield's flight to Louvain in 1550, where he lived with members of the More family and where he began to understand more clearly the thought of More, and his undeniable foresight in the matter of the divorce. This was the experience which brought home to him, as to those bishops deprived of oversight and under house arrest or imprisonment, the essential nature of the papal supremacy. As such, it indicates the extent to which, without apology, Marian Catholics saw the need to understand the Edwardian heresy as rooted in Henrician schism, and to draw on medieval notions of the Church to rediscover integrity.[29] His horror at England's swift descent into schism and deepening heresy underlay both his unstinting participation in the Marian restoration, and

27 See above, Chapter 2, pp. 41–7.
28 Quoted by MacCulloch 1996, p. 492.
29 *Pace* Betteridge, therefore; see above, p. 76. It also suggests that more was at stake than a campaign to have More canonised, as suggested by Elton 1984, p. 171.

his writing of the definitive history of the disastrous preceding years, through the 'lens' of the martyred layman, Thomas More.

As we have also seen, such a conviction informed and motivated all the Marian religious authorities, most of whom, unlike Pole, had acquiesced in the royal supremacy, only later to realise the truth of More's resistance and the significance of his death. They thus articulated their complete rejection of any future royal supremacy, together with the agreement that the Henrician and Edwardian experiments had been an unmitigated and dangerous disaster; such were the agreed foundations upon which they built. Far from finding a disparity between their world view and the 'changed environment of Marian England' which undermined them,[30] they saw, rather, that their world view, in terms of orthodoxy and orthopraxy, *needed* the policies of a Marian England if it was to resist heretical advance and survive intact. It needed a rootedness and a connection with the continued consensus of all Christendom which only obedience to Rome could provide. This was the lesson of bitter experience. And to record this bitter experience for posterity, to ensure it was never repeated, Nicholas Harpsfield undertook his project concerning Thomas More: for More's work, preserved through the very exile in which Harpsfield had shared, resonated for post-Edwardian Catholics with a new authority and truth.

The beliefs and insight of Harpsfield's More

Harpsfield's *Life of More* was based upon the short account of More's life provided by William Roper, More's son-in-law. Harpsfield augmented it, with letters and reminiscences from Erasmus, Bonvisi and others, with his own observations and stories from other sources, and, above all, with allusions and quotations taken directly from Rastell's forthcoming edition of More's works. The focus of the *Life*, occupying approximately a third of its length, is More's 'passion': detailed accounts, taken from More's correspondence and contemporary accounts, of the trials and interrogations of More in his final months, of the thought and convictions which underpinned his stance, and of his final condemnation. His purpose in the preceding pages is to provide a survey of More the family man, scholar, and statesman, including sections devoted to his public life, his wit, his writings, and, most briefly of all, his circle of friends. In all of this, the express purpose is to be as accurate about the subject as possible, as Harpsfield states to Roper in the preface: and he shows anxiety about his ability to do so. Indeed, it should be borne in mind that for seventeen years after his death, the memory of Thomas More

---

30 Macek 1996, p. 165.

was held in scorn by England's religious authorities, and his reputation attacked. The task of bringing to light the true nature of his resistance to the king and his religious and political convictions was not as straightforward as many suggest, and significantly rewrote what was by then the established view. Harpsfield's claim to be publishing 'things now come to light of this worthy man'[31] makes more sense in such a context. Indeed, he specifically deals with the claims of Henrician councillors and reformers alike at More's trial, that More made money from the clergy, that he was a 'busy body', and that he was involved in sedition and treachery in cases like the Nun of Kent. Far from a myth-making falsification of the record, Harpsfield saw his task as the recovery of the truth, both about Henry's divorce and More's resistance to it.

The *Life* breathes a remarkable air, a mixture of a traditional description of a holy man ('hagiography' is a word best avoided) and a political biography of a great statesman; its purpose is to show More's possession of both qualities. More's great legacy becomes his insight, and his ability to see, where most did not, to what a royal supremacy would lead: and that is the sharp focus of the book; interludes about his family life, his scholarship and even his career serve really only to embellish that purpose. Harpsfield makes clear his conviction that More was indeed a great statesman, a shrewd judge of events, perhaps even the most glorious lay man of any age,[32] but also that this ability was profoundly rooted in his religious life. More saw the way things in England tended; he saw the heart of the king and those around him; he saw the motivations and secret desires of their hearts; he saw, supremely, that separation from the rest of Christendom for the sake of private lust or cherished ambition would spell disaster. In this lay his distinction as a statesman as well as the seeds of his martyrdom. So, Harpsfield describes More's distrust of the king's overwhelming affection for him, his conviction that, nevertheless, 'if my head could win him a castle in France ... it should not fail to serve his turn'. So he foresaw to where Cranmer's introduction of oaths would lead in the matter of the Pope's non-involvement in the divorce; so he realised that Anne Boleyn merely served to scratch a transitory itch of the king, and would herself suffer a savage end when he so decided.[33] So, supremely, he handed down, in the Tower works, the raw materials of religious faith which would 'stir and prepare the minds of English men manfully and courageously to withstand, and not to shrink at, the imminent and open persecution which he foresaw, and

---

31 *Life*, p. 6.
32 A claim made in the *Life*, pp. 11–12, 209.
33 *Ibid.*, pp. 25, 72.

immediately followed, against the unity of the Church and the Catholic faith of the same'.[34]

Harpsfield goes further, though, in his discussion of More's powers of foresight. Talking of More's views on Anne Boleyn's inevitable demise, he reflects that the knowledge came by 'some private and secrete revelation and divine information' as much as from 'any worldly and wise conjecture or foresight'. He quotes directly from More's *Supplication of Souls*, a passage in which More seems to predict exactly the kind of descent through heresy and into anarchy which had characterised the Marian understanding of the Edwardian years, as exemplified by Christopherson.[35] More had written:

> then shall all virtue be had in derision, then shall all vice reign and run forth unbridled, then shall youth leave labour and all occupation, then shall folk wax idle and fall to unthriftyness, then shall whores and thieves, beggars and bawds increase, then shall unthrifts flock together and swarm about, and each bear him bold of other, then shall all laws be laughed to scorn, then shall the servants set naught by their masters, and unruly people rebel against their rulers. Then will rise up rifling and robbery, murder and mischief and plain insurrection, whereof what would be the end ... only God knoweth.[36]

Given such a remarkable parallel, it is hardly surprising that More's prediction of the consequences of the royal supremacy took on such a crucial importance in the Marian task of preventing another one. What Harpsfield calls his 'grounded and profound judgement ... deep foresight ... and, as it proved ... sure aim of the lamentable world that followed'[37] amply demonstrates the qualities which made More such an icon for post-Edwardian English Catholics.

More's allegiance, or lack of it, to the pope is nevertheless a vexed subject. Scholars of his writings and thought have difficulty in teasing out from his works the precise nature of his views in this area. Certainly, he lacked the apparent ultramontanism of John Fisher, but the fact remains that his convictions were in the end strong enough to lead to his death for the cause of a continuing English obedience to Rome. Harpsfield elucidates some of More's intellectual struggle in this area, his efforts to come to an accommodation with Henry's wishes, and his

---

34 *Ibid*, pp. 132–3.
35 See above, Chapter 2.
36 *Life*, p. 71; Rastell 1557, p. 313.
37 *Life*, p. 67; Pole described More's foresight in similar terms, in his 1557 sermon, as an 'instinct that the fear of God had put in his minde, when the unity was not yet broken', Strype 1721, vol. III, p. 244.

eventual, even reluctant, failure to change his own conscience. There are even hints and clues in Harpsfield's work which ought to help us to see the acknowledged reluctance of More's eventual commitment to the papacy as part of his attraction to the Marians. There is certainly no sense of what one scholar breezily calls his 'papalism', to which he clung, even in its corruption, as a force for good.[38] Harpsfield makes it perfectly clear that More did not 'cling' to the papacy, but rather to the importance of unity and consensus within Christendom. Only at the end did he come to see that the papacy was a *sine qua non* of that unity.

One might look, for instance, at Harpsfield's description of More's dealings with Henry over the pope. It is a passage which reveals More's innate uncertainty about how to treat the subject, and his willingness to agree with the king if he could find any worthy precedent. Most famously, perhaps, Harpsfield asserts that More had urged the king to be more cautious on the subject of the pope's authority in the writing of the *Assertio Septem Sacramentorum* in the early 1520s. He was accused, along with having helped and abetted the Nun of Kent, Elizabeth Barton, of 'unnaturally procuring and provoking' the king to write the book, thus putting into the pope's hand a sword with which to wound Henry later. More's reply had been interestingly nuanced, and Harpsfield bases it on Roper's own account:

> I was ... after it [the *Assertio*] was finished, by His Grace's appointment and consent of the makers of the same, only a sorter out and placer of principal matters therein contained. Wherein when I found the Pope's authority highly advanced, and with strong arguments mightily defended, I said unto His Grace: 'I must put your highness in remembrance of one thing, and that is this. The Pope, as your grace knoweth, is a Prince as you are, and in league with all other christen Princes. It may hereafter so fall out that your grace and he may vary upon some points of the league, whereupon may grow breach of amity and war between you both. I think it best therefore that that place be amended, and his authority more slenderly touched.'

Henry had refused, however, and surprised More by going on vigorously to assert that his own 'crown imperial' was derived from the see of Rome, a view, More is supposed to have said, that he 'never heard of before'.[39] Marius for one sees no reason to doubt this story, and adds that Chapuys reports that, after More's repetition of it in the interview about Barton, his pension was stopped.[40]

38 Wooding 2000, pp. 7, 120.
39 *Life*, p. 159; see also pp. 150–1 on the divorce.
40 Marius 1984, p. 454.

Harpsfield provides, also, some evidence that More made serious efforts to accommodate himself to the king's wishes, out of loyalty to and affection for him. In his account of More's final trial, he draws on the Paris News Letter version, as well as Roper's versions and the accounts offered by More himself, and the end result, as Chambers notes, though something of a mere conflation, seems to bear the stamp of authenticity.[41] Challenged by Audley about his own obstinacy in refusing that which the bishops (Fisher excepted), universities and learned men of the realm had accepted, More replied that 'these seven years seriously and earnestly he had beset his studies and cogitations upon this point chiefly, among other, of the Pope's authority'. Trying hard to find a precedent for a temporal ruler taking supremacy over the Church, or for any patristic backing for such an endeavour, he had drawn a blank. Any number of living bishops and learned men were as nothing compared to the thousand thousands of those departed who had never contemplated such a breach with tradition.[42] On any reading of his own writings, this is classic Morian thinking: a decision reached by careful consultation of patristic authors in particular, a decision mindful of his twin mantras of unity and consensus of time and place, and a decision undertaken at all out of loyalty to his prince. It also reflects Pole's sermon, which drew on Bonvisi's account in describing More's gradual recognition of the centrality of the papacy, and is therefore indicative of the broader Marian strategy suggested above, to win over the people step by step. More's decision was an important model, displaying a real willingness to change his view, but offering compelling reasons to a Marian audience about why he did not, and about why their own acceptance of a royal supremacy had been folly.[43]

It is in his description of More's trial that Harpsfield reveals most clearly both the theological bedrock of his hero's stand, the unity of Christendom, and his consequent reasons for rejecting Henry's divorce. In so doing, he clearly saw himself as contributing an important plank of the strategy in Marian England for re-educating the populace with regard to the reintroduction of the papal supremacy. The basic belief to which More came is faithfully preserved by Harpsfield, namely that 'a

---

41 *Life*, pp. ccii–cciii.

42 *Ibid.*, pp. 195–6; More's final opinion is reflected also in the *Recantacyons*, p. 44.

43 Strype 1721, vol. III, pp. 244–5; Pole was more dramatic, recalling the account of Bonvisi, that More, having first described the papacy as a human institution 'for the more quietness of the ecclesiasticall body', discovered after twelve days' study that it 'holdeth up all'. This need not conflict with More's declaration of 7 years' study at his trial: he had been concerned with the King's divorce over a long period. On the Marian strategy, see above, Chapter 2.

man is not by the law of one Realm so bound in his conscience where there is a law of the whole corps of Christendom to the contrary in matter touching belief'.[44] Coming to the end of the *Life*, he promises the *Treatise* to set straight the issues surrounding the divorce, claiming that, concerning papal supremacy the people are now 'riper and more fully instructed'.[45] He goes on to assert that the divorce from Queen Katherine set in motion what More, and eventually those who disagreed with him, came to see as 'the ... open persecution ... against the unity of the Church and the Catholic faith of the same'. It remains an event concerning which 'there is nothing in the world done in the English tongue to satisfy the English nation', an oversight he intends to rectify.[46]

The *Treatise* is a larger and less immediately appealing book than the *Life*, dealing in the first half with detailed and tedious rebuttals of authors like Wakefield and their defence of Henry's position. It also demonstrates in formidable, if sometimes bewildering, prolixity, Harpsfield's own colossal expertise in civil and canon law. In it, however, Harpsfield also presses home the convictions which underlie the experiences of Catholics after Edward's death and the priorities of the Marian authorities, and the debt those convictions owe to More. He crafts a carefully argued statement of his position, of the pope as the guarantor of orthodox faith, a bastion against the individualistic whims of princes and nations that would cut them adrift from the mainstream of belief. The Henrician alternative, ultimately, was for the 'wilful pleasure' of men to direct the law. Claiming that some later Henrician legislation, to enable Henry's marriages, actually undid some of the laws passed in order for him to be rid of Katherine, Harpsfield remarks that 'whereas laws were wont to be made for the times and things to come, [Henry made] a law to undo things already well passed, and the laws of the whole Catholic church withal'.[47] Harpsfield even repeats in his own words the very argument More put to his final prosecutors, whether 'the Parliament of this realm, being but one member of the whole Church, may break this decree ordained by this Great Council [i.e. the Lateran] representing the whole Catholic Church'.[48] The whole Church is one body, he argues, and England 'but a small member of the same'; Parliament may not take it to itself to alter, abolish and corrupt the law of the whole universal Church. His polemic exhibits the fire, and the ecclesiology, of the More of the *Responsio* and the *Confutation*, as he thunders against those who

44 *Life*, p. 177.
45 *Ibid.*, p. 213.
46 *Treatise*, preface.
47 *Ibid.*, p. 263.
48 *Ibid.*, p. 265.

claim that the law about affinity, and the Pope who first upheld it, were in error:

> What! Was the whole Church also all this while deceived that so religiously and devoutly, before his time and ever since, abstained from such marriage? Or was the Holy Ghost deceived that teacheth and instructeth the Church? Or was Christ deceived that biddeth us to obey the Church and to take them that disobey for no better than Publicans and Ethnicks?[49]

The acknowledgement of Henry's divorce and the acceptance of the royal supremacy cut English Catholics off from this viewpoint. They denied that the beliefs handed onto their age from the past were any longer applicable, and they entrusted the government of spiritual matters into the hands of the King. In so doing, they lost every aspect of the faith of the past which they wished to retain, and found themselves adrift and threatened with punishment for any element of continued Catholicism in their lives. Harpsfield, having lived through this devastating experience with many who were governing Mary's church, spelt out its nature and effect. In Thomas More, the English lay statesman who in the end could not tolerate such a disjunction with the past, he found the ideal focus for his message. More was the layman whose legacy was to inform the conscience and stir the collective memory of all English laymen after him.

The Christian humanist More and the fight against heresy

It is certainly not a coincidence that Harpsfield conceived his comprehensive project to shine light on the Henrician and Edwardian periods through the person of Thomas More at a time when he himself was in the thick of organising and implementing the Marian attack on heresy. Nor is it coincidental that More himself had been so assiduous and implacable an opponent of heresy. Yet Harpsfield's writings on More were not simply designed to assuage popular unease about the burnings, if indeed such unease existed in the manner and on the scale assumed by many writers, influenced by Foxe.[50] Rather, the importance to Marian England of More the tackler of heresy was to foster a sense of connected-

---

49 Ibid., p. 268; see, for example, Rastell 1557, pp. 506–7; CW, vol. VI, pp. 116 ff., 146–7, 152–3, 178, for evidence of More's agreement with this, and Gogan 1982, pp. 156–7, 271, 296, 301 ff.; Headley 1974, for modern scholarly confirmations that More thought this way about the Church: but the list is not exhaustive.

50 See, for example, the brief discussion in Duffy 1992, pp. 559–60.

ness to a previous, unashamedly Catholic, English age. It was to use More, whose judgement ought to be in no doubt, to prove the ongoing importance of the eradication of heresy, and to present him once more as the man who provided Mary's religious leaders with their inspiration and lead. This, again, was a project re-iterated in Pole's sermon of 1557, in which he had said of heretics, in a phrase which could have been More's own, that 'there cannot be a greater work of cruelty against the Commonwealth, than to nourish or favour any such'.[51] Connected to More's role as supreme statesman, but separate from it, was his guise as the promoter of orthodoxy. His fight against heresy, and thus schism, and his responsibility as a prime figure in the government of the realm were interlinked.

Amid the turbulence of his own times, and the variety of new doctrines which the wind of new learning swept in, Thomas More had seen continued adherence to inherited faith as the only guarantor of meaning and purpose. It goes some way to explaining his personal detestation of heresy, and Harpsfield's presentation of it as central to his own, Marian, project. Richard Marius has written of More's work against heresy that it was 'perhaps the most effective policy More pursued while he was Lord Chancellor'. He goes on to elaborate that, for all its dubiousness in modern eyes, it represented the proof of his mettle, 'for his moves against heretics required a courage that has seldom been recognised'.[52] It was certainly a hallmark of his career, the focus of much of his writing and the end of much of his daily work. In collaboration with and at the request of Cuthbert Tunstall, he had written against Luther, Tyndale and Barnes, voluminous works of sometimes tedious polemic which at their heart expressed the same basic conviction. That was amply expressed in the *Dialogue concerning Heresies* of 1530, in a passage which illustrates the heart of his thought and the roots of his opposition to the King's great matter:

> it best becometh a lay man to do in all things lean and cleave to the common faith and belief of Christ's Church. And thereby do I plainly know it for an heresy if an heresy be a sect and a side way (taken by any part of such as been baptised and bear the name of Christian men) from the common faith and belief of the whole Church beside. For I am very sure and perceive it well not only by experience of mine own time & the places where my self hath been with common report of other honest men from all other places of Christendom but by books also & remembrances left of long time with writing of the old holy

51 Strype 1721, vol. III, p. 241.
52 Marius 1984, pp. 392, 394–5.

fathers and now saints in heaven that from the apostles' time hitherto this manner hath been used taught and allowed and the contrary commonly condemned throughout the whole flock of all good Christian people.[53]

More's belief in the Church as the body of Christ, constantly guided by the Spirit, who forges consent and agreement amongst all truly Christian people, led him to fear and condemn the actions of those who cut themselves off from that consensus: the heretics. Much of the argument of the *Dialogue* revolves around the messenger's assertion of the sole sufficiency of scripture, and More's reply that, without the continued presence of the Spirit, 'the scripture stand them in as good stead as a pair of spectacles should stand a blind friar'. The position of the heretic, in standing outside tradition and rejecting consensus, involves having to set aside patristic authors and the established consent of the Church, and 'rebuking' the priesthood and the prelacy. Besides scripture, More continually and strongly asserted the presence of other signs and guarantees of truth within the Church. Traditions are handed on from the apostolic age to the present one; the papacy exists as an authority under Christ for the government of the Church; there is visibility (*pace* Luther) in bishops, priests and people and a known Church; most of all, there are continued miracles in the life of the Church, infallible signs of the unity and continuity within Christendom which was the bedrock of More's world.[54] So his adherence to the *consensus fidelium* can be described as the 'leitmotiv of all More's polemical works', and so he judged heresy to be the most dangerous crime in Christendom, the extermination of which, whatever the methods, was more important than allowing it to spread and infect the greater number.[55]

Such insights, and the works in which they were expressed, became the bedrock also of the exiled Catholic community in Louvain, which had smuggled out with it what of More's works they could lay their hands on.[56] He spoke directly to the crisis of their situation, in a way which must have made an indelible impression upon their attempts to learn the lessons of the previous twenty years. So, in his own exploration of the foresight and insight of Thomas More, Nicholas Harpsfield drew on

---

53 *CW*, vol. VI, pp. 37–8.
54 Ibid., pp. 62, 79–80, 111–12, 117, 122–3, 152–3, 192, 198–201, 242–3.
55 Rastell (ed.) 1557, pp. 866, 901 (from the *Apology*); Marc'hadour and Lawler in *CW*, vol. VI, p. 501.
56 See Moore (ed.) 1978, p. 142, for an account of Rastell's keeping out of trouble and thus his avoidance of property confiscation, which enabled him and Clements to take their copies of More's works to Louvain where others of More's circle (Heron, John More, Roper) had not been so circumspect.

his close contact with William Roper, his knowledge of the period, and his close acquaintance with More's writings, to re-present these hard-won truths to the age in which he, in his turn, was charged with the examination, adjudication, and, where possible, conversion of heretics.

Harpsfield's description of More's whole religious world, though clearly polemical, manages also to be touching and profoundly human. He roots his presentation of More's campaign against heresy in the Oxford education of his youth, his early reading of and lecturing upon Augustine, and his own acceptance of the devotional world into which he was born, the vital legacy of earlier generations. His own religious life, Harpsfield admits, always had a sense of struggle.

> Surely it seemeth by some apparent conjectures that he was sometime somewhat propense [i.e. disposed towards] and inclined either to be a priest, or to take some monastical and solitary life; for he continued after his foresaid reading four years and more full virtuously and religiously in great devotion and prayer with the monks of the Charterhouse of London, without any manner of profession or vow, either to see and prove whether he could frame himself to that kind of life, or at least for a time to sequester himself from all temporal and worldly exercises.

Marriage was eventually his preferred option; Marius spends much of his biography carefully exploring the psychological and sexual aspects of this decision. Harpsfield seems rather less willing to offer an explanation, except that, though More felt an inclination to monasticism, he was not 'bound so to do', and that his calling was higher than to be sequestered away from affairs of state. He was to save the realm, and men's souls, from perdition. In the making of this decision, though, More ordered himself and his household well, and in a fashion which Harpsfield remarks set an exemplary model to 'the residue of the laity, but even to many of the Clergy also'.[57]

Indeed, Harpsfield's presentation of More's high reverence for the priestly office serves to illustrate the accuracy of his portrait and his preparedness to reveal his subject in his true, reformist, colours. Fox in particular has suggested that this side of More's life is airbrushed out of Harpsfield's work, and others have lent some weight to his case, seeing a particular denial of More's intellectual outlook and character in Harpsfield's alleged detachment of him from his old friend and intellectual brother, Erasmus.[58] As for the clergy, Harpsfield makes his

---

57 *Life*, pp. 17–18.

58 On the accusations of the suppression of More's reformist ideals (particularly by 'detaching' More from Erasmus), see for example McConica 1977, p. 148, though he does attempt to shield Harpsfield from the worst of his criticisms. Fox

case for More as a clerical reformer when he describes More's reverence for the sanctity of priesthood. Accused by the Protestants of improper partiality toward the clergy, and of having written against heresy in order to profit from them, More had, in fact been self-evidently poor. Further, his respect for their office was based purely on the fact that it is through them that 'we are made christen men in Baptism, and by whom we receive the other blessed Sacraments'. And it was for this reason, in fact, that clerical ill-doers feared no-one's jurisdiction more than his.[59]

The *Life* offers ample evidence also of the friendship between More and Erasmus, and, indeed, the accounts and opinions of Erasmus are one of the major additions Harpsfield makes to Roper's biography. Thus, Harpsfield offers a series of *vignettes* of the ways in which Erasmus and the More family interacted, Erasmus praising the Latin of More's children, and especially the learning and good sense of Margaret, and acting as the bridle on the literary battle with Brixius becoming too fierce. Erasmus, Harpsfield reports, 'of all men in the world most delighted in the company of Sir Thomas More, whose help and friendship he much used'.[60] Quoting Erasmus's *Ecclesiastes*, Harpsfield records the favourable judgement of 'the great excellent Clerk' of Rotterdam in the matter of More's wit and pre-eminence amongst Englishmen. The only note of criticism comes in the observation that More's 'learned friend' Erasmus was less willing than More to see the wisdom of suppressing or retracting intemperate material: a view not entirely without basis. And Harpsfield uses Erasmus frequently as a source when describing the remarkable humanist academy which More established within his own family, whom he 'trained up ... in virtue and learning and the knowledge of the Latin and Greek tounges'.[61] Far from suppressing More's credentials as a humanist reformer, then, Harpsfield seems to see them as another of his virtues; nor does he obviously detach More from his humanist colleagues. The *Life*, finally, is not an intellectual biography, and it seems a misplaced criticism to object to it on the grounds that it fails to chart the development of More's thought, especially when the precise nature of that development has proved elusive to contemporary historians.

More, though he opted to marry, nevertheless structured his living in a semi-monastic fashion. Harpsfield carefully describes the regular pattern of his devotion, in confession and Mass in particular. No important duty or task of state was undertaken without seeking godly counsel and the

---

1982, p. 3, is stronger.
 59 *Life*, pp. 109–13.
 60 *Ibid.*, pp. 3, 78–83, 101, 136.
 61 *Ibid.*, pp. 77–8.

consolations of penance and communion. Roper's delightful story of More's choral activity is elaborated by Harpsfield, who describes how, when Lord Chancellor, he would don a surplice and sing in the local church choir. Challenged by Norfolk about the dishonour this might imply toward the king, More replies that the king would rather delight to see his own master, God, so honoured. It is a story with particular resonance in the Marian church, in which, for example, the reluctance of choirmen to serve needed to be challenged.[62] And, beneath the superficiality of such modesty, Harpsfield acknowledges a deeper, profounder and rather more costly side to More's sense of his own humanity, in the hair shirt that he tried (unsuccessfully) to conceal from his family, and his solitary Fridays, spent in the New Building at Chelsea, away even from his loved ones and devoted to prayer and study.[63] We are not shown a man for whom holiness was easily achieved, nor one who took it lightly, but rather, one whose spirituality and commitment to traditional religion in an age of innovation and change stood as an example for others later. He learned to harness the excitement and dangers of the age to an unaltering and unshakeable commitment to traditional expressions of a unifying faith, rather than allowing the impetus of the times to sweep those inherited expressions away. In this presentation of More's private devotional and spiritual world lies the key to understanding the public role he adopted: England's foremost opponent of heresy.

Harpsfield's close friendship with More's son-in-law William Roper leads to his inclusion of the story of Roper's brush with heresy in his narrative, a story omitted in Roper's own account. It lends a note of realism to the biography, in its admission of More's powerlessness to help and as a motive for More's belief in the infectiousness of heretical belief. Harpsfield outlines the spiritual and psychological breakdown which accompanied Roper's despair: immoderate personal devotion led to emotional and spiritual burnout, and his inability to accept divine grace, to the point of '*taedium*'. Into such a desperate mind and heart Luther's teaching found its way, and had its convert. Like all heretics, Roper fell prey to 'ignorance, pride, false allegations, sophistical reasons and arguments' and came to his own private rejection of his connection with the unity and consent of Christendom, in his eschewing of sacraments and ceremonies, his abandonment of 'fasting, praying, his primer and all his other prayers' and his reliance on his faith, and the acquisition of Lutheran learning. In some despair, More admits to his daughter Margaret his failure to 'call him home'.[64] There were

62 See Duffy 1992, p. 559 for Harpsfield's concern over this.
63 *Life*, pp. 64–5.
64 *Ibid.*, pp. 87.

undoubtedly resources here for Harpsfield's own daily contact with the lapsed and their families, some of whom were surely in despair for their relatives. The story of Roper's arrogant detachment of himself from the sacramental channels authorised by the Church and his obstinate choosing of schism reflects the fact that Harpsfield was writing in 1557; many were facing the same issues of a return from heretical belief and the right response of the Catholic faithful. The figure of Thomas More, armed only with prayer where reason had failed, was designed to offer hope.

The description and elucidation of More's fight against heresy in these works is much more concerned with his written polemic than with his active prosecution of individual heretics, and represents another addition to Roper's work, which had omitted a survey of More's writing. In his reconstruction of this thought world of Thomas More, a world he had come to see as crucial to continuing Catholic self-identity, Harpsfield uses More's monumental *Confutation of Tyndale's Answer*, by no means the most elegant or effective of his works of polemic, but containing many of his most characteristic concerns. Harpsfield describes More's objections to the heretical implications of Tyndale's biblical translations: 'congregation' for 'Church', 'senior' for 'priest', 'idols' for 'images', and so on. And he categorises More's major concerns faithfully, as: the defence of tradition, the infallibility of the Church, his horror of predestination, and the championing of the notion of free will. On the necessity of belief in the validity of tradition, Harpsfield shows himself alive both to the divisions within Protestantism and to the line of argument adopted by More:

> These and many other strong reasons to prove the common known Catholic Church, and none other, to be the true Church of Christ, and that seeing we do not know the very books of Scripture (which thing Luther himself confesseth) but by the known Catholic Church, we must of necessity take the sound and true understanding of the said Scriptures, and of all our faith, of the said Church (which understanding is confirmed in the same Church from the Apostles' time, and by infinite miracles, and with the consent of all the old fathers and holy martyrs) with other substantial reasons that Sir Thomas More layeth forth, have so appalled and amazed Tindall that he is like a man that were in an inexplicable labyrinth.[65]

He further emphasises More's fierce defence of an open, known, unified Church, against Barnes's of 'the Church secret and hid in hugger mugger'; and he dwells on the description in the *Apology* of the heretics as

---

65 *Life*, p. 117.

like those who raise a Babel to heaven, reversing the unity of Pentecost as they attack and undermine the Spirit's work with their own various and competing *ersatz* versions of truth.[66]

The entire presentation of the public, literary aspects of More's fight against heresy in these works therefore seeks to provide some sort of continuity in the theological undergirding of the Marian policies. It is, indeed, vital to see this theological continuity, shared between the Catholicism of the Henrician period before the formulation of the royal supremacy and the later faith of Mary's reign. Harpsfield is attempting to construct a bridge of theological and ecclesiological unity across the yawning chasm of the royal supremacy, and the Edwardian destruction of authentic practice. From More's constant sense of outrage that the unity and consensus of Christendom should be broken, and from the consequences of England's breaking it, comes the Marian policy of the reintroduction of papal supremacy. From More's passionate belief in tradition as the provider of authenticity, and from the loss of that authenticity in the abolition of the Mass, comes the Marian emphasis on the sacraments and certain extra-scriptural articles of belief. There is a great divide being outlined here, but it is not between humanists and scholastics, nor between reforming Catholics and conservative ones. It is a divide predicated upon the essential insights of Thomas More, the divide between the continuity, connection and consensus symbolised by obedience to Rome, and the arrogant preference for private judgement symbolised by Henry, Edward, Cranmer and their abandonment of tradition. More and, later, Catholics of all kinds, had come to see it as the divide between orthodoxy and heresy. Harpsfield intended More's life and writings, as well as his martyrdom, to act as a permanent reminder to the English of the dangers of religious isolation. More's wisdom, intuition and foresightedness were to be the bedrock of English Catholic self-understanding.

Hero and villains:
More and the supporters of the divorce

There is every reason to believe that Nicholas Harpsfield learned his historiographical understanding from Thomas More. In the preface to his *Dialogi Sex* of 1566, he asserted that history was the necessary starting-point for all theological enquiry, a view enunciated by More in his earlier historical works, though not uncommon at the time.[67] More's treatment of King Richard III, whether accurate or not, was in many

66 *Ibid.*, pp. 118–20.
67 *Dialogi Sex*, preface; Fox 1982, p. 75.

ways an exercise in exploring the relationship between the vagaries of human nature, and thus the course of human history, and the ongoing providential guidance of God. So too More's great work of imaginative philosophy, *Utopia*, can be seen as a historical exercise, an examination of how human responses to the events and disasters of history actually determine the providential purpose undergirding that history's course. Utopus, like Christ, left to his followers and descendants an institution which they were free to adapt, provided they remained true to his intentions.[68] This was certainly More's understanding of the Church's continued evolution, an essentially optimistic view which was vociferously opposed by his Protestant enemies for whom the witness of scripture and thus of the primitive Church was enough.

It is More's *Richard III*, though, which can be seen as Harpsfield's most direct model for his Marian writings. His study of a monarch whose decisions are essentially made on the basis of private desire, and whose ambition and greed corrupt so completely his own judgement that the realm in turn is threatened mirrors closely Harpsfield's merciless attack on Henry and his advisers in the affair of the divorce and supremacy. Alastair Fox characterises More's view of Richard's reign as one of 'passion': Richard makes a series of disastrous lapses, the product of his own free will, distorted by his lust and greed, and his decisions bring instability on England. Yet even these errors of judgement are part of a providential end; God's restoring and guiding hand is revealed through the 'renovation and amendment [Richard's lapses] induced in men of good will'. Thus, a very Augustinian picture of the workings of human history emerges, derived from More's own thorough knowledge of the *De Civitate Dei*, of a wider 'divine comedy' in which the individual triumphs and disasters of human action are woven into the greater canvas of God's ongoing purpose.[69]

It is at this point too that Harpsfield is reflecting a Marian perspective absolutely central to Cardinal Pole's own convictions and understandings. We noted earlier the easy and natural contempt felt by everyone, including the Queen, towards the events of her brother's reign. What had sometimes been a little harder to drive home with her had been the necessary level of contempt towards her father, not only in addition, but in fact as one worthy or the more opprobrium, as the instigator of schism and heresy. In the early days of her rule, Mary had adopted customary language about the blessed memory of her father in speaking of Henry; Pole had, from afar, fiercely rebuked her. If his memory was indeed blessed, he wrote in fury, the martyrs like More and Fisher had

---

68 Fox 1982, pp. 69–71.
69 *Ibid.*, pp. 77, 93–6.

given their lives for nothing. It was to be a central belief, and reflected nowhere more than in the work of Pole's key lieutenants and allies. Duffy has noted that thereafter a gradual shift is noticeable in writing of the Marian era, towards speaking more openly and diagnostically about the bestial lust, cruel passions and tyrannical savagery of the late King, and of their terrible consequences for England and her people.[70]

Writing from the vantage point of the Marian restoration, Harpsfield's own perspective becomes clearer in this light. His history, written to draw the lessons of recent English history and to act as a warning to future generations never to repeat those errors, is cast in the same mould. At its centre, besides the godly wisdom of Thomas More, are three monarchs: Henry, Edward and Mary. The first two, and especially Henry, are latter-day Richard IIIs, susceptible to the kind of disastrous lapse which endangers the commonwealth. The third is the symbol of the restoration of providence and the ineluctable outworking of God's good purposes. If Harpsfield felt any difficulty in attacking the memory of Mary's father, he did not show it. Indeed, he most likely reflects a growing bitterness in the queen's own feelings towards her father, in denouncing a man who 'would disinherit her and dishonour himself as it were by open proclamation, declaring and proclaiming himself to all the world to have lived in grievous incest about twenty whole years'.[71] His ferocious assault on Henry indicates the standing in which the Marian religious authorities held him, as the perpetrator of the schism which nearly forced England into spiritual suicide.[72] The outworking of providence through the cataclysm Henry initiated is seen in '[God's] blessed minister and Queen, Lady Mary', for it is by her that England has been restored 'to the unity of the Church that we had before abandoned'.[73]

The complicated assortment of motives which contributed to Henry's desire to divorce his queen only serve to add piquancy to Harpsfield's narrative. Writing of the king's desire for a 'goodly male child', he comments that the one he eventually fathered brought more disaster upon the realm than any other, and wryly remarks that the heir Katherine had produced, although female, turned into a splendid ruler.[74] Henry's all-consuming sense of his need for a son, though, was only one strand. The objections, whether his own or the result of scruples planted in his

70 Duffy 2009, pp. 40, 49; see also Mayer 2000b, p. 210.
71 *Treatise*, p. 208.
72 I have found, neither here nor in any other Marian writing, no evidence to support Wooding's assertion that Henry was described by the Marian writers as a 'godly and reforming prince' (Wooding 2000, p. 10).
73 *Life*, p. 218.
74 *Treatise*, pp. 280ff.

mind by his courtiers, to his marriage to his brother's widow grew in their effect on him. In the *Treatise*, Harpsfield examines in painstaking detail these objections, their roots in scripture, the treatment of them in patristic writings and their basis in the law. He goes through the arguments put forward on Henry's behalf during the long and tortuous process of the divorce. He pays lip service at least to the concept that Henry's conscience was troubled because he longed to please God, but finds his case lacking in law, and ecclesiological precedent. Then, turning from the role of lawyer to that of prophet, he takes the gloves off:

> albeit the King's doings and proceedings hitherto may seem somewhat tolerable and to have proceeded from a timorous fearful conscience to offend God, and that he grounded all his doings upon the fear of God and to satisfy his blessed will and pleasure, as it was pretended; yet now I think God saith as well to us as he said once to Ezekiel ... : 'Dig a hole in the wall to see and behold the great abominations done in the Temple', which temple is every man's heart, and for this present matter the King's own heart. Let us, I say, dig the said wall; let us search and examine the secrets of his heart; then will at length many abominations appear. Then will appear the idols, which the King did secretly worship.[75]

The true idol, he goes on to say, was Anne Boleyn, the object of Henry's adulterous lust, the illegal wife of his dishonesty, and the focus of his 'inconstant, wavering, carnal sensuality'.[76]

The basic inconstancy of that carnal desire of the king leads into a savage account of his marital career after the divorce, and a narrative which bristles with contempt. Henry's real disregard for the strictures of the law, beneath his pretence at honouring it, is revealed by the illegality of his relations with Anne, with whose sister and mother he had already slept. The libidinous excess of his serial marriages stands revealed especially in the Anne of Cleves affair.[77] His penultimate marriage, to Katherine Howard, which ended so disastrously amid the revelations of the queen's promiscuity, Harpsfield constructs as divine retribution for the king's behaviour. The 'raging wind' of the affair ought to have been evidence enough of its error.[78] Returning to his Old Testament typology, Harpsfield casts Henry as his Ahab, the idolatrous king whose blood the dogs had licked up as it seeped from his resting coffin at Syon. It is in this idolatry, the worship of his own

75 Ibid., p. 185.
76 Ibid., p. 234.
77 Ibid., pp. 260, 296.
78 Ibid., pp. 277–8.

Nicholas Harpsfield

lust and carnal desire, that Harpsfield places the root cause of the king's 'passion', and of the nation's religious, moral and spiritual demise.[79]

There are other idolatries at work in Harpsfield's history, however, even more closely akin to those More had attributed to Richard III. At the heart of them is ambition, the emotion whose power More had so carefully tamed, and the grasping individualism of which had overturned any sense of the commonwealth and the common good. Henry had been aided and abetted by those whose lust was for power. In the early days, chief amongst them was Cardinal Thomas Wolsey. Harpsfield makes significant additions to Roper's sketch of Wolsey's part in the divorce, and therefore portrays him as a prime mover in it. At the heart of Harpsfield's animus against Wolsey is the suggestion that he was the source of Henry's crisis of conscience over his marriage to Katherine. He allows for some doubt in the matter, tempering Roper's version of the story by reporting John Longland's view that the scruple had been Henry's to start with, and that he had merely been Wolsey's instrument for fostering it. Longland said that he came bitterly to regret it. For all that, Harpsfield declares it 'most credible' that Wolsey was all along the main inspiration for feeding the king such suggestions, and he declares himself in no doubt about his motives. Sharing the universal condemnation of the cardinal after his fall and death, Harpsfield gives vent to a fierce denunciation of his ambition, his thirst for power and his extraordinary love of the trappings of greatness; he describes Wolsey's almost uncontrollable desire for the papacy. It was, thus, an ambition which dispensed with true or wise counsel and told Henry what he wanted to hear, 'preferring [Henry's] sensual appetite and [his] own worldly advancement before God's blessed will'.[80]

This presentation of Wolsey and his fatal flaw is based largely on More's own account of the man with whom he had had so much to do and whom he succeeded as Lord Chancellor. Wolsey swaggers into Harpsfield's narrative early on, initially a champion of More's evident gifts, but swiftly, in his ambition and arrogance, offended by the threat they posed. Harpsfield preserves the historically questionable account of Wolsey's arrival at the parliament of 1523 of which More had been Speaker; More made a speech to the Commons mocking the prelate, 'with all his pomp ... with his maces, his pillars, his poleaxes, his Crosses, his hat and the great Seal too' but advising his admittance.[81] He repeats a story from More's *Dialogue of Comfort* also, a wonderful account of one of Wolsey's dinner parties. The cardinal's own idea of after dinner enter-

---

79 Ibid., p. 203.
80 *Life*, pp. 40–2.
81 Ibid., p. 31.

tainment was to hear his guests trying to outdo one another praising his latest speech. There is a neat but unforced parallelism here. On the one hand, there is the story of the grasping and power-thirsty cleric, telling the king what he wants to hear and unwittingly unleashing 'hideous schisms and heresies' on the kingdom; on the other is the teller of the story, the foresighted More, reflecting from the Tower on the events which have led to such an outcome. Small wonder that Harpsfield thinks Wolsey to have distrusted More, and wonders whether he ever 'entirely and from the heart loved him'.[82]

The tragedies of the different passions of Henry and Wolsey and their disastrous co-operation towards England's breach with Rome, with her history and with truth, are a necessary part of the historical story Harpsfield wishes to present to his late Marian audience. They are, for all that, predominantly in the background, narratives largely derived from More and useful for understanding properly the extent of his wisdom and the nature of his martyrdom. Another anti-hero stands nearer to the foreground of his canvas and is the major focus for his vituperative ire. Wolsey, Harpsfield agrees, was no heretic; if he unleashed heresy on the country, they were events 'which things, though he never intended, or once, I suppose thought should so chance'.[83] When he comes to the figure of his greatest villain, he makes clear that his history is dealing with an evil of a different kind altogether. The true enemy of the state had been the 'Devil's Jackanapes' himself, the man who as Archbishop of Canterbury took upon himself the power of the pope to dispense with Henry's marriage, the heresiarch who 'everted, extinguished, and abolished, not only the rights and ceremonies of the Catholic Church, but divers articles of our faith, and the chief sacraments withal'[84]: Thomas Cranmer.

Uxorius Pontifex: Thomas Cranmer through Marian eyes

The trial and execution of Thomas Cranmer had been intended as a great public show of the basic outlook of the Marian church. It was to prosecute the shaper and principal director of England's period of schism, and in so doing, it was to demonstrate the renewed energy and vision England's political and religious leaders had for the continuation of Thomas More's fight against heresy. The ablest interrogators and the finest minds were deployed to bring the former archbishop to a state of repentance, and, as the *Recantacyons* indicate, some effort at least was

---

82   Ibid., pp. 38, 40, 86.
83   Ibid., p. 40.
84   *Treatise*, pp. 281–2, 291 ff.

made to capitalise on the propaganda coup which Cranmer's capitulation would represent.[85] Reginald Pole took a great interest in the proceedings from a distance, writing detailed letters to Cranmer whilst his associates, including Juan de Villagarcia, Pedro de Soto, Edmund Bonner and John Harpsfield kept up the pressure on the prisoner.[86] In Cranmer, the authorities felt they had the symbol of all that had been wicked about the previous twenty years; in his fall, they intended to glorify England's religious renaissance under Mary.

The events of his final days did not provide them, in the end, with such an easy task. Part of the reason for the failure to publish the *Recantacyons* may have been Cranmer's ultimate refusal to play the part offered him. Despite the pathetic nature of his final submission, his subsequent galvanisation in his last speech and at the moment of his death looks heroic, even in Harpsfield's supposedly polemical account. Harpsfield is forced to rely on the words of Cole before and after the burning, and a historical account of Cranmer's career to spell out the evil of the archbishop's life. Despite the disappointment of the events of Cranmer's death, Harpsfield's unrelenting zeal to unveil and interpret Cranmer's life's work continued, from the day of his execution until the end of the reign. So, in the end, it was in his historical accounts of Cranmer's diabolical achievements in the *Life* and the *Treatise* that he is forced to make his case. Along the way, though, the *Recantacyons* adds elements which illuminate the Marian construction of heresy and the authorities' continued efforts to spell out to the English the true nature of their recent past.

In many ways, it seems that Harpsfield saw Thomas Cranmer as a figure who embodied all that More opposed. Cranmer, the heresiarch, is the object of Harpsfield's anger, because of his part in the horrors of the schism and its attendant heresy and anarchy. Subtly, Harpsfield in all three works contrasts the marks of orthodoxy and sanctity, witnessed in More, with those of heresy and schism, witnessed best in Cranmer's vacillation and inconsistency under fire. More and Cranmer thus appear in frequent contrast throughout the works. In the *Life*, More foresees immediately the effect of Cranmer's declaration on the divorce, and prays that 'these matters be not within a while confirmed with others'. As Cranmer presses on with the divorce in the manner desired by Henry, More withdraws from public life, 'foreseeing the tempestuous stormy world that indeed afterward did most terribly insurge'. But he

---

[85] The lack of such orgainsed publicity has been a criticism of the Marian regime (see for example Loades 1991b, p. 288); the difficulty was not so much lack of will as the question of how to deal with Cranmer's inconsistency, as the text of the *Recantacyons* shows.

[86] Mayer 2000b, pp. 232–5; MacCulloch, pp. 561–605 *passim*.

does make every effort to come to the king's mind, even in patient dialogue with Cranmer himself, 'howbeit, finding in all this conference no substantial and sufficient matter to remove him from his first opinion'.[87] Their final confrontation comes in More's questioning at Lambeth, a scene in whose dialogue Harpsfield manages to encapsulate the whole doctrinal question of the royal supremacy, and the Marian view of the folly of princes deciding doctrinal matters. Cranmer asks More, who has refused to judge the consciences of others, why he does nevertheless judge the King's by his refusal to swear the oath: 'and therefore he should therein obey his Sovereign Lord and King, to whom he was certain he was bound to obey'. More's reply, drawn from his account of it to his daughter, was devastating in its directness and sarcasm:

> Sir Thomas More answered that he thought that was one of the causes in which he was bound not to obey his Prince. And if that reason may conclude, then have we a way to avoid all perplexities; for in whatsoever matters the doctors [i.e. teachers of the faith] stand in great doubt, the King's commandment, given upon whether side he list, solveth all the doubts.

It was a view re-iterated to Cranmer when the Archbishop visited More in the Tower, and More told him that he preferred the destruction of his body than that of his soul.[88]

The *Treatise*, because of its different genre and more wide-ranging style, has less opportunity to place Cranmer and More side by side in order to contrast their qualities; though Harpsfield uses the book to underline Cranmer's character and wickedness, as will be seen. In the more straightforward narrative of the *Recantacyons*, however, More speaks to Cranmer as it were from beyond the grave, and the telling contrast between the two men is made again. Harpsfield quotes the sermon of Henry Cole after Cranmer's execution; he drew a stark contrast between the tenacity of Fisher and More and the inconsistency of Cranmer and Northumberland, in saying that the deaths of the latter pair were needed to atone for those of the former.[89] The most telling moment by far, and a masterstroke in Harpsfield's polemical narrative, occurs when, after his final submission to orthodoxy, Cranmer is reported as being given the *Dialogue of Comfort* to support and strengthen him: Cranmer responds with praise for the martyr: and the (correct) assertion that he was not among those who demanded More's execution.[90]

 87 *Life*, pp. 70, 148–51.
 88 *Ibid.*, pp. 169, 176.
 89 *Recantacyons*, pp. 96–7.
 90 *Ibid.*, pp. 80–1; as MacCulloch observes, a crucial piece of evidence in ascribing the book to Harpsfield.

Nicholas Harpsfield

In dealing with Cranmer as a heretic, not merely an able man led astray by a consuming flaw, Harpsfield roots his account in a different genre than his biographical treatment of Wolsey and the king. It had become a commonplace amongst the continental Catholic apologists to trace a heretical succession, and link Luther and his associates to the long line of those prosecuted and excommunicated throughout the Church's history for their challenge on truth. This had been a characteristic of writers such as Eck in his *Enchiridion* (a work dedicated, ironically, to Henry VIII in his pre-divorce phase) and *Obelisci* and Cochlaeus in the *Philippics*, as well as More himself, whose contact with his German anti-heretical counterparts had been extensive and warm.[91] In works like the *Confutation of Tyndale's Answer*, More had drawn the parallels between the current heresies and their historical predecessors by describing their lack of the marks of the true Church, and especially the attestation of miracle.[92] The idea of a discernible heretical succession had been central to John Fisher too. He had charted the course of Eucharistic heresy in his *De Veritate Corporis et Sanguinis Christi in Eucharistia* of 1527 with a view to the exposure of the error of the reformers by drawing out the similarities between their thought and that of previous schismatics. In the earlier *Assertionis Lutheranae Confutatio*, he had fiercely rebutted Luther's claim that heretics should not be burned, littering his polemic with references to previous heresiarchs, and their attack on tradition. Fisher's great sermon against Luther, originally from 1521 but reprinted twice in the Marian period, portrayed Luther as the latest and worst manifestation of an ongoing heresy which sought to destroy Christ's Church, offering his listeners a series of 'instructions' for identifying the true Church, a set of the marks of the heretic, and a vigorous defence of a sacrificing priesthood and the ultimate sign of authenticity, the Mass.[93]

---

91 Cochlaeus had dedicated his edition of Cassiodorus's *Chronicon* of 1528 to More, and the *Fidelis et Pacifica Commonitio Joan. Cochlaei, contra Infidelem et Seditiosam Commonitionem Mart. Lutheri ad Germanos* of 1531, and the two corresponded frequently. For their correspondence on this topic, see More (ed. Rogers) 1947, pp. 167ff. For the creation of a heretical succession, see for example Cochlaeus (ed. Keen) 1988, pp. 103–4; Bagchi 1991, pp. 176ff. and p. 240, where he discusses Eck's charge to Luther of 'Bohemianism' in the *Obelisci*, and its consequent development into this sense of a 'spiritual genealogy', and the fight between the *ecclesia Dei* and the *ecclesia malignantium*. As Bagchi remarks (p. 192), such work was intended to show that 'the new heterodoxies were ... merely the most recent manifestations of a single, organic heresy that from time to time assailed the Church'.

92 *CW*, vol. VIII (1973), pp. 243–6, 341, 991ff.

93 Fisher 1523, fols. 179ff.; his *Sacri Sacerdotii Defensio* (1525) posited a methodological link between Arius and Luther, that both relied excessively on the spoken words of Christ alone, without reference to the inspired and tempering voice of tradition (fol. 21). For his sermon, see *Revised Short Title Catalogue*, nos. 10896, 10897.

It was within this frame of reference that Harpsfield constructed his portrayal of Thomas Cranmer, and thus it was for the Edwardian abolition of the Mass that he was most reviled. All through his writing, Harpsfield is at pains closely to interlink the divorce to the English schism, and the religious innovation made possible by the royal supremacy with the sacrilege and social decay he had perceived under Edward. So, dealing in the *Treatise* with Henry's third marriage, he remarked that Queen Jane's death in childbirth was a sign that 'very nature seemed to be loth and as it were to abhor of his coming forth into the world'. Edward's reign was characterised by sedition, the tussle for power around the king, the attempt to deprive Henry's legitimate daughters, revolution in religion, and in particular the abolition of the Mass. He takes a diametrically opposite view to Cranmer's in calling Edward the exact reverse of the reforming biblical king Josiah he had sometimes been said to be.[94] The *Reacantacyons* describes Cranmer as 'fouled with the stain of the Lutheran heretics', a sacrilegious despoiler of holy places, who sheltered Lutherans, read their books and married their daughters.[95]

More than for mere heretical leanings, Cranmer receives Harpsfield's vituperation for the fundamental inconsistency of his theological views, and his relentless evolution into what Harpsfield clearly sees as a 'left wing' reformer, who moved from the traditional orthodoxy of seven sacraments to a heretical two, 'and those two only barely recognisable'. The evidence of Cranmer's writings on the eucharist makes the point for him; he points to the *Answer to Gardiner* of 1551 as a breach with his previous positions, and describes the process by which the archbishop interfered with the Mass as received by the Church from previous ages: 'it happened through the same man, that first, adoration was removed from the Eucharist, then the Eucharist itself from the altar, and finally the altar from the Church'.[96] Making explicit Cranmer's connection with previous versions of his Eucharistic error, Harpsfield records that his views certainly derived from Berengar of Tours, the eleventh-century denier of transubstantiation who was the archbishop's 'magister' in these

---

94 *Treatise*, pp. 280–2; MacCulloch 1996, pp. 364–5: though we should note that the source which claims that this language was used at Edward's coronation is now proven to be much later; it was, nevertheless, a biblical parallel which was in currency at the time: Marshall 2013, p. 304.

95 ['Lutheranae sectae macula foadatus'], *Recantacyons*, pp. 6–8; Cranmer's second wife had been the niece of the wife of Andreas Osiander, the reformer of Nuremburg; little is known of her parentage; MacCulloch 1996, pp. 69ff.

96 *Recantacyons*, pp. 9, 10, 14 ['accessit eidem, ut adoratio primum ab Eucharistia, deinde Eucharistia ipsa de altari, postremo altare de templo tolleretur.'].

matters, a view possibly put to him at his trial.⁹⁷ It is, indeed, with the issue of Cranmer's abolition of the Mass and his destruction of altars in England throughout the *Recantacyons* that most polemical capital is made: it is cited early as the major reason why he was an enemy to the commonwealth, who denied the 'potentia' of presence of Christ in favour of a Zwingli-derived slander on truth.⁹⁸

A second feature of Harpsfield's presentation of Cranmer in common with that made by Catholic controversialists of all heretics at the time concerns his morality and hypocrisy. The continental Catholic writers had constantly and often tediously laboured the point that heretics were moral inadequates, men whose lifestyles declared their evil nature. Figures like Cochlaeus, Dietenberger and Blich had produced whole works devoted to proving Lutheranism's moral failings.⁹⁹ Fisher and More in their turn dwelt upon the marriage of Luther to Katherina von Bora and other Protestant scandals as evidence of this trait, Fisher saying of Luther that 'the coupling of him and his mate together is a very 'brothelry' [i.e. act of prostitution] and a detestable sacrilege'.¹⁰⁰ So, to pick a couple of examples from a veritable plethora of possibilities, Thomas More had written of the 'nepharias ... nuptias' (translation is surely superfluous) which Luther had pioneered.¹⁰¹ With his customary horror and sensitivity in the area of sexual sin, he cited it as a clear characteristic of the reformers to indulge libido against the Church's consensus. Of their 'discovery' of a scriptural command to clerical marriage he had written:

> Is it not now a wonder with what spectacles Luther & Tyndall have spied this thing now in these words of Saint Paul? In which of so many great cunning [i.e. intelligent and insightful] fathers and holy saints as have often read and deeply considered those words before there was never none that had either the wit or the grace to perceive that great special commandment this 1500 years until now.¹⁰²

Harpsfield based his view of Cranmer in such a genre too, and clearly felt he had got to the heart of the man.

---

97 *Ibid.*, p. 39.
98 *Ibid.*, pp. 18–19, 76; he further comments (p. 41) that Cranmer's error, in common with all heretics, was to approach sacred truths not as to a rule of life, given with authority, or as a mule to its source of nourishment, but as an over-inquisitive child whose curiosity leads it into life-threatening peril.
99 Bagchi 1991, p. 169.
100 Quoted by Marc'hadour 1989, p. 105.
101 See for instance the *Responsio ad Lutherum* (*CW*, vol. V), pp. 868–8, and the *Confutation of Tyndale's Answer* (*CW*, vol. VIII), pp. 109, 716.
102 *CW*, vol. VI, p. 304.

Supremely, the details of Cranmer's illicit marriage were ones which Harpsfield took pains to unearth. So he tells the very Morian witty tale of the archbishop's painstaking secrecy around his wife, in a time when clerical marriage was still officially illegal. Margaret Cranmer was carried around in a trunk drilled with air-holes like a piece of valuable cargo. Amid the pretence of a celibate life, he soiled the holy space of the Lady Chapel at St Paul's, chairing sacrilegious discussions in Convocation in a place in which the real presence of the host had been venerated. Harpsfield describes him as the 'uxorius pontifex'.[103] As bad as his marriage was his lack of courage in owning up to it, and his pusillanimity, supporting the official ban on clerical marriage whilst keeping his disregard of it closely under wraps.[104]

This hypocrisy, and lack of moral fibre, haunts every word uttered by Harpsfield against his *bête noire*. The essence of his wickedness, and therefore his damage to the religious and societal integrity of the realm, was his self-seeking opportunism, which sought only to accommodate itself to the whim of two monarchs and their courtiers, and to win favour for itself by its willingness to pursue their agenda as its own.[105] Primarily, of course, it was his bending himself to procuring Henry's divorce which got him noticed, and secured his archiepiscopal status. Harpsfield unfairly excoriates Cranmer as a scholar whose academic talent had been 'more flattering than insightful', backed by hard work and an eye to the main chance. Driven by a measure of Wolsey's ambition, he pushed his meagre intellectual talents to the limit to secure the divorce, leading the grateful Henry to overlook his unsuitability for Canterbury and urge him to accept the high office a token of his thanks for enabling the marriage to Anne Boleyn. As Harpsfield later put it in the *Treatise*, he was 'made Archbishop of Canterbury for the good service he had done and should do for the breaking of the first marriage'. Indeed, he suggests that this was the first and devastating breach with Catholic unity, the taking of the matter from the hands of the pope and placing it into the partial and willing judgement of Cranmer.[106]

---

103 *Treatise*, p. 275 *Recantacyons*, pp. 8, 15; Harpsfield may have in mind the Convocation of winter 1549, at which the revision of the Prayer Book had been discussed, including saints' days, the calendar and the evolving doctrine of the Eucharist. MacCulloch (1996, pp. 504–5) says that little is known of the discussion, but that it was 'the only occasion on which Convocation was given any say in the making of the English liturgy'.

104 *Treatise*, pp. 223–4.

105 The horror of the clergy following the desires of the laity had been a theme of Pole's treatment of the schism in his St Andrew's Day Sermon; Strype 1721, vol. III, pp. 244–5.

106 ['magis blandum quam acutum']; *Recantacyons* pp. 3–4; *Treatise* p. 254.

Cranmer's willingness to change his view to suit the will of a misguided monarch did not stop there, Harpsfield adds. When Henry wished to have the marriage to Anne, in its turn, pronounced illegal, the archbishop found reasons: she had slept with others, before and after the wedding; and she had been betrothed to the Earl of Northumberland: facts known well before the event. Similarly, much of the legislation for the divorce had subsequently to be undone to allow Henry's later marriages.[107] The *Recantacyons* said more in this area, accusing Cranmer of having been led on by a desire to please Somerset into deeper heresy and schism. His final denial of the real presence had come from a similar longing to give the young Edward the doctrinal changes he wanted. Perhaps the greatest proof of his inconstancy and unreliability comes in the series of events the *Recantacyons* set out to elucidate, the repentance and subsequent defiant return to heresy which Cranmer demonstrated in his final weeks and months under pressure in Oxford. Even as he broke down, he could not accept the responsibility for his own actions, lashing out at Nicholas Ridley in his search for a scapegoat.[108]

In all of this, Cranmer is classed as a typical, if particularly dangerous, specimen of the kind of heretic against whom More wrote and laboured, an especially virulent and pernicious spokesman for the insidious kind of error that dispenses with continuity, eschews unity with Christendom, and acts unilaterally for the fulfilling of private desire and individual greed. And this apparently excessive treatment is based on a basic insight shared by Marian Catholics: that, as the Archbishop of Canterbury, Cranmer had been most responsible for the fundamental break with history, tradition, and authentic faith against which More had fought and for which cause he had died. It had been, secondly, a break whose effects on the English had been not merely religious, not just about the denial of the power of the Mass and the rejection of authority, but also social. Sedition, revolt, treason, despoliation, insurrection and widespread greed had followed the heresy which the royal supremacy had nurtured: and More had seen it coming. Thus, Harpsfield is a Marian Catholic to his fingertips when he describes the 'the slaughter of good men ... the ransacking of the Church ... the massacre of noble men ... the oppression of the people'[109] of the Edwardian period. Like Pole, he saw them all as the direct result of the over-promotion of the heretical disaster, the 'pernicious pestilential prelate', Thomas Cranmer.

107 *Treatise*, p. 259.
108 *Recantacyons*, pp. 9, 10, 21.
109 ['bonorum caedem ... spolia ecclesiarum ... cladem nobilitatis ... populi oppressionem'].

Conclusion

The fact that Harpsfield drew so much of his material from More himself rather underlines the view of a much more recent biographer that his work on More constitutes 'a big book that feels reliable'.[110] Even his most polemical exercise, the reconstruction of Cranmer's last months, assuming it is his work, has proved useful to contemporary biographers of the archbishop; it allows Cranmer a good run at his arguments, and does not shirk the difficulty (for a Catholic author) of his end, even though the result is weaker, as a piece of controversial literature. And although Harpsfield's 'hagiographical' and polemical purpose inevitably leads to some deliberate falsification and some exaggeration of character, it does not cloud the fundamental importance, or the essential accuracy of the books. They are a window onto Marian Catholicism just before its untimely death, a glimpse of a church with a vivid historical sense, a profound understanding of an earlier, cherished time, in which England and Europe shared faith, and a keen debt to the theology of that time, personified in the figure of Thomas More.

The corpus of Harpsfield's Marian writings adds strength to the arguments of Chapter 2, in demonstrating the rediscovery in English Catholicism at the time of a humanist learning combined with a commitment to the wider unity of Christendom under the pope, a marriage of ideas held together in More himself as in his Marian descendants. It shows further that such a marriage, as witnessed in Mary's reign, had noble and thoroughly English roots in More and Fisher, and was therefore by no means at odds with patriotism or the devotion due to the state. Indeed, More's deepening and gradual papalism ideally matched Marian concerns to overcome popular resistance to the papacy. Arguments by critics of Harpsfield's writings, that he traced the roots of the English schism to secular events and ignored their spiritual import, are thus far wide of the mark. It was at the heart of the More project to demonstrate that the two spheres were necessarily coinherent. Most powerfully in the *Treatise*, Harpsfield described how Henry's deeply irreligious motives gradually foisted on England schismatic and sacrilegious changes which in their turn produced catastrophic economic, social and moral outcomes. In this, Harpsfield was absolutely, and explicitly, in the business of defining the Marian Church by comparison with the Henrician and Edwardian versions: a comparison which he felt confident would leave the Marian Church looking integrated with the commonwealth and uncompromised by heresy.

Perhaps the most striking difference between Roper's study of More

---

110 Marius 1984, p. xvii.

and Harpsfield's augmentation of it is the extraordinary assessment of his subject with which Harpsfield ends. Roper does include the story of Charles V, repeated by Harpsfield, who, on learning of More's death, expressed the view that the loss of an entire city would have been preferable to that of 'such a worthy Counsellor'.[111] Whereas Roper, however, kept mostly to the plain facts of his father-in-law's life, Harpsfield constantly draws the moral from them; he concludes with a glowing celebration of More's virtues and wisdom, and his 'special peerless prerogative' as 'the first of any whatsoever lay man in England that died a martyr for the defence and preservation of the unity of the Catholic Church'. It is a martyrdom which places him, says Harpsfield, above any captain of the army, as the most learned layman in England's history who, though he never went to war, yet fought against heresy for the soul, which is 'incomparably above the price and estimation of the body ... there be no greater enemies in the world to a common wealth then wretched and desperate heretics'. In More's actions, England's very history was defended, as the country which was the first under Roman rule to accept the Christian faith through Lucius, but which, under Henry, was the first to deny it. So it is that More is, because of his foresight and understanding, the 'blessed Protomartyr of all the laity', and so it is that Harpsfield defends his martyrdom as the most glorious kind, accepted in the defence of the Church's unity.[112]

In this remarkable conclusion, Harpsfield was not alone, but echoed not just the language of polemicists like Miles Hogarde, but also the public rhetoric of Reginald Pole himself. Pole had long advocated what Mayer calls a 'martyrological theory of the papacy', whose God-given primacy had been proven again and again by those, like More, who had given their blood for the truth of the doctrine. In 1557, he called More a 'great Defender of the Catholic Faith', in the line of the patriarchs themselves, and he asked of his remarkable stand over the Supremacy: 'was not this a great Miracle?'.[113] Pole, Harpsfield and the architects of the Marian restoration saw that, in More, the fundamental religious convictions of Marian Catholicism had already been writ large, convic-

---

111 *Life*, p. 205; Reynolds (ed.) 1963, p. 50.
112 *Life*, pp. 206, 209, 211–13.
113 Hogarde's *Displaying of the Protestants* of 1556 described More as a 'second Cicero, a man endewed with heavenly eloquence', who opposed Cranmer, who 'continued in promoting of heresy, and divorcing this realm from a godly wife called unity, preferring heresy that strumpet to match with this noble commonwealth' (fols. 60v and 96r). Pole saw More's 'Love, that charity he bore to Christ, to his Church, to the body of the commonwealth of this realme' as the 'mortar' which held him into the 'sure stone' of the Church, governed by the pope; Strype 1721, vol. III, pp. 243–4, 250; Mayer 2000b, p. 205.

tions which in his own day had been prophetic, and which at the time of Harpsfield's writing were seen as the foundations of future stability. They were enunciated and celebrated as a sequel to the reintroduction of traditional forms and patterns of devotion, and as the ecclesiological underpinning of them. The project which centered on More, championed by Pole, and involving Roper, Rastell and especially Harpsfield was meant to describe and define for a considerable time the foundations of English Catholicism, and the disaster which Henry, Edward and Cranmer represented.

Perhaps the best and most vivid illustration of this whole understanding comes in the *Life of More*, a passage which indicates how Marian Catholics had come to see the effects of the royal supremacy, and how they had come to venerate the godly foresight of More. Harpsfield retells the famous tale of More's meeting with his disappointed friends, Gardiner, Tunstall and Clerk, on the day of Queen Anne's coronation. They had been to it; he had not, despite their entreaties and their financial help. In reply to their remonstrations, who saw the danger in which he had placed himself, More told a story. A virgin had offended a king, and he desired to execute her. But the law forbade the execution of virgins. A quick-thinking courtier saw the solution: 'Why make ye so much ado, my Lords, about so small a matter? Let her first be deflowered, and then after she may be devoured'. So it was decided.[114] More knew he would be devoured; he refused to be deflowered, as his colleagues had been. He saw, unavoidably, that a royal supremacy would mean a creeping process to the destruction of Catholic faith itself, and those who worked from within such a system to retain traditional expressions of faith would inevitably lose. The foundational and ineradicable conviction of all the Marian religious leaders, Gardiner and Tunstall among them, was that More had been right. The realisation led them to retell the story of his life and death, realise the ongoing importance of his convictions and mine the treasure trove of his writings, edified by his commitment to the unity of Christendom and his grasp of the danger of heresy. On this bedrock they built their church.

114 *Life*, pp. 150–1.

✢ 4 ✢

Furthering God's Service
The Canterbury Visitations

In recent years, new local surveys of the Reformation period have given us an increasingly granular and variegated sense of the ways in which religious change was received and implemented in towns and villages across England. This has often reinforced our pre-existent knowledge of regional diversity in religious sentiment, but also challenged assumptions by showing how, even in small local communities, disputes about shifts in religious life could be sharp, bitterly divided, and combustible. So, to offer one small illustrative example, a Christmas Eve gathering in Linkinhorne, Cornwall, in 1553 went badly wrong. For some, the new Queen's edict reinstituting the Mass was a cause for great joy: the host of the party, John Combe, in some genuine excitement, reported that he'd just returned from church, where 'he had heard and seen that thing he saw not in four year before'. 'I have, thanked be God', he declared, 'heard Mass and received holy bread and holy water'. Not everyone was thrilled by this development, and Combe's exultant brag was cut short by the curses of another reveller, Sampson Jackson, a confirmed Protestant. Jackson expressed himself indeed in language rather hostile to female monarchs in general and to Mary in particular, violently condemning her policy and the plan to reintroduce the papal supremacy. Matters swiftly degenerated and ended in official denunciations flying around the village during the Christmas season. Perhaps out of an abundance of festive spirit, no action was taken.[1]

Things were apparently much the same 300 miles east, in the Canterbury diocese. As the metropolitical see, it was often a particular focus for the examination of the behaviour of its people in religious matters, and, especially given its proximity to London, a place of sharp divisions and intense rivalries in theological and ecclesial debates. Those responsible for the oversight of the diocese naturally took very seriously their duty to

1 Quoted by Duffy 2003, pp. 153–4.

ensure its conformity to current policy, given its heightened profile. During the reign of Mary Tudor, the person more responsible in that regard than anyone was Nicholas Harpsfield, acting as the close confidante and chief emissary of the Cardinal Archbishop and papal legate himself, Reginald Pole. In a series of sweeping, detailed and painstaking visitations in 1556 and 1557, Harpsfield conducted a rigorous examination of all aspects of the life of the diocese, on a scale and with a scope that made them models of their kind. Nor were these merely enforcement exercises, as we will see. Harpsfield did indeed restore the fabric of churches and the material infrastructure required for the re-introduction of the old services and patterns of devotion; but he also enquired after, and sought to amend, the moral and spiritual lives of the people of Kent. His presence in a community was no mere act of surveillance, but also a sweeping attempt to reform the health of a county, and to give weight and effect to Queen Mary's desire for 'charity' to characterise all human affairs in her realm.

Returning from his exile in Louvain at Mary's accession, Harpsfield seems to have been chosen quickly as an effective, scholarly, thorough and reliable overseer of parish reform, a role subsequently further increased by his work as a historian and polemicist, whose fruit we have already seen. By tradition, the diocese of Canterbury had only one archdeacon: it was therefore already a prominent and significant role.[2] The Archdeacon had particular functions, beyond those normal even for the role, including the installation of suffragan bishops, the reconciliation of penitents, and the holding of monthly courts for the examination of the laity and their priests. Along with Pole and Gardiner, Harpsfield was given the peculiar authority to absolve other clergy; given Pole's forced absence from the diocese because of his role at the centre of national government, the Archdeacon found himself acting even more in place of his Archbishop. He was installed in March 1554, replacing Edmund Cranmer, the nephew of the imprisoned Archbishop, Thomas. Harpsfield, in addition, worked closely with two other key allies in his diocesan duties: with his brother John, as Vicar General of the diocese of London, in which John was Archdeacon, and with More's son-in-law, William Roper. Roper as Sheriff of Kent reported directly to the Privy Council and thus in tandem with his friend, Harpsfield. During this time of their collegial activity, presumably, they also honed the twin biographies of Sir Thomas for which they are now known.[3]

---

2 There are now three archdeacons in the diocese: an abundance which Harpsfield would likely have found surprising.

3 On the duties of the Archdeacon of Canterbury in general, and Harpsfield in particular, see: L. E. Whatmore (ed.) 1950, p. 4, Mayer 2000b, pp. 214–15, 248; on Roper's role in Kent, see Duffy 2009, p. 92.

The Canterbury Visitations

This crossover of roles between the religious and secular authorities is important to note, revealing a level of intent and efficiency not always credited to Mary's government. Local constables and ecclesiastical leaders like Harpsfield sometimes found themselves getting in one another's way, but in general they seem to have worked in reasonably effective harmony. This co-operation at grassroots, local level reflected also the kind of authority given to Pole by the Queen, who relied on him to undertake responsibilities and oversee reform beyond the reconstruction of the English Church. We should see the work of the legatine synod of 1555, therefore, as a project not only about the reconstruction of Catholicism in England, but also directed towards the kind of moral and spiritual renewal in the lives of English people in general which, as we have seen, was seen as one major outcome of such religious reformation. In other words, in Pole's mind, it was impossible to separate the weekly worshipping life of a parish church from the welfare, charity and concord of the whole community which it served, in matters which flowed from religious behaviour: the local economy, marital harmony, inter-personal relations, and a sense of connection to the commonwealth and to Christendom. Article XII of the synod's injunctions firmly underscored the centrality of the role of the Archdeacon in the visitation of diocese which was now underway: as Mayer reminds us, the maxim that 'the Archdeacon is the eye of the Bishop' was nowhere more true than in Canterbury. It helped that the Archdeacon also shared the heart and mind of his Bishop. This visitation was not merely for the refurbishment of churches, vital though that was: it was about the re-creation of community life itself, through individual transformation and the rekindling of charity.[4]

The list of articles for Archdeacon Harpsfield's 1556 visitation of the diocese of Canterbury reflects the kind of concerns we would by now expect of him, as a leading implementer of Marian religious policy. The articles also reflect his characteristic attention to detail, not least by their length and number: fifty-four in total. There are separate sections and questions for clergy and laity. Those for priests are a somewhat haphazard combination of matters of church fabric, personal morality, pastoral care, public piety and efficient record-keeping. Those for the laity focus naturally enough on regular attendance at the Mass and other public services, the ability to articulate orthodoxy, obedience to the rules of the Church and the kind of bonds of mutual charity already mentioned, including care for the parish's poorer members, well-functioning hospitals, and the carrying of the Sacrament to the sick and

---

4 Mayer 2000b, p. 307 on Pole's duties and pp. 289–90 on the Legatine Synod and Canterbury visitation; also Duffy 2009, p. 134.

housebound. There is also a particular regard for behaviour, both private morality and public comportment, to which, as we will see, Harpsfield paid close attention. 'Walking talking and "jangling"' while in church was especially forbidden, along with the kinds of matters not peculiar to Catholic faith: swearing, infidelity and marital propriety, refusal to pay taxes, 'drunkenness, ribaldry, evil living and lewd pastimes' and witchcraft. Harpsfield's returns show commitment to all these priorities, and also include the vital data about each parish: the patronage and value of the living, the names of those with responsibility, and the number of parishioners and communicants, alongside the particular issues which he and his team might have identified. The pace of it all strikes even a modern reader as punishing: sometimes more than six churches in a single day, which must have been gruelling for both visitors and the visited. But it was hardest work of all for Harpsfield himself, who visited every single parish in person, eschewing the custom of most archdeacons, of either visiting by proxy or examining a whole deanery at a time, in one central location.[5]

The visitation records, then, offer us a fascinating glimpse into the reality of the Marian restoration of religion in a diocese where its success was vital. The reputation of the Cardinal Archbishop himself, and his authority as a key face of the government, was on the line but, more than that, so was the truth of his claims for the papal supremacy as the guarantor of peace and concord. Neither was Kent an easy, unchallenging proposition at the beginning of the visitations: Cranmer too had seen its spiritual life as essential in his own work as Archbishop, and his nephew's appointment as Harpsfield's predecessor witnessed to that. In many parts of the diocese, and especially across the Weald, Protestantism was flourishing in local communities. Monitoring the life and behaviour of people in these places was not always simple, as they relied on distance from the centre and sympathetic local officials in carrying on their Evangelical activity. For Harpsfield, as for Pole, then, a great deal hung on these visitations. They were the practical outworking of the regime's whole project in religion. If local communities could not be brought, not only to conformity, but to some sort of sense of profit from that obedience, some feeling that communal life had indeed improved by it, then the Queen's own moral authority was in peril. The lofty claims for papal supremacy and traditional religion which Harpsfield was making in writing through the *Life* and the *Treatise* had to be mirrored in the reality of parish renewal. That was the ambition behind the visitations, and the weight of responsibility on the Archdeacon's shoulders as he led them.

5 Whatmore (ed.) 1950, pp. 5–7.

Material reform and repair

The detailed lists of instructions given to parishes and their priests and churchwardens may seem to us predictable enough, if possessed of formidable attention to even the smallest elements. The paraphernalia of traditional devotion, in various guises, are to the fore and often repeated in various places: albs for use during the Mass; the returning of statues of patron saints to their prior place on a side altar, which is to be reconstructed if necessary; the proper decoration of the chancel, so that the restored high altar might once again be a proper place for so holy a rite; cloths and frontals and veils to be restored for use in worship and especially the Mass; the refashioning of Easter sepulchres; restoring the Blessed Sacrament, with a lamp, to its place as the focus of the church. The new chrism oils needed proper housing in suitable aumbrys, and again and again Harpsfield's keen eye noticed and recorded even the smallest obstacles to the proper re-ordering of his churches. Sometimes the obstacles were quite literal, as at Kingsnorth, where it was 'commanded that Giles Brett do remove his stool out of the procession way'. Some parishioners clearly, then as now, needed steering away from an arrogant sense of entitlement and their own individual rights, when those came at the cost of others' inconvenience and the disruption of corporate worship.[6]

The restoration of the main altar itself occupied a great deal of time, expense and attention. No part of the church, of course, more reflected the devastations, to Marian eyes, of Cranmer's liturgical agenda, and nothing was more important to rectify. It was an urgent need for the restoration of the Mass, of course, but also highly symbolic as the focal point of parish devotion and piety. Shadoxhurst near Ashford is a typical example of a common direction, that 'they make an altar of stone' in place of the wooden table set length-wise down the church which the introduction of the 1552 Prayer Book had prescribed. Here too, there was a dispute about erecting a side altar, another frequent issue in the visitation records. 'They sayeth there is no room', a side note comments, as explanation for the failure in this area at a subsequent archidiaconal visit. Doubtless, this was an insufficient answer for Harpsfield. At River, near Dover, conversely, the locals were apparently only too happy to inform on their previous priest, one Patrick Brown, a convinced Edwardian in religious matters who was squarely blamed *in absentia* for the destruction of their altar, even as they set to in rebuilding it as ordered.[7]

6 Ibid., p. 103.
7 Ibid., pp. 66, 99–101.

The other main and most obvious focal point in medieval parish churches had been the rood. In many places, the screen had not survived the Edwardian violence; where it did, Harpsfield ordered, as at Eythorne, that the figures of Mary and John on it be repainted and liberated from their enforced Protestant obscurity, if not in this case literally whitewashed, certainly erased from the notice and devotion of the parishioners. In other places, some elements of it remained; at Tenterden, the front had been destroyed, and here again the parishioners were only too happy to inform the Archdeacon of the identity of the Evangelical hooligans who had committed the sacrilege: John Bailey, now removed to the comparative safety of Rye, and George Castlyne. The order was given to rebuild it again before Easter, and to furnish it appropriately with lights. At Throwley, the name was given of the destroyer of the loft, but with a clear sense that he was merely acting on another's orders; Harpsfield notes that the suspect is now in Canterbury again and should be questioned further about 'who caused him to pull down the rood loft'. He was slowly unpicking the knots of Protestant resistance in his jurisdiction.[8]

The sense of sacrilege of the destruction of altars and roods is reflected everywhere in the visitation returns, in relation to both property and people. At Hurst, things had deteriorated enormously, such that Harpsfield judged that the villagers needed to travel to nearby Aldington for Mass. Faced with the non-residency of the priest, John Wall, for twenty years, and the apparent lack of care exercised by his errant flock, creatures of another kind had taken up residence. As the record tersely states in Latin, 'the church is absolutely in disrepair and is now being used in profane ways: namely by pigs'. At Sutton Valence, the altar had not only been destroyed, but its stone repurposed for very mundane use: the notes recorded that it 'lieth in the chimney of Master Harper'. The absence of a priest and the deterioration of church buildings often go hand in hand: at Bewesfield, this had been compounded by the fact that Master Cumberford, who received the parish income even whilst non-resident for fourteen years, had made no provision for maintenance of any property. The vicarage had been let and then sub-let for eight years, to his private benefit and at a cost to the parish, while the church fell deeper into ruination: the chancel was then 'utterly fallen down' and the nave was not in a much better condition.[9]

Reading the returns, one notices on many occasions instructions which are nothing really to do with Catholic faith, but in fact more focused on having a parish church which is fit for any kind of purpose

8 *Ibid.*, pp. 41, 134, 332.
9 *Ibid.*, pp. 48, 203, 262.

of public worship. Frequently, windows are open to the elements and need reglazing; walls have started to crumble and peel and require plastering and painting; 'rubbish' is noticed, cluttering up holy spaces; the area around the church is unkempt, overgrown and unsightly. A visitation on this scale and with this attention to detail draws attention to all manner of restoration which is required. It is fascinating to contemplate too, given our lack of much evidence, how it all was received by local people, especially those whose churches were in some disrepair. The return of colour, ceremony, lights, altar cloths, a sacrificing priesthood, patron saints, holy water stoops, chrism oils and rood screens in front of re-erected altars, in glazed, repaired and re-painted churches must have seemed like an extraordinary renaissance to many without particular Evangelical commitments, and perhaps even to some who held them, if they had been used to a cold, damp, crumbling church. The candles at Buckland, which it was commanded needed to be 'more comely' seem to stand for much more: churches across the diocese sprang back to life and vibrant worship.[10] The next step, though, was more fraught: reforming the manners and morals of priests and people to match their renewed places of worship.

Living like a heretic: renewing behaviour

The Marian authorities took very seriously indeed the need to ensure that local parishes were served by a literate, competent, and orthodox priesthood. Years before the completion of the Council of Trent, and its decree founding seminaries across the Catholic world for priestly formation, Pole's Legatine Synod had commanded that such a seminary be established in every English diocese. By the time of Mary's death, four had already done so. The Archbishop was adamant that priests should be resident in their parish, up to the job in hand both theologically and pastorally, and effective as teacher, preacher and guardian of community morality.[11] This was to be especially the case, and particularly closely enforced, in his own diocese of Canterbury. It was also axiomatic that guardians of morality had to live impeccable lives of piety and charity themselves. Harpsfield therefore made a searching inventory of the lives of his priests as an integral part of his great visitations.

The visitation returns themselves reflect very clearly the kinds of emphases already noted in the articles. The Edwardian relaxation of the laws against clerical marriage, an issue on which King Henry himself

10 *Ibid.*, p. 67.
11 On the establishment of seminaries under Article 11 of the Synod, see Duffy 2009, pp. 25, 196–7, 206.

had been very conservative very consistently, had resulted in the need for Mary's government to ensure that such wives were now 'put away' again, and not resorted to in a clandestine fashion. Even worse were those clergy who had decided to forsake their role altogether and merge with the crowd of the local community, failing to uphold themselves as obvious exemplars of virtue or sources of comfort. Where no vicarage was provided or available, the temptations apparently were sometimes very great, as at Ash, where the priest was given a 'commandment to board in some convenient house and not in a common ale house'. Absenteeism was another great problem, and residence, or some other form of solution, was often enjoined. At Crundale, the priest was a minor canon of Canterbury Cathedral and had neglected things greatly whilst still taking his stipend. He was ordered to provide a curate in his stead, or face losing his income. He is, as we have seen, but one example among many.[12] It is worth noting that absentee priests were always a source of angst, for both Protestants and Catholics; the visitation returns rather suggest that it was possible to get away with a great deal, unless and until the Archdeacon got serious. There was no more serious archdeacon about such matters than Nicholas Harpsfield, and his clergy, of all stripes and convictions, were soon feeling the force of his presence.

Cardinal Pole's emphasis on the need for good sermons, and on the preaching ministry at the heart of the priestly vocation, is also reflected in Harpsfield's concerns and records. This is perhaps of particular interest, given that until very recently it had often been sweepingly asserted that preaching was of a very low priority in his work, and in the Marian Restoration in general. The Legatine Synod, though, was very forceful about the need for more and better sermons, and that 'the gift and talent of preaching', in frequent, thoughtful, helpful and diligent sermons, drawing on a wealth of continued ministerial development and study, should be central in every priest's life and work. That direction is very clearly echoed in Harpsfield's own work on the ground of the Kent parishes he oversaw. At Bekesbourne, site of Cranmer's new archiepiscopal palace, there had been no sermons for a year, but merely the 'exhortations' of the vicar, Marmaduke Smythe, presumably rambling, unfocused diatribes about his preferred topics, and entirely founded upon his own opinions. Pluckley was even worse off, where the priest quite literally seems to have made use of a bully pulpit: 'there hath been but one sermon this year, except such as the parson made wherein he doth chafe with his farmer'. Maybe it was the one time in the week when the farmer felt unable to argue back.[13]

12 Whatmore (ed.) 1950, pp. 73, 107.
13 On preaching in the Marian restoration, see Duffy 2009, pp. 17–21, 50–5;

The Canterbury Visitations

When he wasn't baiting the locals from the pulpit, William Barker, the priest at Pluckley, doesn't seem to have been very much occupied with necessary parish responsibilities. He represents also a great number of clergy rebuked and reprimanded in the returns for their inattention to and incompetence around straightforward matters of record-keeping and orderly conduct of the parish's life. He is ordered to present himself at Canterbury on the Tuesday after Michaelmas, accused of the most basic of failures, namely that he 'cannot be found many times for christenings and burials by means whereof sometimes children have remained unchristened'. Whatever was said to him as he presented himself on that fateful October Tuesday obviously worked: a note is added in the margin from the subsequent return visit the following year: 'reformatus'. Many priests and wardens are asked to come to Canterbury for further examination and investigation, and often required to bring with them further evidence of ongoing reform.[14]

Even if priests were viewed as the founts from which moral renewal ought to flow, and even if Harpsfield was clear that it was impossible to legislate for good behaviour if the priests themselves did not set a good example, a huge amount of attention was also given to the lives and proclivities of the laity. Here again, we see evidence of the kind of close co-operation between the religious and secular arms of government, which seems to have been especially well-developed in Kent. The Archdeacon and his entourage looked for all manner of dissolute, licentious and impious behaviour, as well as evidence of selfishness and dereliction of duty to the church. Among examples of the latter we find Christopher Nevison of Goodnestone, who had claimed a part of the churchyard as his inheritance, but then allowed it to fall into 'ruin and decay': the good people are offering to maintain it, if they can simply 'enjoy as their churchyard'. Someone of the same name, presumably the same man, interestingly is mentioned just a couple of miles away at Adisham, where he is rather scandalously buried under the high altar, despite 'living like an heretic and so dying'.[15] Several marital disputes emerge during the examination of the parishes too, and reconciliation is enjoined upon the parties with care.

More than anything else, it is for non-attendance at divine worship that the people of Kent are criticised, and commanded to do better. At Barham, the Brook family were particular miscreants and had very obviously failed to appear for the Easter sacrament. At Herne Bay, the local singer James Nottingham is told to put his own self-absorption

---

Whatmore (ed.) 1950, pp. 99, 120.
  14 Whatmore (ed.) 1950, p. 120.
  15 Duffy 2009, p. 106; Whatmore (ed.) 1950, pp. 76, 81.

behind him and give something back to his community, sorely in need of a decent musical lead: he 'hath in commandment to be in the choir to help further God's service with singing on Sundays and other holy days'. In Wye, the butchers were a particular cause of dissent, and are commanded to close their shops on Sundays and attend the service; John Mantell of Stockbury was more a lover of hunting than of praying, and is told to reform by presenting himself on a Sunday more often. The denizens of Maidstone, a larger settlement, gave Harpsfield plenty with which to occupy himself, including the non-attendance of Johanna Drowley, the alcoholism of Richard Elsmere, the disruptive behaviour of Joyce Taunton, a 'common scold', and the marital desertion of Thomas Mapisden. Here, the wayward butchers were told to put their souls before their purses, and close on Sunday mornings. Here too, the churchwardens are given a list of those whom they need to cajole back to church.[16]

In all this, the returns give us a fascinating glimpse into the daily life and work of a leading official in Mary's religious project, and a compelling on-the-ground glimpse of the kinds of challenges the government faced. The interconnectedness of the religious restoration and the renewal of private morality and public charity is everywhere on display: the legislation which reinstituted the Mass was only the first step, and seen as a part of the wider ambition of national renaissance. But there was an even more difficult and potentially more intractable problem faced by Archdeacon Harpsfield in these conversations with locals. More hidden than churches in disrepair, less easily mended even than marriages that had failed or butchers wanting to maximise profit, more stubborn than simple non-attendance at church, was the issue of the heretical views which had crept in and taken root in parishes all across the diocese. Given the vitriol aimed at the Marian policy on heresy, and given Harpsfield's own centrality in the execution of that policy – and of heretics – we need to face it squarely. For the visitations also give us better picture of what it looked like at local level, and of what, for Harpsfield and his associates, was at stake.

'All the spoil of the house': monastic possessions

It is in Harpsfield's efforts to untangle the Gordian knot of the former monastic lands and incomes, and their redistribution after the Dissolution, that we encounter perhaps the most intractable issue of these visitations, and one often overlooked. Kent was a particularly difficult place in which to try to ensure that justice was served in the arrange-

---

16 Ibid., pp. 77, 92, 109, 216–17, 243.

ments which were made at that time, and often being ignored by those who benefited from them. One major factor in the complication was that the booty had not, of course, enriched Protestant families only: many Catholics, who otherwise welcomed Mary's accession and supported her religious policy, were equally determined not to be impoverished by giving up any of their recent lucre to the Church again. It had always been clear that this would be intractable; indeed, as we have seen, it was one of the major sticking points in Pole's long-delayed return to England, and Mary had had to take a conciliatory position on it to make any progress at all. But she had also tried to set a good example, and hope that others would be persuaded – or shamed – to follow it. She had devolved to dioceses and their bishops more say over appointments within their jurisdiction, and forfeited many of the Crown's rights to fees and incomes, in the process restoring lands to the Church which had come to the Crown during the Dissolution. She was also, of course, of one mind with Cardinal Pole about the need to re-introduce monastic houses to the realm; but even she knew that this would likely be slow, even glacial, work. It was work done also in the wake of a papal dissolution of all those houses which had been disbanded and plundered under Henry: all Marian monastic foundations were new and from scratch. The seven which were re-founded by 1558, with about six more in train, were in themselves a tribute to her and Pole's good work amid a changed environment, and not the failure which it is often claimed.[17]

The visitation records reveal both the complications all this had left behind, and also a sense of the failure of the Dissolution as it had originally been sold and conceived. In place of monastic houses which had too much money, influence and power, there were the cronies of the King and their descendants, or those to whom they had parcelled off and sold their lands. Such people were even less accountable to the local communities which the monasteries had sought to serve than those religious houses had been. Indeed, it was no part of a private land-owner's duty in many cases to do anything at all for the local population, its parish church, or its communal life. At West Langdon, Harpsfield struggled, as he did elsewhere, to untangle the threads of the mess through careful detective work. A local landowner, Mistress Auger, had the lease of the lands, but was not paying the stipend for a curate, as it had been agreed with Archbishop Cranmer she would do, once the parishioners repaired their church. Meanwhile, a Mr Spillman, also in receipt of significant former monastic income, was allowing the parish to fall into poverty – they had already had to sell the bells to

---

17 Wizeman 2011, p. 159; and Freeman 2011 p. 188; on the Marian foundations of monastic houses, see Marshall 2017, pp. 402–3.

raise a little capital – while he sat on a stash of ecclesiastical wealth.[18]

Elsewhere, the failures and selfishness of those made rich through monastic resources was even more egregious. At St Lawrence's Hospital in Canterbury, otherwise known as the 'King's Hospital' because of its original foundation by King John, 'for blind and lame', no trace could be found of the original endowment and no sign of continued charitable work through the foundation. A Mr Tipsall in London was eventually tracked down as the recipient, after several deaths and inheritances, of 'all the spoil of the house', with the outcome that further investigation was required, that the sick might be tended and the house properly financed. At Jacob's Hospital, similarly, a man named Dartnall was both the agent charged by the late King to force the community of sisters to give up the endowment, and the lucky beneficiary of the King's dispersal of it. It is not clear whether any sisters survive nor whether they are in receipt of their promised pensions. At St John's Hospital, a poor, devastated group of brothers eke out an existence with no priest, no ornaments for worship and no help from neighbouring parishes. Their claim that 'they are of no parish but a parish of themselves' is upheld by the Archdeacon, and the subsequent visitation record attests to the re-equipping of the parish and its worship.[19]

Harpsfield's on-the-ground experiences in these visitations influenced very clearly his writings, both at the end of Mary's reign and in his work during the Elizabethan years. It is important that we understand his perspective, and that of his peers and colleagues, on the dissolution of the monasteries. Good Catholic humanists like him, and like Thomas More and Reginald Pole, were clearly in favour of reform where power was too unbridled or wealth inequitably held, and especially when religious principles were at stake. But the wholesale destruction of the entire monastic life of the nation, the closing of the houses, the dispersal of their communities, the ceasing of their activities and the distribution of their material assets to make wealthy landowners yet wealthier had in their mind been an act of unprecedented, horrifying vandalism and cruelty. Medieval monastic foundations occupied a critical space in the societies of their day, before welfare systems, accessible health care and any sense of nationalised services. The lands which they owned were carefully tended and husbanded, largely for the common good, through agricultural practices and wisdom of which these houses were the guardians. They were reliable centres of hospitality and vital power houses of scholarship and education, before state schools or state-sponsored universities existed. This was all quite before any question of

18 Whatmore (ed.) 1950, p. 39.
19 Ibid., pp. 136–8.

the value of having places of prayer and worship so frequently dotted throughout the land.

Writing his *Treatise on the Pretended Divorce*, perhaps at around the same time as his visitations were finishing their second iteration in 1558, Nicholas Harpsfield, in examining the various elements of the sacrilege with which he charges King Henry, seems in some ways to save the gravest for last. Having dealt with the 'Great Matter' in excruciating legal detail, and having then quite salaciously described the whirlwind which the realm subsequently reaped, including the biblical 'abomination of desolation' of the royal arms set up in churches and the altars torn down, he turns to the monasteries. Henry's greed and covetousness, he claims, 'never ceased until it had eaten up and devoured' every religious house, about 8,000 of them, in the land. In so doing, Henry further defiled himself, impoverished the realm both materially and spiritually, and insulted the pious memory of his predecessors who had established many of them. Building to his peroration, Harpsfield sees this act of sacrilege as the worst of all, fundamental to the dissolving of any sense of English community itself, and thus the bonds of charity that held people together. The result has been disastrous in ways Henry and his ministers ought to have foreseen:

> the only loss of the monasteries was not only for the decay of virtue, prayer and religion, but also of the politic commonwealth inestimable and importable. I say they were the very nurseries not only of piety and devotion, but also of the happy flourishing of the commonwealth. Where were the blind and lame and other impotent poor people fed and succoured, but there?... Where were the noblemen's, gentlemen's, and other men's sons so well, so virtuously, and so mannerly brought up as they were there?...Who found so many needy scholars and poor men's sons at the universities as they did?...It is come to pass that where before there dwelt many a good yeoman able to do the King and the realm good service, there is nobody now dwelling but a shepherd with his dog ... What is the decay of tillage but the suppression of the abbeys? What is the decay of the woods and the cause of the excessive price of wood, but the suppression of the said abbeys ... ?[20]

The anger is palpable: but also based on the empirical evidence of his archidiaconal work. The loss of the religious houses was a disaster: not only religiously, but educationally, environmentally, economically, and, above all in the erosion of Christian charity and unity. It is a theme which resonated very deeply with him, and to which he would return.

20 Harpsfield (ed. Pocock), *Treatise*, pp. 282, 298-9.

Uprooting heresy

In returning to the difficult question of heresy and its treatment by the Marian authorities, it is important to build on the kind of understanding of how it was viewed and encountered which was earlier sketched. Nicholas Harpsfield, as both Vicar General in the diocese of London and Archdeacon of Canterbury, was perhaps more directly engaged in this struggle for the soul of the nation (as he saw it) than anyone else. We should remind ourselves at the outset, too, of what was at stake (no pun intended) for Harpsfield as his allies, and of the sixteenth-century understanding which underpinned their response. For there was no post-modern commitment to freedom of religion, either among Catholics or Protestants: both felt that to permit heresy was deliberately to give sedition and treachery room to grow, and to endanger the immortal souls of anyone tempted to embrace it. They 'simply' disagreed about what constituted heresy: Catholicism, or an 'Evangelical', or Lutheran, belief. Nor are we talking about particularly covert resistance from Kentish Protestants: as Thomas Freeman reminds us, in openly mocking the Blessed Sacrament they were openly mocking God and as such could not be winked at.[21] The Queen and her ministers, facing an increasingly entrenched, obdurate and resolute Protestant population, felt their only possible course of action, if the Restoration was to succeed, was to enforce it. In examining Harpsfield's dealings with Protestants and other heterodox individuals during the visitations, we actually discover a great deal about the ways in which the policy was implemented, in ways which frequently challenge Foxe's later depiction of it as merely bloodthirsty, tyrannical and cruel.

The first thing to note in relation to the visitations returns is that, in some cases, the diocesan officials were dealing with issues which would have been heretical to Catholic or Protestant. For instance, there were those among those questioned who denied the Trinity, or refused to confess the divinity of Christ. Equally, many local communities harboured those suspected of witchcraft and enchantment. Alicia Bowerman of Wye, for instance, was accused of the use of both spells and unusual potions in her efforts to bring relief to those with long-term illness, such as the unfortunate brother of Thomas Pratt, suffering from a persistent ache in his arm. After careful enquiry, and her denial of anything untoward, she was committed to penance and the promise to watch her future behaviour. In Maidstone, the aged Mr. Cowdale, allegedly 100 years old, was similarly accused of enchantment, but quickly defended himself by saying that he merely prayed for the sick, and was an entirely orthodox

---

21 Freeman 2011, p. 204.

Catholic. No further action was taken, and it must be assumed that his own longevity was a good advert for his methods, however suspicious they were for some of his neighbours.[22]

The process which pertained in the examination of Protestants followed very similarly that which Sir Thomas More had espoused and favoured twenty years earlier, and which his own son-in-law, Harpsfield's county colleague Roper, had described after his own brief skirmish with Lutheranism. It was painstaking, and scrupulously fair. The executions rightly shock our modern sensibilities, but they were not done hastily or without every effort having been made to bring about a different result. In other words, only the most determined Protestants, who could find no way to square their inner conscience with an outward conformity to the law, had to worry about paying with their life for their convictions. Just as More had sought, with patience and determination, to argue Roper out of his heresy, so the visitation returns demonstrate Harpsfield and his associates devoting a great deal of time, care and attention to their examination of and conversation with those suspected of error. The returns from Ulcombe, just outside Maidstone, illustrate the general *modus operandi*. In the case of Peter Fowle and Johanna Adams, whose non-reception of the Sacrament was but the surface of their nonconformity, the Archdeacon specifically offers a gentler approach and a second chance, because, as the note-taker remarks, 'he hoped for their reform'. It seems to have worked in her case, and she is recorded as having complied and openly recanted. Fowle is detected again in the 1558 returns: but his name does not appear among the lists of those executed, we do not know whether because he conformed or simply escaped further action. Often, rather than dig over the past, a simple act of confession and compliance wipes the slate clean and Harpsfield's work is done. This is, as Eamon Duffy remarks, 'thorough and determined rather than bloodthirsty'. It may seem absurd to say so, but it is also quite clearly pastoral: like his hero More, Harpsfield sees his task as doing whatever he can to assist others to evade eternal damnation and to enter the fullness of the life of the Church.[23]

Elsewhere, the detection was often more concerning an individual's outward behaviour as about their espoused beliefs. The pattern of such infractions was common and predictable: refusal to receive the sacrament, or to attend confession regularly, or to have their children confirmed; participation in key liturgical practices such as creeping to the cross on Good Friday; and, occasionally, an open blasphemy which needed more stringent attention. Sometimes, Harpsfield recorded what

---

22 Whatmore (ed.) 1950, pp. 109, 216.
23 *Ibid.*, pp. 208, 327; Duffy 2009, p. 153.

he felt was the intertwining of heretical belief with immorality, as at Marden, where a small growth of disobedience had also led to a number of adulterous liaisons. The constable here was ordered to attend to several of those guilty of minor misdemeanours, before they took hold; the Evangelical leanings of the parish meant also that it required an unusually large amount of equipment in order to be properly equipped again for Catholic worship. Several had not received communion in three years and were to be brought to conformity and those with explicit and outright hostility especially carefully guarded. These included the disruptive William Randolph, who had made a public nuisance of himself protesting at the elevation of the host. For quieter protests which nevertheless smacked of insolence, disobedience and error, priests were told to instigate the sorts of penalties which might encourage a return to orthodoxy. The three villages of Sandhurst, Hawkhurst and Benenden, near Tunbridge Wells, shared not only geography but also a rather trenchant Protestant-leaning population: their priests are instructed not to bury those who have refused to receive communion, especially at Easter, or take part in parish devotions like creeping to the cross. At Staplehurst, just up the road, the lack of Catholic devotion and proper liturgy often went the other way, as those hostile to them simply carried on refusing to participate in the rites and rituals associated with baptism, death and burial. Harpsfield had his work cut out here: and it is no surprise to find among the names of those executed in Canterbury in 1557 at least three names of Staplehurst parishioners.[24]

There is much evidence in all this of the kind of hardening in the views of many Protestants at this time which Thomas Freeman posits: they were less likely now to recant or to be quiet than had been their predecessors under King Henry. Similarly, as we will see, there was no going back for Catholics like Harpsfield either, and he spent the last seventeen years of his life incarcerated because of his resolute conviction of the necessity of a papal supremacy and Catholic belief. As Freeman says, though, the open, irreducible opposition of increasing numbers of Protestants both made the burnings inevitable and ensured that some would die, however many chances they were given to recant. We meet that reality in these returns. We meet also the detailed work of organising, scrutinising and follow-up which made these more than mere spot-checks, but rather a diocesan-wide programme of (as Harpsfield saw it) the re-Christianisation of the people. Men like William Hawlet of Herne Bay, having been detected and sentenced, would not get away in future with hoping to keep their heads down. Sent to Canterbury to give

---

24 Whatmore (ed.) 1950, pp. 177, 179, 180, 190–4; Doran and Freeman (eds.) 2011, pp. 250, 253–4.

assurances of his penance and continued obedience, he found himself caught up in a network of surveillance and concern which made any decision to persist, either in public protest or private nonconformity, both absolutely intentional and increasingly courageous.[25]

During the reign of Mary Tudor, fifty-two men and women went to the stake, and to a horrid and horrifying death, in the diocese of Canterbury. Nicholas Harpsfield was a prime mover in the detection of these offenders, and in the insistence that those who refused to conform or recant should be executed. In this, he was carrying out his own best judgement, but also the orders of his superior Cardinal Pole and the policy of the government and Queen. There can no attempt to legitimise the barbaric killing of others for their beliefs by any modern world view, of course. In surveying the lives and deaths of those who paid the ultimate price as part of Harpsfield's visitations, however, we must try at least to bear in mind the world view of those who executed them. Mary and her ministers viewed these people as the 'devil's agents', and they believed that there was a very well-proven track record of their insurrection, sedition, violence, treachery and hatred. There was no safe way to tolerate such people or their views; and it was folly, they believed, to allow them to live unchallenged in local communities where their views and toxic beliefs and behaviours would spread like a cancer. They were not martyrs, either: Nicholas Harpsfield passionately held to the tenet of Augustine and the teaching of the Church in believing that it is the cause for which one dies, and not the death itself, which makes the martyr. In executing these men and women, he believed, rather like those who remove from society the operatives of various contemporary extremist groups like ISIS or National Action, that he was simply protecting England from a very fearsome fate, whose dire consequences, utter sacrilege and appalling instability had already been glimpsed in the six short years of Edward's reign.[26]

More context to all this cruelty is also offered by the reign which followed. Elizabeth's policies, spared the uncompromising eye of a John Foxe whose work was placed in every parish church and became the standard view of centuries of English people, were possibly even crueller. She and her father executed over 300 Catholics, including the Irish monks indiscriminately killed by her troops without even a trial. Seizing on the mistake of a papal bull against her, she executed non-conforming Catholics straightforwardly as traitors, rather than as heretics, but with a method quite as brutal as burning and even more painful. Her network of surveillance and detection is legendary. This

---

25 Freeman 2011, p. 190; Whatmore (ed.) 1950, p. 93.
26 Houliston 2011, p. 43; Loades 1991b, p. 101.

is not to try to play a tit-for-tat game of whose monarch is crueller: but simply to plead for the policies of the Marian authorities to be seen in the light of their own best wisdom, too. Part of the appeal of Thomas More for men like Nicholas Harpsfield was actually his unwillingness to exact the ultimate punishment, even if he was determined to eradicate heresy itself as utterly ruinous to the realm: his careful, measured approach, which allowed for second chances and sought to reconcile people to the Church long before sending them to their death, was a model for them to follow. Peter Marshall notes that more people were burned for heresy in 1535 alone, long after More's fall from grace and power, than had suffered similarly in the previous decade, which had included Wolsey's and More's chancellorships. Something of a similar caution about the hunt for heretics underpins Harpsfield's visitations and examinations: the editor of the published returns comments that excommunication was a very rare penalty in his work. But he was working in age much more confessionally divided, and in which sides, now irrevocably chosen, were less easily changed. Still, as Edward Jones said, before his execution in 1590, Mary and her authorities believed they worked 'in all charitable sort' to save heretics from the consequences of their own beliefs, following ancient laws also in place throughout Christendom; Elizabeth simply 'butchered' Catholics, following laws without precedent or equivalent anywhere else.[27]

In the end, the progress of Harpsfield's work was affected by factors beyond his control: epidemic, failure of the harvest, economic downturn and a disastrous foreign war. Ultimately, it came to an end with the extraordinary deaths of Mary and Pole on the same day. We glimpse in these visitations returns, then, what might have been, and what was in fact slowly coming to be in the areas of Kent which fell within his jurisdiction and oversight. The changes in the physical appearance and material apparatus of the churches in the diocese were great and significant; the restoration of Catholic liturgy and devotion was within reach; there is even evidence that some changes of heart and mind were under way as the old faith re-established itself, a sacrificing priesthood re-emerged, and the colour, vibrancy and vividness of the churches was recast. Amid all the evidence that the Marian policies were in fact effective, then, that of Archdeacon Harpsfield's grassroots activism must not be ignored in reassessing the period. Through hundreds of often highly pastoral conversations, minute attention to detail, unwearying efforts all across his diocese, and a superbly well-organised system of oversight, he had made great strides in a very short time towards his goal.

---

27 Richards 2011, pp. 208–9; Marshall 2017, p. 222; Houliston 2011, p. 42.

PART III

Forging an English Catholic Community

✢ 5 ✢

'Holy, venerable and sacred'
The *Dialogi Sex* and Early Elizabethan Catholicism

The catalogues of printed books indicate that Catholics had little to publish in the months and years immediately following Queen Elizabeth's accession. Anne Boleyn's daughter, for reason of her parentage alone, was likely to have wanted a recognisably Protestant settlement; but the precise nature of the Queen's own religious preferences seem to have remained a mystery, even to those closest to her. The mood of England at her accession is perhaps less mysterious; Dickens's judgement that Elizabeth was 'deeply committed' to reversing her half-sister's Catholic restoration, and that the 'domestic situation was largely favourable to such a design' seems now to be overturned.[1] Mary's mistake, as Haigh suggests, was to die inopportunely[2]: she and her ministers seem actually to have bequeathed a fairly settled religious state to her successor, and a populace largely reconciled to Roman Catholicism, the Pope, and traditional expressions of what they certainly saw as the 'old religion'. Another few years of Marian Catholicism, and her religious legacy would have been rather harder to undo.

Yet it was a Protestant settlement which Elizabeth oversaw, and it was achieved with cost and difficulty, to all sides. The months of the development of the legislation for the Settlement, well-catalogued and much-discussed, were months in which Catholics too took great thought for their own response. Critically, virtually none of the Marian episcopate, and certainly none of note, were prepared even to countenance another royal supremacy, and they did not weaken in their determination. The lessons of the Edwardian period had been hard learned, but they were indelibly printed in Catholic memory and consciousness,

---

1 Dickens 1964, p. 401.
2 Haigh 1993, p. 236.

in terms which we have already encountered in the words of Stephen Gardiner. Only finally by depriving the bishops of office did Elizabeth secure her Settlement, and the machinery of ecclesiastical government to implement it. These men were resistant to all attempts to secure their assent; they thus thwarted the regime's desire to secure their co-operation in the implementation of a new settlement of religion.

For those who refused such co-operation, the penalties were stiff. Nicholas Harpsfield, after apparently attempting to escape,[3] was confined to the Fleet, one of a number of prominent Marian clergy deprived and imprisoned for their obstinacy. Others, more fortunate, fled to the continent, and took up residence in Louvain and elsewhere, among them some of the finest minds of Marian Catholicism: Thomas Stapleton, Thomas Harding, and Nicholas Sander. The connections between such men and those back home, especially Harpsfield, remained; apart from anything else, Harpsfield shared a common educational background with many of them, the alumni of Winchester and New College. Copies of Harpsfield's *Dialogi Sex* were amongst the libraries of Harding and Sander; many of them made reference to his work in their own.[4] After his prominent and effective role in the Marian restoration, as archdeacon, author, polemicist and opponent of heresy, there is every reason to suppose that Harpsfield assumed an important status for this group of exiles. Indeed, as the only Marian author of note also to publish under Elizabeth,[5] he represented a figure of continuity and stability, a source of inspiration and encouragement to those formed under Mary but beginning their literary careers under her Protestant half sister.

All these Catholic voices, though, were silent until the 1560s. In those years, definition was being given to the Elizabethan Settlement, through literary work which simultaneously challenged the Catholics to defend their own position. John Jewel's *Apology*, following his Challenge Sermon of 1559, set out more clearly than ever before the Elizabethan church's assertion of its authenticity, through laying careful claim both to scripture and the Early Church. Jewel made a strong case for the character and integrity of the Elizabethan church, based on his declaration that 'we … have returned again unto the primitive church of the ancient fathers and apostles, that is to say, to the first ground and beginning of

---

3 See Pollen (ed.) 1905, p. 41, for Sander's report to Morone on Harpsfield's escape bid.

4 Coppens 1993, p. 174; Harding 1568, fol. 180; Sanders 1567, fol. 137v, and 1571, fol. 724.

5 Haugaard (1968, pp. 323–4) states that Bishops Bonner and Watson were particularly closely guarded, and thus probably lacked the facilities to write, the strictness of their position 'directly related to the government's suspicion … of their propensity to encourage others to emulate their non-conformity'.

things, as unto the very foundations and headsprings of Christ's church'.[6] Such work was mirrored and supported by the kind of research being published by Flacius Illyricus and his colleagues abroad, compiling their *Magdeburg Centuries*. At the same time, but in a somewhat different vein, John Foxe was producing and publishing his own history of the succession of those who had opposed papal supremacy and preached scriptural faith in the face of Catholic persecution. It was in reaction to these works and their like that Harpsfield and his co-religionists in Louvain wrote, in fierce denunciation of the ideas expressed in them. By the mid 1560s, English Catholics finally had something definite to attack.

The works produced by Harpsfield and the exiles in the 1560s are important therefore, not only as the initial responses to the emerging Elizabethan ecclesiology, but also for what they demonstrate about the continuity of English Catholicism in this transitional period between Marian dominance and Elizabethan minority. The assumption underlying much writing about Elizabethan Catholicism, from John Bossy to Lucy Wooding, that the Catholicism which eventually existed in England by the late sixteenth century assumed a radically different form from that under Mary will be examined in Chapter 7. On this reading, the 1560s represent the last hurrah (if even that) of an outdated form of religion much in need of renewal: and, indeed, works dealing with English Catholicism after 1570 pay the works of the 1560s little attention, apparently on the basis that they represent only the dying embers of Marian Catholic fire. So it is that the works of this period have been little studied, particularly the Latin writings of Harpsfield. Closer examination of them reveals something more than the frail death throes of an outdated medievalism, however, and demonstrates a body of material which exhibits considerable dynamism and confidence, in clear continuity with the Marian emphases already described, and with a more fully formed understanding of the strength of the Catholic case than many have acknowledged. This is especially true of their clear and forceful delineation of the theological gulf which yawned between their beliefs and the those of the Elizabethan Church. As such, these works, and especially Harpsfield's *Dialogi Sex*, seem also at times to be steeped in the Counter-Reformation which Queen Mary allegedly did not discover.

The *Dialogi Sex* in particular, indeed, is an important book, demonstrating the continued vitality of the Marian Catholic outlook in the 1560s and the fight against the Elizabethan Church. In scholarly terms, this makes a study of it overdue. Alison Shell, studying Elizabethan literature, has noted that poets and playwrights wrote 'a literary response

6 Booty (ed.) 1963, p. 135.

to an agenda set by theologians', and that that agenda lacks much serious study.[7] Others, like Booty, have paid attention to small sections of this material in their work on Jewel and the Protestant writers of the day. Many have taken the view of the 1560s outlined by Dickens and Bossy, seeing English Catholicism in that decade as merely awaiting the re-creation that seminarians would bring in the following one, a view characterised by McGrath as being about a Catholicism which was 'out of date, passive, inert and geriatric'.[8] Where scholarly attention has been given to the Catholic work of this time, it has tended to be only for works in English, and with questionable results, as with Wooding's recent appraisal, which, in attempting to trace a move from a reformed humanist Catholicism under Mary to a re-scholasticised one in the 1570s tries to make the works of the 1560s face in two ways at once. English Catholics, she claims, were forced, by clever Protestant propaganda and by the pressures of the Counter-Reformation, into a position at odds with their Marian past which they did not wholeheartedly endorse. This view will be examined in greater detail later: but such a summary serves to underline the need for a fuller assessment of the works of the 1560s. Their major concerns and ideas are reflected in the *Dialogi Sex*, which is used here as a prism through which to view them.

That said, the *Dialogi Sex* is a difficult book to summarise, because of the wide-ranging nature of its subject matter and the somewhat protean character of its dialogue, despite the organisation of the material.[9] However, across the whole sweep of the first five dialogues, which are the concern of this chapter, three main areas of argument stand out. They are: Harpsfield's firm defence of the papacy; the book's self-consciously traditional evocation and espousal of the holy, including the cult of the saints, prayers to the dead and participation in the Mass; and its profound interest in and advocacy of the events of the Catholic Reformation, which was under way at the time of its writing. In particular, Harpsfield clearly saw Trent, and the papal establishment of missionary orders, as signs of the renewal of Catholicism along lines consonant with its past. In dealing with these three main areas in turn, a clearer idea may be gained of the extent to which the *Dialogi Sex* carried forward the Marian understanding of religion, and indeed Harpsfield's own Marian writings, and also made a significant contribution to the wider Catholic task, in England and abroad, of fighting Protestantism on its own, historical, ground.

---

7 Shell 1999, pp. 1–2.
8 McGrath 1984, pp. 414–28.
9 For an outline of the book's contents, see below, Appendix II.

The *Dialogi Sex*: structure and form

Harpsfield's *Dialogi Sex* was a publishing event in its own lifetime. It was published in Antwerp in 1566,[10] under the pseudonym of Alan Cope, another Marian priest in exile abroad, to protect the book's real author, in prison in England, from the inevitable backlash by the Elizabethan authorities. It is a massive book, 1000 pages long. The six dialogues deal in turn with the matters most hotly disputed between Catholics and Protestants: Dialogue One discusses the saints, the papacy and clerical celibacy; Dialogue Two deals with monasticism; Dialogue Three tackles prayers for and to the dead, including the saints, and with miracles. The fourth Dialogue constitutes a lengthy investigation of images in Christian practice and behaviour, and the fifth moves from this theme to that of martyrdom, leading in the sixth and final dialogue to the first sustained attack on Foxe by an English Catholic, which requires a discussion in its own right.[11] Along the way, the discussions digress, taking in the history of general councils, emperors, kings and popes, and containing a wealth of historical material and vivid stories.

The genre Harpsfield chose for his work was not accidental. The dialogue form had not notably been employed under Mary, but had a considerable pedigree. Betteridge has noted its value as a literary and polemical genre in an environment in which the writer seeks urgently to persuade his readers of his case. In the 1530s, he claims, it was used to place the discussion firmly in the public sphere, between 'two concerned members of the polity', that the work as a whole might be conducive to what he terms 'active reading', by which he seems to mean a level of engagement in the reader more likely to produce conversion than mere diatribe.[12] Harpsfield thus self-consciously adopted the favoured and most successful literary form of his favourite Englishman: the *Dialogi Sex* is, in effect, a *Dialogue concerning Heresies* for the 1560s.[13] The dialogicians are Irenaeus, an Englishman, and, as his name suggests, the defender of Catholic orthodoxy, and Critobolus, a German Protestant

---

10 It was reprinted in 1573, with very minor additions, for which see Appendix II.

11 See below, Chapter 6.

12 Betteridge 1999, pp. 41, 44; Bagchi 1991, pp. 193ff. also notes the important humanist credentials of the dialogue form in the early work against Luther, and Macek 1996, p. 140, adds that English writers such as Tunstall, Bonner and Gardiner used it as 'the vehicle best suited to express the value they placed on human communication and persuasion'. For Elizabethan Catholics, that value, as a plea for the right to personal expression, would have had added poignancy.

13 See above, pp. 86–7.

committed to his religion and to its establishment in England.[14] Harpsfield also chose to write in Latin, a feature which reflects the international character he hoped the book would have, as a permanent theological resource, and a record, at home and abroad, of the intellectual character and calibre of the English opposition to Protestantism in general and the Elizabethan Settlement in particular. Whereas Harpsfield's Marian works, in English, had a specific and urgent purpose in inculcating a Catholic mindset in the people, the *Dialogi Sex* had a wider, and less immediate object. The book thus works on a number of levels: as the dialogue between English Catholicism and continental Protestantism, as the debate between Englishmen about their religion, and as a form of the questions about loyalty and conformity which seem to have torn the soul of every English Catholic in two, even before any wider debate with others.

Several characteristics of the dialogues stand out. One is the way in which they seem to mirror the realities of human conversation, wandering, at times apparently randomly, from subject to subject, despite the professed subject titles of the dialogues. It is a realism which can be difficult for the reader. In terms of its subject matter, however, it is Harpsfield's ambitious historical breadth which stands out. Throughout the book, Harpsfield deploys a remarkably wide range of authors, from Augustine of Hippo to Erasmus and Thomas More. He cites patristic authors, scholastic thinkers, papal bulls and conciliar decrees. In so doing, of course, he challenges Jewel's thesis, of the unfaithfulness of Catholicism to scripture, by attempting to trace a continuity of practice and belief from the earliest days of the church to the present day. As such, the third major feature of the book becomes clear. The *Dialogi Sex* is a profoundly practical book; that is to say, it is a book about the authentic practice of the Christian faith, a book pointing its readers towards orthopraxy, in reception of communion, devotion to the saints, a proper understanding of the importance of the papacy, and so on. It is, thus, also a book about the holy, a massive theological and historical exercise in identifying genuine points of contact with the divine, places where holiness has always been encountered and faith properly exercised. Harpsfield worked on this material earlier in Elizabeth's reign, the only remaining trace of which is a manuscript claiming to be a

---

14 Interestingly, also the name of the Pelagian dialogician in Jerome's *Dialogue against the Pelagians*, a work of which Harpsfield must have been aware: see Kelly 1975, pp. 319–20. I suggest that he took the name from it, in a turning of the tables on the Protestants, who normally charged Catholics with an excessive reliance on works. The *Dialogi Sex* certainly accuses the Protestants of relying on human reason and invention for salvation, in place of true and received faith; see, for example, below, pp. 148–9.

translation of a Latin *Life of Christ*. The material, though repeated, was thoroughly reworked for the dialogues.[15] Like Jewel, but in defiance of his *Apology*, Harpsfield placed much confidence in the power of history to demonstrate truth; in the opening preface, he warns of the dangers of tearing historical study away from 'sacred and theological matters', and quotes Cicero on the ability of history to be the 'witness of the times'.[16]

Omnium Ecclesiarum caput: the defence of the papacy

The introductory meeting between Harpsfield's two characters introduces the nature of their historical disagreement on precisely the lines outlined above. Irenaeus finds Critobolus reading Jewel's *Apology of the Church of England*, convinced by it that evangelical doctrine marks a return to primitive and pure Christianity. Having warned him about the dangers of trusting too much those who distort and mangle the historical evidence for their own ends, Irenaeus immediately begins a stout defence of the nature and place of miracle in this discussion, as that which indicates a place of truth.[17] Almost immediately, however, Critobolus turns his attention to the part of the *Apology*'s argument he has found the strongest, and the area of Catholic doctrine he finds the weakest: the papacy. So, it is here that the discussion really begins, a confident, unashamed strategy on Harpsfield's part to make a strength of what his opponents felt ought to be his weakness. If the Marian view of the papacy was less tentative than Wooding and others suggest, and indeed was argued with vigour, as I have claimed, this area of the book represents a clear continuity between late Marian and early Elizabethan Catholic thought.

Critobolus bases his criticisms of the papacy on his belief that the model of royal supremacy possesses greater historical authority, pointing to Constantine, Theodosius and Martian, rulers beloved of many a Protestant polemicist. The first dialogue therefore begins almost where Harpsfield had left off at Mary's death, with an argument about the very issue for which Thomas More died. Irenaeus's counter-attack begins there also, with his argument that British Christians cannot suddenly divorce themselves from centuries of consent and agreement with the rest of Christendom about the role and place of the papacy, nor should they diminish the status of that office with the kind of 'little lightweight arguments' they are producing. Their discussion on this subject leads from the theological basis of Thomas More's opposition to the royal

---

15 See Appendix I for a short treatment of the *Life of Christ*.
16 ['rebus sacris et theologia' ... 'testis temporum'] Harpsfield 1566, Preface.
17 *Ibid.*, pp. 6, 11–18.

supremacy, to its consequences for England. The language is remniscent of Harpsfield's *Treatise*, sketching the evil, schism and heresy which was suffered as a result. Irenaeus, surveying what for him represents the abominable results of royal supremacy, deploys the old argument that, in the case of a ruler like Nero, the royal supremacy is a doctrine of appalling implications.[18] Supremely, it is an act of spiritual suicide to cut a national church off from apostolic continuity, a point made to undermine all the reformed churches:

> For sure, nothing vexes and pulls apart the Evangelicals more, than the question which the Catholics demand of them, that they should explain the Apostolic and continuous succession of their churches.[19]

Finally, when Critobolus pours scorn on the possible existence of Pope Joan, Irenaeus points out that the story is in any case false, but no more absurd than the all too real, flesh and blood, woman currently governing the English Church. And at least, according to legend, the female pope had the decency to attempt to disguise her gender. Pope Joan is introduced, both to undermine Protestant historiography, and to point to the unprecedented scandal now happening in England:

> I ask you then, which is more sordid, a woman, who nevertheless presents herself as a man, and covers her gender, in order to be thought by all to be a man; or one rather, who does nothing to conceal her gender, and takes the place of the Pope and is the Supreme Head of the Church?[20]

English Catholic writers in the 1560s speak with one voice on this mat-

---

18 A point devastatingly put to Cranmer at his trial by Thomas Martin; MacCulloch 1996, p. 577.

19 ['leviscula ... argumenta' ... 'nulla certe res Evangelicos magis pungit et lancinat, quam illa Catholicorum interrogatio, qua ab eis postulatur, ut Ecclesiarum suarum Apostolicam et continuatam successionem explicent'] Harpsfield 1566, p. 139.

20 ['Ego vero te rogo, utrum turpius, feminam, quae se tamen pro viro gerit, sexumque tegit, quaeque ab omnibus pro viro habetur; an eam potius, quae sexum nihil dissimulat, pro Pontifice ac supremo Ecclesiae capite habere?'] *Ibid.*, pp. 46–9, 659; other authors noted not only Elizabeth's gender but also Edward's youth, in similar fashion. See, for example, Sanders 1567, preface (no pagination); Stapleton 1567, p. 254, a passage which seems to add weight to the view that Harpsfield was involved in the content and argument of the *Counterblast*: 'ye list to wonder at your selves, which do place the Pope's supreme authority in princes, be they men, or women: Yea and children too. And in so few years you have had all three. Man. Child. And woman. The less marvel had it been, if in so many hundred years, we had had one woman pope, which yet as I said, is utterly false.'

ter. Though they often address Elizabeth herself respectfully and avoid personal invective against her, they unanimously reject her assumption of a lay supremacy, however it is expressed. So, Harding, in a book dedicated to Elizabeth, yet claims that the pope has responsibility for 'bearing the charge and taking care of the church in lieu and stead of [Christ]'; so Dorman says that, in relation to Christ, the pope is 'supplyng his corporal absence for the time'; so John Rastell stresses that the spirit, guiding the Church through an unbroken papacy, ensures the Church's inerrancy; so Stapleton sees the papacy as the maintainer of apostolic consistency of doctrine and praxis, and 'schismatical disobedience toward the See of Rome' as the essence of English policy. Sanders, most of all, wrote voluminously on the historical and doctrinal importance of the pope throughout Christian history as Christ's vicegerent as head of the Church.[21] The careful though resolute Marian appeal, made specifically to an English audience, has now developed into the confidence and power of these works, often in Latin, for a wider European readership, but the underlying conviction is the same.

Harpsfield in the *Dialogi Sex* thus continues to assert the fundamental insight of Marian papalism, of the criticial importance of the pope for the maintenance of orthodoxy across Christendom. With the wider audience of the 1560s in mind, however, he seeks to demonstrate, through Irenaeus, that the papacy is indeed the only thing which can guarantee unity of belief and the eradication of heresy across the believing world. As he puts it, Rome alone has stood firm against the heresies which have afflicted other churches, a phenomenon he attributes to the guardianship of the papacy:

> We embrace this blessing with thanks, just as much as our mind is able, that it has been accomplished that, while the churches of Alexandria, Antioch, Jerusalem, Constantinople and other Apostolic foundations have been tossed about more often by different heresies, like great storms ... only Rome by the great mercy of God, has never up to now taught even one point contrary to the orthodox Catholic faith, nor felt the goads of Turkish slavery.[22]

Irenaeus does point back to the works of the Marian priest John Chris-

---

21 Harding 1565*b*, fol. 46; Dorman 1564, fol. 15; Rastell 1566*a*, fols. 144–5; Stapleton 1566, fol. 122; Sanders 1566, 1571, *passim*.

22 ['Hanc felicitatem cum gratiis, quantas mens nostra capere potest maximus, amplectimur; qua factum est, ut, cum Alexandrinem, Antiochenae, Hierosolymitanae, Constantinopolitanae, ac aliae Apostolicae Sedes variis heresibus, quasi vastis tempestatibus saepius sint iactatae ... sola Roma summa Dei benignitate, numquam hactenus vel unum apicem contra rectam, & Catholicae fidem promulgarit; neque illos Turcicae servitutis aculeos senserit.'] Harpsfield 1566, p. 52.

topherson, 'a man of most holy memory, and the great glory of our England', to demonstrate the growing authority of the papacy in bewildering and difficult heretical times, an authority which has come to demand that the pope must approve the canons of the councils, and to be the sole bulwark against schism and disunity after the demise of the Roman Empire. In matters of the definition of doctrine, 'there is no consensus without him, or at any rate, nothing whatsoever can be decided against his opinion'.[23]

The extent and detail of Harpsfield's historical analysis in this is, for the period, typically thorough. Patristic authors, ecumenical councils, and the opinions of subsequent scholars and saints are examined and teased apart to furnish evidence of their assent to the papacy; the works of heretics are brought as evidence of their contumacy and protean inconsistency.[24] This is not, however, merely an exercise in piling up historical proof until one's opponent is buried beneath the weight of accumulated evidence. Harpsfield uses the thought of the Church, established in custom, to point to the divine authority and Christlike sanctity of the Popes. It was no new concept, particularly to those steeped in the works of Thomas More, but it was deployed here with a new vigour. Thus, it is in fact the presence of 'divine law' which Harpsfield most cites to bolster his argument, a law revealed in history but transcending it also, in offering to the contemporary world and Church the headship of Christ himself through the pope. Using imagery derived from Cyprian and Leo, Irenaeus's picture is, again, one of a stream or channel, by which life is given. Cutting off the flow will inevitably bring death. There is a flow of authority, from heaven to earth: just as the earth derives its life and light from the sun, so the Church shares in the life and sovereignty of God himself through the mediating figures of Christ, in heaven, and the pope, Peter's successor, on earth. Seen this way, the papacy is not about temporal control and ecclesial authority as much as an institution which is the life blood of the Church, the earthly and visible channel by which divine authority and grace are kept alive within the Church; the gates of hell cannot prevail against it.[25]

These views about the procession of authority from heaven to earth, rooted in Ignatius, enable Harpsfield to make the further point that the channels of grace do not stop with pope, but continue to flow outward

---

23 ['sanctissimae vir memoriae, & magnum Angliae nostrae decus' ... 'nihil est contra eius consensum, vel certe nihil omnino contra eius sententiam constituendum'] *Ibid.*, p. 119.

24 Especially Calvin, whom Irenaeus accuses of having accepted Peter's presence in Rome in the *Institutes*, and then later to have retracted it; *ibid.*, p. 95.

25 *Ibid.*, p. 125.

into the Church, at every level and in every place. They flow out to the Church's priests, who minister and make sacrifice not in their own right, but as the representatives of Christ; they derive their authority to do so from bishops and pope, who mediate the priesthood of Christ. Every believer who experiences the sacraments is participating in the life of God, and receiving grace as from Christ himself:

> And so Christ is the Chief Shepherd, and Supreme Head of his Church. But just as it is Christ, who alone baptises, who alone forgives sins, who alone is the priest, by whose merit his body is consecrated and offered at the altar, all this nevertheless he does through his visible ministers, in an invisible way: so he alone, who is removed from the sight of all, rules his Church, unchanging in its manifest form; he rules it through ministers who may be seen. Over all of whom he has placed Peter and his successors as head.[26]

It is only in understanding the force and wonder of this argument that Protestants will come to understand the extent of their apostasy, by which they have divided themselves from any sense of a proper succession, any notion of apostolicity and authenticity, and a share in the ongoing and all too tangible outpouring of divine grace within the Church's life.

Harpsfield's attempt to imbue the papacy with this level of authority, as an office mediating not less than Christ himself, leads to a more surprising strategy, pointing to the sanctity of the holders of the office over the centuries of Christian history. Such a strategy, of course, flew in the face of an overwhelming mass of Protestant criticism, from Luther to John Bale and John Foxe, basing its critique on the belief that the Pope was Antichrist, with all the diabolical moral and spiritual turpitude that that involved. Through printed word and picture, Protestants had made a powerful case; the work under examination here attempts to reinvest the papacy with innate and inherited sanctity. So, for instance, Harpsfield moves on from the ecclesiological foundation already described to trace the kinds of sanctity exhibited in the popes. Liberius stood almost alone and against the emperor in resisting Arianism; Leo notably modelled holy living and orthodox thinking; Charlemagne respected Adrian for the conduct of his life; Augustine of Canterbury, sent with the authority

---

26 ['est itaque Christus summus pastor, & summum Ecclesiae suae caput. Sed quemadmodum Christus est, qui solus baptizat, solus remittit peccata, solus est sacerdos, cuius virtute corpus suum in altari consecratur & offertur, & ea tamen omnia per suos aspectabiles ministros, non aspectabili modo, operatur: ita licet solus hanc Ecclesiam apparente forma constantem, ipse ab omni oculorum sensu remotus gubernet; per ministros tamen oculis subiectos eam gubernat. Quibus omnibus Petrum, Petrique successores praefecit.'] *Ibid.*, pp. 128ff., 142.

of Pope Gregory and ordained to mission by him, was able to perform miracles and signs by which the heretical English were returned again to orthodoxy. For Gregory at least, it was God's means of showing to the people Augustine's papal authority.[27] Harpsfield's contemporaries on the continent adopted a similar line, even extending their argument to the present day; Nicholas Sanders dedicated his *De Visibili Monarchia Ecclesiae* of 1571 to Pius V, praising him for his sanctity of life and championing of truth, not least in his sponsorship of the Tridentine breviary, missal and catechism.[28]

Irenaeus drives his point home in the strongest terms:

> And so, this is the plea, which we Catholics make to Evangelicals like you with all our energy, that they should not uproot the old faith against the authority of the Roman See, nor rob that see of the power it possesses from God himself.[29]

There is nothing in Harpsfield's defence of the papacy, nothing in his presentation of it as instituted by dominical command for the preservation of Christian unity and as the only bulwark against heresy, to suggest a moribund Marian Catholicism struggling to find a voice almost ten years after its time was over. Yet such is the impression given, both by the lack of scholarly attention to the *Dialogi Sex* and other English Catholic works of the period, and by what recent study there has been. Most notably, the analysis of Wooding, cited above, misses the character of this work as the continuation of Marian beliefs, because she has misunderstood the Marian period itself. Wooding's belief that Marian Catholicism saw the papacy as fulfilling only 'administrative' functions is carried forward into her reading of the English works of the 1560s, and her claim that 'the subject which had been conspicuous by its absence in the Marian works still held quite a minor place in these works'.[30] That said, she attempts to make these works face both ways by adducing a simultaneous and enforced realignment on English Catholics from Counter-Reformation Rome: they were gradually forced to reject their Marian Catholic outlook for the new scholasticism of a return to papal obedience. As she puts it, 'the head of the Church, no longer Christ, but the Pope, was the chief glory of that Church'.[31]

---

27 Ibid., pp. 55ff., 602, 675–6.
28 Sanders 1567, Preface (no pagination), and p. 721; see also Stapleton 1567, fols. 477–8.
29 ['atque, hoc est, quod nos Catholici a vestris Evangelicis potissimum postulamus, ne contra illius sedis auctoritate religionem veterem invertant, neve potestatem divinitus illi attributam intercipiant.'] Harpsfield 1566, p. 59.
30 Wooding 2000, p. 198.
31 Ibid., pp. 225, 244.

Both the *Dialogi Sex* and the English works of the 1560s point in a different direction, one which is only made clear by understanding the works of the Marian period. By starting the *Dialogi Sex* with the defence of the papacy, Harpsfield showed his commitment to the subject. In writing against their Protestant enemies on the divine institution of the papacy, English Catholics were not ignoring or denying Christ's headship of the Church.[32] They were, rather, restating for a different time in their history the fundamental conviction of Thomas More which underlay both their eventual rejection of Edward's supremacy and their undertaking of the Marian restoration. They insisted on the need for obedience to the papacy if heresy was to be avoided and the authentic practice of Catholic faith retained. The date of English Catholicism's return to a deeply held belief in papal supremacy after a dangerous experiment in lay headship was not the 1560s, but late in Edward's reign, when the consequences of a royal supremacy became universally clear. Nor was it enforced by *diktat* from Rome, but rather by bitter experience in Edwardian England, the destruction of altars, the abolition of the Mass, the end of English monasticism, the rise of social upheaval and seditious uprisings, and the marginalisation and imprisonment of key traditionalists. That had been the point of Harpsfield's work during Mary's reign, and that was the conviction which underpinned not only his work in the 1560s, but that of his co-religionists in exile abroad as well. As such, these works transmit a vital and hard-won conviction to a later recusant age.

The presentation of the holy in the dialogues

Though the importance of the papacy has clearly to be established in the book, Harpsfield's overriding concern in the dialogues is to defend traditional Catholic teaching on holiness and patterns of devotion. Reflecting Marian concerns, he is at pains through Irenaeus to direct his readers especially to the sacraments, the Mass and penance in particular. There also much on the cult of the saints, the sign of the cross, images and relics, points of contact with God and sources of nurture in the truth.[33] As has already been observed, it is an exercise which he conducts with vividness and power, through an enormously wide range of historical material and with a feel for a telling story or a compelling argument. That this is the area in which Harpsfield sites his

---

32 When Wooding takes Sanders's 'ruled by one head' to mean the pope (p. 249) she mistakes his meaning: he is clearly, in the context, referring to Christ.

33 For the comparative lack of non-sacramental areas in Marian writings, see above, pp. 58–9.

main line of attack in the dialogues is interesting and important. In the first place, it gives the lie to the view that 1560s Catholicism in England was grounded, and had been from the 1530s, in a reformist humanism not so very different from its Protestant opponent. It has already been suggested that such a view of English Reformation Catholicism misses important facts, and Harpsfield's presentation of traditional devotion in the *Dialogi Sex*, especially when viewed alongside other contemporary works, offers further evidence for that view. Indeed, what Harpsfield does in his discussion of these things is to use them precisely to point out the enormous *difference* between Catholicism and Protestantism, the one possessed of authenticity and offering access to the heavenly, the other grounded in apostasy and conveying only error to humanity. Secondly, the discussion of the holy undermines the criticism of 'survivalism' sometimes aimed at English Catholicism of this time. In fact, the *Dialogi Sex* can be seen as one of the earliest works by an English Catholic to draw from the decrees of Trent and to root its rediscovery of traditional religion in Counter-Reformation impetuses.

These points are made, for example, in the discussions on monasticism, which opens book two, and the cult of the saints, which occupies much of dialogues one and three, and crops up elsewhere also. In the face of Protestant criticism that the tales surrounding these institutions and beliefs were 'superstitiosus' and merely 'lies and tricks of the Devil',[34] Harpsfield asserts the traditional value of the lives of the saints as being revelations of the holy life and thus encouragement to struggling believers. Attempting to meet Critobolus on his own ground by finding scriptural precedent for monasticism, Irenaeus reflects on Christ's words to the rich ruler in Mark 10 that 'with these few words, Christ sums up the whole monastic way of life, which is entirely defined in perfecting chastity, poverty, and obedience.[35] But he places a good deal of confidence also in the patristic witness: reeling off a huge list of those holy men, often bishops, who have written lives and histories of monks and the monastic life for the edification of other Christians, he asks:

> There is no-one, either from these writers, or from all the other Fathers, in the whole sweep of these 300 years, who criticises the monastic life, who teaches that it is contrary to the Word of God; there is no-one from these I have named, who does not approve of the institution of monasticism, and does not extol it with the highest praise.[36]

---

34 ['mendacia et Diabolicae praestigiae'], Harpsfield 1566, p. 174.

35 ['quibus paucis verbis Christus totam vitam Monasticam complectitur, quae in castitate, paupertate, et obedientia excolenda, tota ponitur.'] *Ibid.*, pp. 195 ff.

36 ['Nemo enim est, vel ex his, vel ex ceteris omnibus patribus, toto hoc tre-

Here is a feature that Harpsfield will use again and again, as indeed he does concerning the papacy, to demonstrate the difference between a Protestantism that ignores and derides centuries of custom and history in a misguided search for the recovery of scriptural truth, and a Catholicism which sees itself as the recipient of a noble tradition.

Irenaeus furnishes Critobolus with saintly examples of his case, historical examples given as evidence of the continuity of grace and of the changelessness of a revealed God. Antony, the paradigm of the monastic life in its highest form, as a process of growth into godliness, along with Martin and Hilarion, point to the importance of the continuance of monks and the religious, as signs and symbols of God's earthly presence. Figures like Simon Stylites, to whom crowds flocked seeking spiritual direction and the guidance of one whose whole life was turned towards God, model the real benefits to the whole Church of such an institution. Benedict was a new Moses, an heir to the prophets, a seer who led men 'Dei contemplationem', as if from slavery to freedom. And the preponderance of martyrs from amongst the ranks of the religious, at the hands of the Vandals, the Saracens, and even recently in Germany and England under Henry, points to their enjoyment of an illustrious place in the line of succession of the saints. To make his point the more compelling for Englishmen, Harpsfield gives Irenaeus a list of notable English saints, and asks why they no longer deserve English reverence and devotion:

> What hinders us then, that we should not be under obligation [to remember] as well as the other saints, Fugacius and Damanius (who here in England, chosen by Pope Eleutherius, converted King Lucius to Christ), the most blessed martyrs of Christ under Diocletian, Alban, Amphibolus, Auron and Julius; why not later our apostle Augustine in Saxon times with his most holy bishops, Melitus, Justus, Erkenwald, Birinus and Cuthbert, with those illustrious kings and martyrs of Christ, Oswald and Oswin, and also finally those most holy women, Ethelburga, Sexburga, Etheldreda, Mildred, Hilda and others like them so devoted in their calling and station: why should we not honour them, with pious prayers, and especially in those places, either which they occupied while they lived or else, where their holy relics were laid to rest after they had left this life?[37]

centorum annorum curriculo, qui Monasticam vitam improbet, qui eam verbo Dei adversari doceat; nemo ex his, quos nominavi, qui non Monastica instituta probet, summique laudibus amplificet'], *Ibid.*, p. 209.

37 ['Quid enim obstat, cur prae aliis caelitibus Fugacium & Damanium (qui huc per Eleutherium Romanum Pontificem delegati Lucium regem Christo initiarunt) quid cur non beatissimos illos Christi sub Diocletiano Martyres, Albanum,

Nicholas Harpsfield

To deny the importance of monasticism as a divine gift to the Church, Irenaeus claims, is to deny the Spirit's continued inspiration; those who do so prefer 'their own dreams' to divine revelation. Later, he turns on the work of John Bale, who blackens the reputation of English saints like Augustine of Canterbury, Boniface and Bede, preferring his own wild historical assumptions to the witness of continuity and tradition, and as a result despoiling the riches of England's religious past.[38] Harpsfield, in common with his co-religionists abroad, points out that, for a true Catholic, 'in rejecting the honour of these saints, you reject just about the whole Christian religion, and all piety'.[39]

In such description and appeal, Harpsfield is redeploying by now familiar Catholic arguments about the importance of tradition and historical continuity, arguments which had been the watchwords of Thomas More and the foundation of the Marian restoration. Yet he was also attempting something which became increasingly vital to Tridentine Europe, the recovery of universal and local religious history as a means to the encouragement of Catholic believers to return to a form of religion with the sanction of history, and with a power proven in the lives of its adherents. It was in the use of what Simon Ditchfield has called *historia sacra* that Catholics later in the sixteenth century found great resources for the recovery and renewal of their faith. It was a genre which found in England its earliest and even fullest expression in Harpsfield's own *Historia Ecclesiastica Anglicana*. As Ditchfield puts it, the period after Trent 'witnessed the relaunching of sanctity and its role as one of the identifying marks of the true Church'. Harpsfield in the *Dialogi Sex* can even be seen as an precursor to those, Baronius and Campi among them, who did just this; for Harpsfield, who had immersed himself so

---

Amphibalum, Auronem & Iulium; quid porro cur non Apostolum nostrum ad Saxonum tempora Augustinum cum sanctissimis illis Episcopis, Melito, Iusto, Erkenualdo, Bermo Cuthberto, cum illustribus illis regibus & Christi Martyribus Osualde, Osuino, cum sanctissimis denique illis feminis Ethelburga, Sexburga, Etheldreda, Mildreda, Hilda & similibus tam singulari quodam studio & officio, quam piis precibus, idque in illis praecipue locis, ubi aut ipsi dum viverent sunt versati, aut postquam ex hac vita migrarunt, sanctae illorum reliquae sunt repositae, nobis demereamur?'] *Ibid.*, p. 430.

38 *Ibid.*, pp. 257–76, 284, 430, 670–90.

39 ['cum isto Sanctorum honore, omnem propemodum Christianam religionem, omnemque pietatem abiecistis'.] *Ibid.*, p. 430. For Harpsfield's contemporaries' similar espousal of monasticism and the importance of the saints, although these were not major topics in Jewel's Challenge or the *Apology*, see, for example, Harding 1565b, fols. 145, 159 (in which he records Chrysostom's view that monks share 'fellowship with angels'); 1568, fols. 363–4; Rastell 1564, fols. 160ff.; 1566, fol. 147; Stapleton 1565b, fols. 104ff., 121ff. (where he claims that to enter a monastery is 'as it is to passe from earth to heaven'); Sanders 1566, pp. 13–14.

deeply in the works of More, glorying in the power of God revealed in the saints was a familiar exercise. As Ditchfield puts it, the *Dialogi Sex* was 'a substantial and well thought out reply to the Centuriators [which] identified the precise elements of Roman Catholic doctrine and practice that were under threat and marshalled [Harpsfield's] considerable erudition towards their defence'.[40]

Again, therefore, in his evocation of sanctity, Harpsfield was attempting to draw out the gulf of belief and practice which separated Catholics from their opponents. It is in these descriptions on the saints that the methodological difference between Harpsfield and his targets, Foxe, Jewel and the Centuriators, becomes most apparent. In examining Protestant treatment of historical accounts, Irenaeus accuses them in their partiality and reinterpretation of ascribing to the devil benefits which are from God, and of accepting the possibility of visions of evil, but not of what is holy and good. Like the Manichees' use of scripture, they accept whatever in the historical record helps their cause as genuine, and reject what goes against them.[41] There are fundamental divisions revealed in this. Both sides certainly rely on the importance of source materials and, in some senses, a humanistic approach; they use them to vastly different ends, however. Harpsfield is absolutely convinced of the necessity of seeing the history of the Church as a kind of sacred continuum: a knowledge of Christian history points to the things necessary for the advancement and inculcation of holiness and sanctification in Christian people. To any attempt to condemn or reduce elements of the historical record because of a perceived incompatibility with scripture or a 'primitive' Church, he is fiercely resistant. The God revealed in scripture is revealed in identical, unchanging ways through the papacy, through the decrees of the councils, and through the lives of his faithful servants in every age and place. The evil of those, like Jewel and the Centuriators, who reject, mangle or falsify the history of the Church is therefore the evil of the idolator and the desecrator, intent on 'virtually the complete abolition of the memory of antiquity'.[42]

This confident embracing of theological difference by Harpsfield emerges again in the book's discussion of the sacraments, and in particular the Mass. In this, the *Dialogi Sex*, and other English Catholic works of the period, offer a strong challenge to the view that, for early Elizabethan Catholics, 'error, or even heresy, were merely wayward fragments of

---

40 Ditchfield 1995, pp. 49, 283.
41 Harpsfield 1566, pp. 352ff, 406ff., 318.
42 ['totam paene antiquitatis memoriam abolendam', p. 348] *Ibid.*, preface, and pp. 166, 216, 347–8, etc.

an otherwise all-encompassing consensus'.⁴³ Rather, through his very historical and exhaustive research, Harpsfield hoped to demonstrate the horror and sacrilege of those who rejected the practice of centuries. As with his attack on Foxe in Dialogue Six, so with his defence of the traditional worship of the Church in Dialogues One to Five: Harpsfield's aim was to state Catholicism's sole claim to the truth and unmask its Elizabethan Protestant opponent as a dangerous, even diabolical, impostor. Heresy, as Irenaeus says to Critobolus, is idolatry too, and Protestant heresy in particular, setting up ideological idols which are blindly worshipped: two sacraments, *sola fides*, no prayers to saints, no images, Pope as Antichrist: 'this, and other things of this kind, I tell you, every time you hear them, then every single time they are offering you the same old idols, the object of their lust'. He warns his disputant: 'don't let anyone sell you fairy stories'.⁴⁴

The discussion of the sacraments in the *Dialogi Sex*, then, enforces a number of the book's purposes already described: the stark delineation of the difference between Catholicism and Protestantism, a forceful example of the historical authority possessed by Catholicism and therefore a strong plea for the importance of tradition, and, finally, the grounding of the book in religious practice, thus offering the reader clear routes back to authentic faith. The discussion on penance exemplifies this. Irenaeus asserts that the mind of the Church has always been resolutely convinced of the importance and necessity of confession, and claims that Luther himself was the first to reject it. He unashamedly admits that the scriptural and dominical basis for it is sketchy, except perhaps for the command of Christ to Peter about binding and loosing on earth as in heaven. For all that, however, he declares that nothing, no institution in the Church, can claim such a pedigree for its effectiveness at freeing those whose consciences are troubled by the knowledge of sin; nothing else has been and is as useful in making real to humanity the peace of Christ. Indeed, so affirming, so healthful and healing an institution is it, that many are convinced that it must, in an unattested way, have been a direct institution of Christ. To prove his point, Irenaeus tells a story from John Climacus about a thief whose advent at a monastery brings him the inner harmony he had so long sought. Here, Harpsfield reflects a Marian emphasis on the importance of penance.⁴⁵

---

43 Wooding 2000, p. 203.

44 ['haec, inquam, et alia id genus, quoties audies, toties illi tibi totidem idola, quibuscum fornicens, proponunt'] Harpsfield 1566, p. 388; ['nemo vobis fabulas vendat'] *Ibid.*, p. 403; he is quoting Augustine against the Donatists.

45 *Ibid.*, pp. 294–7; see above, pp. 32 ff. on Marian writing on penance.

More than penance, however, the major sacramental discussion in the book revolves around the Mass.[46] The Elizabethan Eucharistic theology against which Harpsfield and the Louvainists wrote in the 1560s has been the focus of much debate, not least because of its lack of clarity. Indeed, its very variegation and obscurity were factors noticed by its opponents at the time. It had been a favourite slogan of the Marians to emphasise the relentless change and innovation in English communion services before Mary's accession.[47] Now, with a liturgy produced by a conjunction of previous services, the comparative traditionalism of 1549 merged with the more radical 1552 Prayer Book, the essential ambiguity remained. One of the advantages, too, of a belief in transubstantiation was that it was a firm, colourful, relatively simple belief. Catholics could, and did, declare it proudly, citing its historical attestation and virtually universal pre-Reformation assent. There was little in technical argument or complex metaphysical theology for the reader to understand. For their opponents, it was more difficult. This is easily demonstrated even by the work of modern scholars, attempting to place English Protestant figures like Jewel or Cranmer on the Luther-Zwingli axis of belief in a Eucharistic real presence, and to tease out from often apparently contradictory statements whether and how they believed Christ to be present at the Eucharist, and how their views evolved.[48] Harpsfield and his colleagues were little concerned with the precise shade of their opponents' varied views: they were interested only in pointing out that diversity and disharmony amongst Protestants and in offering a vivid and firm defence of the belief which all true Catholics shared to a man, that of transubstantiation. In this, again, they were absolutely rooted in the writings of the 1550s; and, again, *pace* Wooding,[49] they

---

46 Though the other four sacraments are not entirely ignored; see for instance Irenaeus's stout defence of marriage's sacramental status, and his insistence that therefore Catholics need no lessons from oft-married Protestants on this score. He also quotes Trent's decree on marriage as authoritative, *ibid.*, pp. 222, 232.

47 See above, pp. 16–19, 41–7; also Duffy 2001, pp. 98–100.

48 See for instance Booty 1963, attempting to define Jewel's eucharistic theology, and in the end (p. 174) asserting: 'the truth is, that Jewel tended toward a "middle position", as did ... Cranmer'. For all Booty's pages of close argument for this view, Cranmer was no holder of a middle position, at least by 1552, and Jewel himself remains difficult to pin down, even though he seems to have allowed for a greater doctrine of Real Presence than did Cranmer, by 1553. See also Brooks 1992 and MacCulloch 1996, esp. pp. 614–17. Hunt (1998) reveals the sometimes complicated relationships in Elizabethan England between 'official', puritan and popular views on the Lord's Supper.

49 Wooding 2000, pp. 204–5, in which she claims that the authors of the 1560s emphasised real presence but not transubstantiation 'in their desire to reaffirm consensus', and focused on 'the centre-piece of late medieval piety' whilst 'expound-

were unrepentant and undeterred in using the language and theology of real presence in its strongest form.

In his attack on Protestant reliance on reason at the expense of faith and truth, Harpsfield's Irenaeus soon brings his line of argument round to transubstantiation. In their denial that this could be the divine *modus operandi* at the altar, he accuses the Protestants of reducing the limitless and inscrutable power of God by their human reason to a tidy, circumscribed, domesticated understanding of his action in the world.[50] Typically, he uses the accumulated wealth of historical material to prove the awesome reality of transubstantiation. He cites especially the miracle of Bolsena, concerning a priest in the time of Pope Urban IV who doubted of the verity of what he was supposed to celebrate at the altar. To mend his doubt, the consecrated host shed blood as he held it. The miraculous and doubt-dispelling event gave rise to the Corpus Christi festival in honour of the blessed sacrament: its continued observance was, for Irenaeus, another sacred link with the witness of past generations.[51] He goes on to talk, rather more vaguely, of miracles, signs and wonders associated with the Eucharist, spread across Europe, divine aids given to help the faithful accept Eucharistic truth. But the challenge is clear. Speaking of all such historical accounts of Eucharistic miracle, Irenaeus demands:

> If your Centuriators should dare to deny all this, then I wonder from which histories their own annals will have been botched together; or how they expect to gain the confidence of others in their own version, when they so shamefully question the trustworthiness of everyone else's books.[52]

Beyond this kind of description, Irenaeus relies on what he presents as the universal testimony of history and of all Catholic writers to argue for seven sacraments and the use of the altar as an altar in all times and places. Figures as diverse as Augustine, Epiphanius, Gildas, Bernard of Clairvaux, Erasmus, and Giovanni Pico della Mirandola are cited as

---

ing ideas which bore all the imprint of a reformed understanding'. But see below, footnote 56, for declarations of a belief in transubstantiation by the major English Catholic authors of the 1560s; nor does Wooding discuss in her final chapter whether this area too was later subject to the forced realignment with Tridentine theology which she posits.

50 Harpsfield 1566, pp. 286ff.

51 On Bolsena and Corpus Christi see, for example, Rubin 1991.

52 ['Quae omnia si Magdeburgenses tui negare audeant, miror ex quibus tandem historiis istos suos annales sint consarcinaturi; aut quam suae narrationi fidem ab aliis habitum iri expectent, qui aliorum libris fidem paene omnem tam flagitiose derogant.'] Harpsfield 1566, p. 288.

those who held to these truths, holders of an unbroken confidence in the Eucharist as the supreme place of Christ's presence and visibility in the world.[53] By contrast, the Protestants have multiplied their variety and nuance of belief in this area, have extinguished unity and 'concordia', and have adopted an 'absurdissimus' doctrine instead of the one most obviously indicated by Christ's words of institution.[54] Irenaeus identifies Lutheranism's greatest weapon against Zwingli as having been the charge that, with no belief in a corporeal presence of Christ in the host, worship itself is lost:

> And so Catholics trust, believe and are certain that the Body of Christ, and not just bread, is present, by God's word and by the Church's authority. The evangelicals follow not God's word, not faith, but the uncertain and untrustworthy judgement of their own senses.[55]

Why, then he asks, could not Luther have gone the whole way in accepting the Eucharist as a supreme place of sanctity, in which God is closely joined to humanity? In strong, almost sexual, language, he regrets the loss of intimacy, and the idea of divine-human conjunction, which is the result of Protestant Eucharistic innovation, 'it lacks the idea that God and humanity are joined together most closely'.[56] Again, Harpsfield defines the utterly opposing beliefs in question, and the key issues at stake, by pointing both to the vigour and power of the Catholic position, and to the Protestant Eucharistic theology, characterised by a Christ who is 'cut in two' by their sacrilege. Once more, the language and argument

---

53 Ibid., pp. 668, 684, 686, 906–7, 910 ff.

54 Ibid., pp. 804 ff.; see also pp. 745–6, in which the varieties of Eucharistic belief among the Protestants are delineated by a discussion of Thomas Cranmer, and his gradual movement 'leftwards' along the scale, from Catholic orthodoxy in the 1520s to Zwinglian memorialism by the 1550s.

55 ['Catholici itaque Christi corpus, nec tamen panem adesse, ex verbo Dei & Ecclesiae auctoritate credimus, scimus, & certi sumus. Evangelici non verbum Dei, non fidem, sed sensuum suorum incertum & infirmum iudicium sequuntur.'], Ibid., p. 882.

56 ['cum Deo et hominibus artissime copulare dereret'] Ibid., pp. 882–3. For the same image, see Sanders's *Supper of our Lord* of 1565, fols. 268, 377: the Eucharist is given by Christ 'to join us to his flesh and blood by real copulation of bodies'. Sanders and the rest echo Harpsfield's approach, especially liking the cry of the deacons in the ancient liturgies of SS. James and Basil of 'holy things for holy people' at the moment of distribution. For the defence of transubstantiation in the 1560s, cf. Dorman 1564, fols. 67–8, 72–3; Harding 1565a, fols. 134 ff., 1565b, fol. 90, 1566, fols. 252, 280, 1568, fol. 340; Rastell 1564, fols. 68, 86–7, 143–4; Stapleton 1565a, fols. 60, 193–6; and especially Sanders 1565, *passim*. These works would certainly bear further study.

owes much to earlier Marian material.⁵⁷

Faith is denied to the believer, and sacrilege committed too, by Protestant destruction of images. Claiming them as sites of miracles and aides to devotion, Irenaeus describes their power:

> Thus images always flood into the eyes and minds of contemplatives, morning, noon and night, and vividly call back to memory the illustrious deeds of Christ and the Martyrs; and they kindle to a blaze in us the wonderful fire of love and imitation of them.⁵⁸

They contain 'the hope of salvation', are indicators of the 'archetypum' which they aim to represent, and thus are signifiers of the 'dwelling place of God' and indicators of the holy ground of divine revelation to humans. They indicate, like Jacob's ladder, a contact point between human efforts to be faithful and divine prevenient grace, a place far removed from the sacrilegious desecration of Protestant worship. Nicholas Sander agreed, quoting Harpsfield and using some of his illustrations; John Martiall, two years earlier in his *Treatyse of the Crosse*, had also characterised the Protestant project as being one of desecration, destruction and the abolition of the holy, their aim towards the Catholic Church being 'to spoil her of her armour'.⁵⁹

Interestingly, in his argument for traditional practice and forms of devotion, Harpsfield plays another very strong suit in the matter of the crucifix and the sign of the cross.⁶⁰ He found in this area a vast store of the kinds of historical backing he relished, and it was something which gave him leave to introduce many of his favourite figures: Helena and Constantine, Chrysostom, Augustine of Canterbury and the Jesuits. Most of all, of course, it was an area hotly in dispute in England, as Elizabeth's stubborn refusal to remove the crucifix from the royal chapel became a notorious point of disagreement between her and her bishops, and an easy object of mocking criticism for their religious opponents. For Jewel himself it was a matter of the deepest concern; writing to Peter Martyr in November 1559, he had predicted accurately that the queen's cross

---

57 *Ibid.*, p. 880; see above, pp. 17–22, 41–7, for the same sentiments expressed in Marian works. Harpsfield's argument about the size of the gulf between Catholics and Protestants perhaps receives strongest expression in the final dialogue. See below, Chapter 6, *passim*.

58 ['Atqui imagines semper in oculos et animos intuentium, mane, meridie, versperi incurrunt, et res praeclare a Christo et Martyribus gestas ad memoriam revocant; et mirum quendam amoris ac imitationis ardorem in nobis incendunt'] *Ibid.*, pp. 454, 543.

59 *Ibid.*, pp. 596, 604; Martiall 1564, fols. 6–7; Sander 1567, fols. 137, 161.

60 Nicholas Sander thought the *Dialogi Sex* said all that was needed on the subject: 1567, fol. 137v.

'will soon be drawn into a precedent', and expressed the fear that, in such affairs, 'the slow-paced horses retard the chariot'.[61] He was quite right. Harpsfield was among several Catholics who appealed to Elizabeth on this issue, or who simply pointed to the internal inconsistency of Elizabethan religion as proof of its rottenness. But they did so carefully, particularly as far as the queen herself was concerned. Their intent was in deadly earnest, however, and based on a far more fundamental difference than Wooding suggests when she claims that their appeals to the queen on the issue 'were a recognition of their shared reformist legacy, and a shrewd attempt to exploit that common ground'.[62]

It is in lamenting England's apostasy in rejecting its Catholic heritage that Irenaeus yet finds hope that 'we find our most noble queen to be an inspiration, who has kept a memorial (i.e. a crucifix) standing in her own chapel for the veneration of the cross'.[63] He later suggests that Helena herself may be the queen's personal inspiration, by whose life and example she is encouraged to hold the forces of heresy and error at bay:

> We hope she will be all the more firm in her clinging to the cross through treading in the footsteps of the most praiseworthy Helena.

In condemning the strength of the language of the *Apology* against Catholic practice, he likens its author or authors to the worst kind of malicious gossips, who sully the good name of their neighbours. Chief amongst that number is the queen herself, whose attachment to Catholic practice speaks for itself. For her sake at least, they should be silent: she is, after all, a learned woman, perfectly able to read and understand the patristic and other sources in their original languages for herself.[64] There is a careful artfulness in this, a studied attempt to remain loyal to Elizabeth which runs throughout Catholic literature of her reign, polemical and imaginative alike,[65] but it is a device intended to cut ice as well. Neither Harpsfield nor any of his peers seriously suspected that Elizabeth was in fact a Catholic: her acceptance of a royal supremacy and the details of the religious settlement she had achieved would have

---

61 Bossy 1963, p. 24.
62 Wooding 2000, p. 196.
63 ['excitatem arbitramur serenissimam Reginam nostram, venerandum crucis in Basilica sua erectum hactenus retinuisse trophaeum.'] Harpsfield 1566, p. 581.
64 ['Quibus laudatissimae Helenae vestigiis eo constantius inhaesuram eam speramus.'] *Ibid.*, pp. 509, 581, 713.
65 A point made by Alison Shell for the poetry and drama she studies. See, for instance, Shell 1999, pp. 110–11, and her observation that 'it does most of [the recusant writers] a disservice to equate Catholicism with subversion', and notes their efforts to 'bring about a situation where Catholics could unreservedly be loyal to the monarch'.

given the lie to that. The point, rather, was one of pointing up division within England, a division felt by Jewel and others keenly enough, and useful as a rhetorical device in attacking the English's Church's ordained leaders whilst claiming its lay governor for themselves. It also reflects, more seriously for Harpsfield, the agony of loyalty which increasingly became the lot of every English Catholic.[66]

As is revealed in the use of Helena and Constantine in the argument for the power of the sign of the cross, Harpsfield again shows his desire to find peculiarly English examples of the importance of the practices he describes; in their case, an example which deliberately inverts a Protestant trope.[67] It is a tendency carried on into the *Historia*, a tendency absolutely derived and drawn from the example of More, to prove the 'Englishness' of Catholicism and the need for catholicity if true Englishness, found in connection to Christendom and membership of a wider Church, is to be rediscovered. So, here, Harpsfield through Irenaeus details the wonders recently witnessed in England, by which he suggests God has been calling Englishmen back to the merits of true faith. He especially cites the image of a cross found in the wood of a fallen tree in Wales, an event well-attested and dating from the night of 13 April 1559. By this, Irenaeus claims, the nation has been recalled to safety, as wandering sheep back to a pasture. As corroboration of the story, Harpsfield includes between the pages of the book a fold-out representation of the prodigy. It leads into one of the most moving sections of the book, a passionate outburst by Irenaeus which surely reveals Harpsfield's own inner anguish, his lack of the 'optimism' which O'Connell describes, normally so well hidden beneath the artifice of his writing:

> If only, if only, my people would be warned by divine miracles like this, and following Saint Paul's example would stop persecuting Christ on his cross, in his image and through his followers. If only they would return from whence they broke away, that is, to the sheepfold of Christ, weeping bitter tears with Peter. But this is easier to pray for than to hope for; although I shall never stop either praying or hoping; for as long as I live, as do they, whom it concerns, I shall not be frustrated in my prayer and my hope.[68]

66 So, for example, Harding dedicates his *Confutation* of 1565 to Elizabeth on the basis of her own hints that she is less than a full-blooded Protestant; he nevertheless warns her sternly that Protestantism is a cancer which will will disturb and disorder her realm, if she does not check it and strive instead for unity, internal to the nation and with Christendom.

67 See for example Foxe's decorated letter 'C', using Constantine, in the preface to the *Acts and Monuments*.

68 ['Utinam, utinam, populares mei huiusmodi miraculis divinitus admoniti,

It will be clear that part of the power of these arguments reflected earlier Marian emphases. Harpsfield hoped that it would be made obvious to his readers that participation in the patterns and practices of devotion authorised and commanded by the Church, and received from the past, was enough to give even the humblest believer access to God and direct experience of the holy. His prose sought to reinvest such practices with sanctity, to renew that sense of their efficacy and wonder which had been eroded by countless Protestant sermons on superstition and pleas to human powers of reason. An act as simple as making the sign of the cross, making confession or receiving the consecrated host brought God vividly into the life of the individual, just as history witnessed it had always done. To that end, Harpsfield and his peers unashamedly spoke the language of the miraculous. Recent examples like that in Glamorgan were merely the latest manifestations of a centuries-old event: the revelation of God's purpose or presence through miracle, which emphasised the value of the symbolic language of traditional religion. From Athanasius and Chrysostom to Gregory of Tours and Hilarion, from Macrina to Thomas More, miracles witnessed to the power of God in the lives of Catholics and the Church. Portents testified against schism, as in Germany in 1501; signs and wonders were always given as pointers towards truth. Their insistence was, Harpsfield, stressed, for his own time and his own readers as much as any before:

> So then, I ask moreover, why God would have confirmed and, as it were, commended to the world, filthy idolatry with such miracle? ... If it is merely superstition, why should so many notable miracles be said by so many venerable sources to have occurred through the Cross, as we have enumerated?[69]

In this vocabulary and tone, again, lies the confident delineation of theological difference. Miracles, affirming the power of traditional devotion, signs of God's presence, belong to Catholics; Protestants, uprooted and disconnected from the wellsprings of orthodoxy and ongoing revelation, are not given authority or offered corroboration by evident signs of miracle or growth. Critobolus is forced constantly to pour scorn or

---

Divi Paolo exemplo desinerent Christum in eius cruce, imagine, membris persequi. Utinam unde exierunt, illuc, id est, ad ovile Christi, amare cum Petro flentes redirent. Sed haec facilius est optare quam sperare; quamquam neque optare, neque sperare unquam desinam; quam diu vixero, et illi, quorum interest, ne ego optatis et spe mea frustratus fuero'] Harpsfield 1566, pp. 504–5; see also Law 1886.

69 ['Quin et illud rogo, quare Deus foedam idolatriam tanto miraculo confirmavit, ac quasi orbi commendavit? ... Si superstitio insit, cur tanta et tam praeclara a tantis patribus ad crucem, quae recensimus, miracula acciderent?'] Harpsfield 1566, p. 499.

Nicholas Harpsfield

cast doubt on the veracity and helpfulness of miracles, unable to produce accounts of their presence within his own side, in stark contrast to Irenaeus. The accusation is just that which Stapleton levelled at his opponents in his preface to Staphylus's *Apologie*:

> Not one of these new gospellers was ever able so much as to cure a lame colt or a halting bitch: so far is it, that these men could ever cast out devils, heal the lame, cure the blind, restore the deaf, or raise up the dead.

In his other work of that year, the *Fortresse of the Faith*, he stressed that 'in the church of Christ, no faith was ever planted, without miracles to confirm it', asking 'what likelihood thereof have we seen in Luther and his brood?'.[70] These are sentiments echoed throughout the *Dialogi Sex*: where purported miracles occur in Protestant life, Irenaeus argues that they are works of the devil, if they exist at all. Corroborative miracles occur only where there is already assent to tradition, connection with Christendom and history, and true Christian charity.[71]

This analysis of the *Dialogi Sex*'s discussion of sanctity and the holy, and in particular Harpsfield's vigorous advocacy of traditional religious practice, rather gives the lie to two views. The first is the notion that 1560s English Catholicism was a hangover from a Marian faith feeble in its self-expression[72]; the second one which sees the essential characteristic of English Catholicism at the time as one of indebtedness to the same reformist impulses as had brought forth Protestantism. Tracing Catholic faith through history, Harpsfield describes its power, its authenticity, and its fundamental difference from its Protestant opponent, particularly in its commitment to continuity and its avoidance of Protestantism's worship of 'filthy idols', in slogans such as *sola scriptura* and *sola fides*, its belief in predestination, and its rejection of the real presence, prayers to the saints, and five of the sacraments.[73] What emerges from Harpsfield's

---

70 Stapleton 1565a, fol. 35; 1565b, fol. 92; in *The Fortresse*, Stapleton (1565b), fols. 98–9, also retells the Staphylus story of Luther's inability to perform an exorcism, and a scurrilous tale of Calvin's trick, by which he hoped to fake a resurrection. His willing volunteer, acting dead for the benefit of the crowd, was found, when Calvin approached him to 'raise' him, actually to have died.

71 On the discussions on Protestant/Catholic differences over miracles in the *Dialogi Sex*, see pp. 233, 401ff., 673, 675–6, 688, 734, 919, 940, 949–50 and especially 972, when a charge akin to Stapleton's is made about the lack of miracles in heretical sects like Protestantism. See also below, pp. 155; 158–61; 182–4; 190–1.

72 Part Two has attempted to challenge this view; if the Marian Catholic corpus was rigorous, there are obvious 'knock-on' effects for Marian writing under Elizabeth.

73 Harpsfield 1566, pp. 388–97.

work then, is a reclaiming of the miraculous as witness to the power of traditional Catholic devotion, as an assertion that Catholicism possesses an indisputable historical pedigree, and a fearless admission that it thus constitutes something entirely opposite to Protestantism. All of this can be seen to build on the convictions of the Marian authors, surveyed in Chapter 1, and on their espousal of the fundamental insights of More against the devastation of the royal supremacy, the subject of Chapter 2. But part of the pedigree Harpsfield asserts in the book, in history and in visible miraculous signs, lies in the final area needing examination, Harpsfield's strong view that the Roman Catholic Church in his own day was still bearing witness, in miracle and renewal, to this line of continuity and authenticity. The Counter-Reformation, in other words, is at the heart of his case.

Defining faith and 'taming' the heathen: Harpsfield and the Counter-Reformation

Just as Harpsfield's dialogues presented a strong claim for the timeless authenticity of the Catholic faith as it had been believed and practised throughout the history of Christianity itself, and just as he adduced certain historical signs of its authenticity, such as miracle and the tangibility of the holy, so also he made the vital claim that such signs were visibly displayed in the Catholicism of his day. In particular, he pointed to the varied movements and instances of renewal then being witnessed, now commonly known as the Counter-Reformation. In his description of Catholic renewal and his commitment to it as a sign of the truth of his belief, Harpsfield demonstrated a considerable knowledge of the Counter-Reformation, and a deep commitment to its form and effect. He saw it as conclusive proof of the continuity of the faith he had always held, and of the error of its Protestant opponent; the God who had revealed himself consistently through the Catholic faith was doing so still through that same faith and its outworking.

Harpsfield's commitment to Catholic Reformation is important, for two main reasons. Firstly, it is a useful reminder of the extent to which Marian Catholics were imbued with the spirit of the age, and attached importance to it. In many ways, Marian England had been a laboratory for the Counter-Reformation, in the attempts to establish seminaries, reinstil traditional devotion and foster a renewed sense of Christendom. However, the Counter-Reformation came to its maturity only after Mary's death, as has been said; the claim that she ought better to have discovered it is therefore historically misplaced. Even so, Harpsfield shows the extent to which the events of Trent and the revival of missionary orders in particular had deeply influenced and even inspired him. This interest cannot date solely from after the accession of Elizabeth: the frequent references to the Jesuit letters in the dialogues are unreferenced and probably indicate an earlier knowledge of them now reduced to memory alone.[74] Nor, in fact, does Harpsfield's use of the Counter-Reformation indicate that he struggled to assimilate it into his celebration of the nature and purpose of the Catholic Church. His vivid espousal of the Catholicism of the time of writing, in all its rediscovery of ancient and authentic elements from its own history, underlines his basic conviction, that true faith is timeless, and that the faith rejected by Protestant England stands in continuity with the apostolic faith of Christ. Harpsfield embraces the Counter-Reformation as an indication of the truth of his claims to authenticity, not as a difficult but obligatory *volte face* from his defence of 'medieval' religion.

That observation leads to the second reason for the importance of this material: neither Harpsfield nor his contemporaries were forced by an increasingly dominant and resurgent papacy into accepting the Counter-Reformation mindset against their will, as has been claimed.[75] The *Dialogi Sex* and other works of the time show that Harpsfield and his colleagues seized on Trent, on the revival of religious orders, and on the remarkable evangelisation of the New World as indications, divine signs, of the continued authenticity and potency of the Catholic faith. The claim that as Jewel and Foxe stole the reformist middle ground, English humanist Catholics were forced back to a more conservative and papist position, is not substantiated by the *Dialogi Sex*: quite the reverse. Pole in 1557 had contrasted the charity of Counter-Reformation Italy with the hard-heartedness of Protestant London.[76] So, ten years on, Harpsfield in the *Dialogi Sex* triumphantly claimed the successes and impact of the Counter-Reformation. This therefore marked not a shift in direction, but rather an ebullient production of the truth of Harpsfield's case, that faithful adherence to the historic Catholic faith, and obedience to its demands, leads to dramatic signs of divine approval, as it always has done. So Irenaeus thunders:

> God, because of his great holiness and providence, in the manner of the best kind of head of the household, in the place of his flock, which is dying off through the impiety of the Turk and

---

74 He could also have relied on Catholic authors living abroad, for example, Thomas Dorman: see below, p. 161.
75 Wooding 2000, pp. 188, 227, 231.
76 Strype 1721, vol. III, pp. 254–5.

the heretic, has substituted for it and supplied in its stead this other world, as a kind of distinguished and noble replacement.[77]

From the fourth page of the first dialogue, the Council of Trent is cited by Irenaeus as evidence of the continued upholding of the inherited apostolic faith by the Catholic Church. When Critobolus accuses the Tridentine fathers of the subversion of truth, Irenaeus immediately agrees to rebut his claim, and Harpsfield adds a marginal note about the 'trivial and feeble calumnies of the evangelicals against the Catholic Church and Council of Trent'. It is Irenaeus's assertion that the Council was called by God under the Pope 'for the calming of these storms in the Church'.[78] Trent, like all true councils before it, is possessed of the universal consent of true Christendom, is backed by papal and episcopal authority, and constituted an authentic exercise of the Church's customary method of dealing with pressing questions of faith and practice. Irenaeus asserts that Ambrose himself would honour its decrees. If not, he would have to rescind every work he had ever written. Such an argument is designed to undermine Protestantism's professed reliance on conciliar government; Critobolus, faced with the weight and effect of Trent and his own rejection of it, is made to comment after Irenaeus's explanation of its authority, 'in the manner of the Early Church, and greatly inspired by the Holy Spirit', that

> I seem to have stumbled into some sort of maze, from which I shall never easily escape.[79]

Trent is thus unobtrusively but no less certainly a confidence-giving foundation of much of Harpsfield's claim to Catholic continuity and truth in the dialogues. He saw Trent as the latest conciliar exponent of true faith, a council convened ecumenically and speaking the settled mind of the Church as all properly constituted councils had done before it. As such, it transmitted orthodoxy and orthopraxy to each age, just as the popes did. Nor was Harpsfield a maverick voice in saying this. Harding, Allen, Sanders and others see the importance of Trent as an authoritative voice in contemporary debate, its decrees promulgated by

---

77 ['Deus pro immensa sua pietate ac providentia, more optimi patrisfamilias, in demortui huius per Turcicam ac haereticam impietatem gregis locum, alterum hunc orbem, veluti egregiam quandam & nobilem faeturam supposuit, ac suffecit.'] Harpsfield 1566, p. 783.

78 ['frigidae & ieiuniae Evangelicorum in Catholicam Ecclesiam et Synhodum Tridentiae calumniae' ... 'ad pacificandas has Ecclesiae tempestates'] Ibid., p. 323.

79 ['in labyrinthum nescio quem incidisse videor, e quo numquam commode me extricabo'] Ibid., pp. 647–8.

papal bull.[80] Their relative preference for defending the papacy probably rests on nothing more than the fact that it was the institution chosen for greatest (and easiest) Protestant attack. If they managed to save the papacy from the accusation and charges made against it, they saved everything else as well. Further, if they seem to rely on the evidence of previous councils as much as or even more than that of Trent, the reason might be their professed aim of demonstrating contemporary consistency and continuity with what has gone before, in papacy and council. There certainly seems no hint of a reluctance to discuss Trent, on the grounds that it represented a new Catholic position from which they, in their English humanist way, were long distant. Irenaeus even quotes in full the Tridentine decree on saints, relics and images, dating from the ninth session of 1563. Critobolus is forced to acknowledge that:

> I cannot fail to yield to such certain and insightful truth, and such great authority.[81]

However important Harpsfield felt Trent to be as a sign of continuity of belief, quoting its decrees lacked a certain glamour, when compared to the colourful stories of miracle and the lives of the saints with which he had bolstered his earlier arguments about the efficacy of orthodoxy. It is in this respect that he seizes on the contemporary stories of the Counter-Reformation as corroboration that, as Trent restates an authentic, apostolic faith against a new heresy, so that faith is also dynamic, both in its missionary spirit, and its fruit in the lives of converts. The witness of the miraculous which backs his evocation of the holy and the whole of Catholic practice thus also permeates his defence of Tridentine Catholicism. In particular, Harpsfield draws the reader's attention to the miracles associated with the great missionary enterprise of the Counter-Reformation, and to the work and witness of the new missionary orders, the Jesuits chief amongst them. In their determination to concentrate on mission and service, and their dedication to the apostolic faith, Harpsfield claims, the Jesuits have unlocked again the power of the faith he has been defending and elucidating.

Harpsfield's knowledge of Jesuit activity raises an intriguing question about whether his knowledge of Counter-Reformation activity had Marian roots. Cardinal Pole had famously refused the Jesuits access

---

80 See, for example, Harding 1565b, Preface to the Reader, which cites Trent as a witness to catholicity, and fols. 294ff.; Allen 1565, fol. 268v; 1567, p. 385; Sanders 1565, fols. 2, 296; 1571, p. 721, for discussions; marginal references and passing mentions of Trent are numerous in all these works.

81 ['Non possum tam certae ac tam perspicuae veritati, tantaeque auctoritati non cedere '] Harpsfield 1566, pp. 707–10.

to Marian England, and it may be assumed that that was a decision of which Harpsfield had some knowledge.[82] By the time of the *Dialogi Sex*'s writing, however, the Society of Jesus was over twenty years old, and had already made substantial progress in their missionary work. The task of chronicling that work, though, was still at a comparatively early stage. Ignatius's secretary, Juan Alfonso de Polanco, played a lead role in drafting and composing official documents, as well as in beginning the practice, early in the 1550s, of sending out a circular letter which summarised the contents of Jesuit letters to Rome and which 'powerfully conveyed to all who read or heard them ... what it meant to be a Jesuit and how 'our way of proceeding' was put into practice around the globe'.[83] But not until 1574 was this turned into the *Chronicon Societatis Iesu*, covering all the society's activities to 1556. Even before Polanco's work, however, letters from men like Francis Xavier had been circulating widely, and were printed even in the 1540s.[84] Harpsfield, in notes to his text, is able only to direct the reader to 'Vide Epist. Patrum societatis IESU', and does not offer a precise reference. This indicates either that he is working entirely from memory on the basis of having read the letters under Mary, or that he is relying for his information on those visiting him in confinement. The former, given the lack of precise references, is perhaps more likely. In any case, the work and stories of the Jesuits assume great importance for the way in which they back Harpsfield's More-based claim that miracle always accompanies the practice of authentic Catholicism.

The early discussion on holy water makes the case. In asserting its value, Irenaeus points to its current value in Jesuit missionary work:

> For, to overlook the other parts of the world, in those which we call the New World, it is said that the fathers of the Society of the holy name of Jesus have brought about many benefits to the sick through holy water, which, when they had given it for drinking to the dumb, the paralysed and the fevered, soon overcame their speech impediment, paralysis or tertian fever.[85]

---

82   See the articles by Loades (1996) and Mayer (1996), and especially Loades's comments that the Jesuits, in comparative infancy and with only one English speaker amongst them, may have been unsuitable for Pole's purposes at the time. See also Duffy 2016.

83   O'Malley 1993, p. 10.

84   See Correia-Afonso 1955, pp. 32–5; Xavier's letters became available in Latin in 1563.

85   ['ut enim reliquas mundi partes praetermittam, in eo, quem novum orbem dicimus, traditur patres societatis sacrosancti nominis IESU per aquam lustralem multa in aegrotos beneficia contulisse, quam cum potandam dedissent muto, paralytico, & febricitanti, ille linguae impedimentum, proximus paralysin, tertius febrem depulit'] Harpsfield 1566, p. 18.

It has also calmed storms, made barren women fertile, and expelled vermin. Irenaeus cites the conversion of uncouth tribes abroad as evidence of the veracity of the faith of the Jesuits, and the 'taming' ('mansuefactos') of them in their heathen practices as a sign of divine grace at work. Brazil and India alike have been places where the efficacy of the sign of the cross has lately been witnessed. He tells the story of a Moorish girl converted simply by witnessing the prayers of a Catholic, and numbers genocide and cannibalism as among the crimes from which the converts have turned. Faced with such divine approval of the Catholic missionary cause, the Protestants have a big problem:

> We can glory indeed in this remarkable mission, the learned young people produced by our Catholic missionaries, this wonderful gift of God and of the Catholic faith, which they (the Protestants) have recently so sordidly cast off having accepted it for a thousand years. Let them then show – this is what I'm looking for – the rocks, which God has moved, the children, whom he has made learned, that they might refute the lies of the Catholics. I hear mighty and splendid words, but all devoid of any action or proof.

In all of this, Irenaeus asserts that this faith, being taught to foreigners and producing such a change in them, is the same Catholic faith which had previously sustained all of Europe, and that its advance stands in contrast to a moribund Protestantism. Critobolus therefore has a choice:

> Either no-one was ever rightly instructed in the faith of Christ ... or this is self-evidently the true and apostolic faith.[86]

Irenaeus ends Dialogue Three with a short biography of the Jesuits' greatest missionary, Francis Xavier. He places him directly in the apostolic succession from St Thomas, the first missionary to India. Dying in his efforts to reach further east into Japan and China, Francis's body was miraculously preserved, and his corpse was discovered months after his death to have been perfectly preserved and uncorrupt. The comparisons between this kind of story and those Irenaeus has told of medieval saints is clear, and the link intentional: the lives and deaths

---

86 ['Haec nos vere de diserta Catholicorum nostrorum infantia, & admirabili Dei dono, & Catholicae fidei, quam isti ante mille annos acceptam nuper turpissime abdicarunt, stupenda propagatione gloriari possumus. Ipsi vero interim ostendant, quaeso, lapides, quos Deus excitavit, & infantes, quos disertos fecit, ut Catholicorum mendacia refutarent. Audio verba magnifica & splendida, sed ab omni re ac demonstratione vacua', 'omnes aut numquam in Christi religione recte sunt institutae ... aut sincera est plane atque Apostolica religio'] Harpsfield 1566, pp. 556–7, 783–5, 940, 952: another echo of Thomas More.

of the Jesuits, like those of their saintly forebears, witness to the marks of orthodoxy in miracle, sign and wonder. The evocation of Francis Xavier, indeed, leads Critobolus to repentance of his ignoring of 'these heavenly citizens of the glorious Kingdom'.[87] The Jesuits are described treading in the steps of all the saints, striving to extend the Christian faith into the near, middle and far East, one of the only good things amidst a Christian world crumbling into error and fractured by schism.[88] In them, indeed, beleaguered European Catholics like Harpsfield and his associates placed their confidence for the recreation of a Christendom with further-flung borders and a renewed orthodoxy. So also Thomas Dorman commented in 1564 that, every Sunday and holy day, thousands across the world were now participating in Mass because of the Jesuits' work, rejoicing in new-found faith while Europe struggled with schism. They were a shaming witness against Catholicism's enemies:

> Look upon those religious men of the society of Jesus, whose chiefest profession is to instruct youth in virtue and learning, to travail about the world to bring in to Christ's fold infidels and heretics. Which they have so done within these few years, with such spiritual fruit and increase, with such exceeding great gain of lost souls ... in Africa, in India, in Persia, and elsewhere, that God hath well testified by sundry miracles wrought now by them in those parties, no less than once in the primitive Church by his apostles, how highly he esteemeth their labour.[89]

Conclusion

In his introduction to the reader, Harpsfield, using his own voice, criticised the Centuriators that, in attempting to clean the Church of what they saw as stains ('maculas'), they had contaminated the whole of its history and thus guided others into the most serious heresies. It was to that history that he wanted his writings to point, and it was the shape and content of history which made his case, mirroring that of Thomas More: authenticity through continuity. So, he quotes Cicero:

> History is the witness of the times, the light of truth, the life of memory, the teacher of life, the herald of posterity. To be ignorant of what happened before you were born is quite simply like eternal infancy.

87 Ibid., p. 447.
88 Ibid., pp. 972ff., 992.
89 Dorman 1564, fol. 99; his comment about the primitive Church echoes Harpsfield's attempt to undermine Protestant appeals to it by locating its essence within contemporary Catholicism.

The *Dialogi Sex*, then, bases its claims and its appeal on that witness of history; when Critobolus is finally and triumphantly returned to the safety of the 'Catholicae Ecclesiae unitatem', it is because of the overwhelming weight of the evidence of Protestantism's breach with the past and therefore of his own error.[90] He is received back, as he sees it, into a Church alive with the presence of the divine, governed and empowered through the headship of Christ himself, mediated through pope and priests, and constantly bearing witness to its sanctity through miracle, sacrament, missionary expansion and doctrinal consistency and unity.

Thus, the *Dialogi Sex* sets about taking earlier English Catholic understandings into a recusant age, and it uncompromisingly portrays the chasm of theological and devotional difference which yawned between Catholicism and Protestantism. In so doing, it is a book which carries forward the insights of the Marian restoration, enunciating beliefs which were themselves the result of the Edwardian experience. There is an unwavering conviction about the manner in which such fundamental English Catholic beliefs, on the supremacy, on the sacraments, on the relative power of faith and reason, and on the importance of monasticism and the cult of the saints, are restated in defiance of the Elizabethan attempt finally and fully to overrule them. There is a confidence in the subject matter and a fiery quality to the language which belies the constrained and presumably difficult circumstances of the book's creation. Neither in the *Dialogi* Sex, therefore, nor in the works of Harpsfield's contemporaries, is there anything to suggest either an 'inert' faith, nor a dramatic change in outlook from humanism to re-imposed scholasticism.[91] Harpsfield and his colleagues, rather, reveal the continued strength of Marian Catholicism, and their own determination to fight for the survival of the old faith, without which they believed, as had More, that England would never find her true identity or purpose again.

---

90 ['historia testis est temporum, lux veritatis, vita memoriae, magistra vitae, nuncia vetustatis. Nesquire quid, antequam natus fis, acciderit, nihil aliud esse quam semper esse puerum.'] Harpsfield 1566, p. 1001.

91 See above, pp. 132; 140.

✠ 6 ✠

'Against Charity'
The Attack on Foxe

> *This great tome is not only a martyrology and history and an encyclopedia all in one, but it is even more a whole library in a single volume, presenting the vast panorama of a centuries-old crusade and epoch-making revolution … There can have been few books in the world like it, few that would give an innocent reader such a sense of being in the know, past, present and future, that would give a simple man so complete a picture of the world in which he found himself and how it came to be so; few books that would so completely furnish forth an untutored mind with a whole intellectual world, so perfectly suited to its tastes and adapted to its powers, so completely to arm it against the challenges and pressures of an age of unprecedented moral and mental aggression.*[1]

> *Cet animal est tres mechant. Quand on l'attaque il se defend.*[2]

Foxe and the inculcation of identity

In 1566, John Rastell excoriated Bishop John Jewel for the pathetic parochialism of his English Protestant outlook, as delineated in the *Apology*. Laying claim to a universal Catholic faith, to be found and experienced outside Europe as well as within it, he advised Jewel to 'keep yourself warm at home … so long as ye may: for if you be once out of your own country, your religion is so universal and catholike, that many miles before ye come to the Mountains of Egypt, you will be taken for a renegate'.[3] He was responding to Jewel's own mocking of Thomas Harding, that his defence of Catholicism had relied on the lives and example of distant and foreign figures, unbacked by English example, in language

---

1 White 1963, p. 192.
2 The verdict of Collinson (1994, p. 166n.) on Harpsfield's work against Foxe.
3 Rastell 1566b, fols. 143–4.

therefore unconvincing to the English. Both were pointing to a key fault line in the ongoing dispute between their religions: precisely how to lay claim to the continuity of their different versions of the Christian faith with the Christianity of the early Church. In this, both, similarly, were attempting to claim for England her proper place and religious birthright; the Protestants, by detailing the likeness of their church to the Early Church, and the Catholics by pointing to a line of succession, through the papacy, across Christendom, of which England was a part.

Catholic opponents had realised that early Elizabethan Protestants were trying to create a specifically English religious identity, grounded in history but with a character all its own. Jewel's *Apology* was the first 'official' element in the propaganda campaign of the 1560s to underpin the Elizabethan Settlement of religion with thoroughgoing ecclesiological credibility. The deluge of Catholic opposition it received is ample witness at the least to its importance, and most likely to its effectiveness. But the *Apology* was also necessarily limited, a book imbued with its author's careful and slightly bookish approach, a product of the Academy which lacked something of the vibrancy and fire needed to set alight the minds and hearts of the people. For that, something different was needed: and it was supplied by John Foxe, in the *Acts and Monuments*. Foxe's work lacked, at least in its creation, the official backing Jewel enjoyed, and set about a rather different task: the creation of an English Protestant martyrology. English men and women who had suffered and died under the oppressive cruelty of corrupted papists for the pure faith of the first Christians were, in Foxe's hands, the most eloquent of voices. They called Elizabethan Protestants to stand firm in the faith they shared with such martyrs.

Foxe's work had gestated during the years of his exile under Mary; as the Marian prosecution of Protestants progressed, he had been increasingly drawn to the idea of a martyrological project. Indeed, the execution of the Marian martyrs clearly marks the high water mark of the book, and the *terminus ante quem* in Foxe's historical conception of his work. He published a Latin 'progress report', the *Rerum in ecclesia gestarum*, in 1559, bringing up to date his description of the persecution and murder of those standing in the long line of the godly across the ages. In 1563, his research was published in English, revised and expanded, covering the time from 1000 to the present, a monumental work of historical detail and captivating incident. In particular, of course, Foxe was at pains to stress the cruelty of the Marian regime, and the tremendous witness of the Marian martyrs to their Elizabethan co-religionists. In the hands of Foxe, the voices of Ridley, Latimer, Cranmer, Taylor and the rest were a remarkable propaganda tool, a great call to courage, steadfastness and faith, a witness that the Elizabethans had received safely the torch of truth. It was intended, as Helen White commented, as a 'rationalization of a victory'; the memory of the terrors of the past became a 'reinforcement for the confidence of the present'.[4]

It is clear therefore that there was a double purpose in Foxe's work and that the *Acts and Monuments* was a two-edged sword. For, as Patrick Collinson has pointed out, Foxe's description of the past sufferings of the godly was not only offering Protestant Elizabethans historical credibility and a connection with true believers in every previous age. It was also focusing on the unchanging character of their persecutors. The fault of the Catholic Church was 'not confusion and division, but malevolent cruelty'.[5] Perhaps this, indeed, was in the long run the more successful of Foxe's purposes: the *Acts and Monuments* set in English minds for generations the character of Catholicism as persecuting, hateful and cruel. Scholars as far from Foxe's first publication as Dickens and Mozley bear witness to the effect of his work, seeing in the book's treatment of the Marian martyrs the definitive picture of the events of those years, and of the moral and spiritual poverty of the queen and her regime. Such was certainly the intention of Foxe himself, and of the Elizabethan authorities.

Though Foxe was in some ways a figure on the edge of the official Elizabethan religious hierarchy, his book was considered vital, and therefore accorded a remarkable prestige, by them. Edmund Grindal had been involved in its evolution all along; indeed, it had been a collaborative exercise between him and his friend Foxe; he was alert, on Elizabeth's accession, to its coming of age as an irresistible polemical force.[6] Bishop John Parkhurst of Norwich expressed his own approval of the book's exposure of Catholic character and his anticipation of its effect on English consciousness. Writing to Bullinger only a few weeks after its first publication, he claimed that 'the papists themselves are now beginning to be disgusted with the cruelty of their leaders'.[7] By 1571, Archbishop Parker, perhaps encouraged by Edmund Grindal, newly enthroned in York, issued instructions for the latest edition of the *Acts and Monuments* to be placed in the palaces of archbishops and bishops, in cathedrals, and in the homes of deans, members of the chapters, and archdeacons. It was to be available to as many as possible, for their better education and Christian formation. Many churches, indeed, seem to have procured their own copies too, and some still remain.[8] Foxe's

---

4 White 1963, p. 141.
5 Collinson 1994, p. 162.
6 Collinson 1979, pp. 79–82.
7 *Zurich Letters*, p. 128.
8 Cardwell (ed.) 1842, pp. 115, 117; Gregory 1999, p. 193.

book soon became important, therefore, for the definition of Elizabethan Protestantism and for claiming continuity with the Christian past. Indeed, in the hands of those responsible for the fixing of Protestant character into English souls, it was an unparalleled resource.[9]

Given that, it is surprising that the Catholic repsonse to it was considerably more muted than that to the *Apology*. In the preface to the second, 1570, edition, Foxe's introduction attacked the 'wasps' who had carped at and criticised the 1563 edition, and remarked in his preface to the Queen that 'no English Papist almost in all the Realm thought himself a perfect Catholic, unless he had cast out some word or other, to give that book a blow'. The barrage of abuse and criticism extended further, 'even to the gates of Louvain'.[10] At a popular level, in discussion, conversation and debate, that may have been the case. And it was in Foxe's own interest to play up the hatred of Catholics for his work, as its professed purpose and Parkhurst's comments reveal. But there is actually little, in terms of printed, published Catholic response to the book, contemporary with its first publication. The *Acts and Monuments* is barely mentioned by Milward, in his comprehensive survey of printed controversy of the age, for, apart from the *Dialogi Sex*, no Catholic responses exist from the 1560s. It is mentioned, by Harding and Stapleton, for instance, and Foxe is attacked: but only in passing. Their work was aimed at Jewel, and stayed on target. No author seems to have published a determined refutation of Foxe's claims and historical method, or anything approaching a comprehensive rebuttal of his project and its ideological underpinning, at the time of its first appearance. It was not until the work of Robert Persons, claim scholars as far apart as Townsend and Parry, that any Catholic seriously attempted to offer a critique of a work whose power to shape English religious understanding and identity had been so strong.[11] Perhaps, for all Foxe's claims, the work did not make its real impact until after the second edition had been published.

All of which makes Harpsfield's work the more important, and the nascent scholarly discovery of it more urgent.[12] A removed, imprisoned observer of the developing Elizabethan church, Harpsfield saw

---

9 Foxe's own response to Elizabeth and the Settlement seems to have been mixed. He was certainly less of an establishment figure than Jewel: see, for example, Betteridge 1997.

10 Foxe 1570, Prefaces (unpaginated); Mozley 1940, pp. 144–5.

11 Parry 1997, p. 295; Sullivan 1999, pp. 154–5, quoting Townsend's edition of the *Acts and Monuments* in 1841, which charged Persons' *Treatise of Three Conversions of England from Paganism to Christian Religion*, published in 1603–4, with being the first serious attack on Foxe and the source of all subsequent ones. In fact, as will be seen, Persons' debt to the work of Harpsfield almost forty years earlier was immense.

12 A point made also by Freeman 1998b, p. 327.

The Attack on Foxe

the force which Foxe's martyrs were exerting, and responded in the sixth dialogue of his book to their claims. His work, where noticed by scholars of Foxe, has received scant attention and dismissive criticism. Mozley thought the sixth dialogue nit-picking and disingenuous, the product of an inhuman personality attempting to hide its past cruelty, displeased 'to see the misdeeds of [his] own party brought to light'. Harpsfield, he claimed, 'shows a singular unwillingness to touch the the heart of the book', and attacks what he does single out childishly and partially. There is no *apologia pro vita sua*, no defence of the Marian persecutions, no appeal to fact and recent history to prove his assertions of Foxe's untruth. Harpsfield is mean-minded, and mealy-mouthed, making much of small errors already admitted by Foxe, and making nothing of the overwhelming strength of the book's holistic case. More recently, Bet described the result of Harpsfield's criticisms as sterility, beginning 'a fruitless bombardment and counter-bombardment that over the next 40 years reduced the history of the Church in England to a cratered wasteland of twisted readings, shattered texts and bullet-ridden egos, as the confessional trenches were dug ever deeper in Counter-Reformation Europe'.[13]

Such criticisms witness to ignorance of, or lack of attention to, those for whom Harpsfield was writing, and they miss the central issues at stake. The sixth of the dialogues is, in fact, a remarkable piece of work. Virtually uniquely in its time, it engages seriously with Foxe's text and with his histories; it offers not just criticism of individual stories but an underlying critique of the veracity of all of Foxe's martyr claims. And it demonstrates again Harpsfield's great claim to historical attention and credit: his ability to take the resources, historical and theological, of an earlier phase of English Catholic life and identity, and reshape, retune and remould them for the pressing exigencies of the present. In the sixth dialogue in particular, Harpsfield transmits to an English Catholic community in retreat, in opposition, in defeat and in deep crisis about its identity a solid guide to its character. It is a formula built upon the insights of the past but relevant to the beginnings of recusancy. Specifically, he sees in their position precisely the fire with which to fight Foxe's own. Just as Harpsfield had emphasised the saintly qualities of Thomas More, standing firm though in a persecuted minority, so in the sixth dialogue he emphasised the faithfulness of English Catholics.[14] He set out to show that the Catholics' difficulties were those of the true

---

13 Mozley 1940, pp. 155, 161, 175–6, 185–6; Parry 1997, p. 295.

14 Gregory (1999, pp. 250–1) notes that only in England in early modern Europe were Catholics executed for their faith: a later development than 1566, but one for which the seeds were sown early in Elizabeth's reign.

church, grounded in continuity and consent, whereas the martyrs of Foxe were rightly punished as heretics and traitors. To do so, he allowed himself a vast historical sweep which outdid even Foxe, and brought to light much about his heroes of which Foxe himself might have been wary. In all this, the dialogue precisely mirrored Foxe's double purpose: it undermined the claims of the Protestants, and in so doing shaped the character and mindset of English Catholics.

The effect of the *Dialogi Sex*'s criticism of Foxe's work went further even than that, however, and it is for this reason too that it is worthy of greater attention. For, in his historiography and his attacks on some of Foxe's martyrs, Harpsfield adduced arguments and landed blows which even Foxe was forced to concede in the second edition of his book, published in 1570. There is evidence to suggest that Foxe was greatly concerned by the power of some of Harpsfield's writing, that he felt it deserved careful reply, and that he even felt forced to make alterations to the 1570 edition of the *Acts and Monuments* as a direct result of a reading of the dialogues. Work on the evolution of Foxe's work in the sixteenth century is now thankfully more fully advanced; we are still discovering the extent of the changes Foxe made in reply to just (or even unjust) criticism, through the remarkable work of the John Foxe Project and its scholarly leaders, especially Thomas Freeman. In the following examination of Harpsfield's arguments against Foxe, as a contribution to that work, his two main purposes and their effects are investigated: firstly, his remoulding of the English Catholic tradition for the beginnings of recusancy, and secondly, the changes such a remoulding, and direct criticism, elicited in the work of Foxe himself.

The ecclesiological nature of the battle

The sixth of Harpsfield's dialogues, his treatment of Foxe's martyrology, is by far the longest of them, occupying the last 265 pages of the book: over a quarter of the total. Its main weakness is a structural one: in common with many examples of dialogue form, it mirrors perhaps too much the reality of human conversation; the discourse moves from argument to argument and back again, dealing somewhat haphazardly with the characters and content of the *Acts and Monuments*, and leaving it largely to the reader to construct the main themes of the attack.[15] However, it is also, in many ways, the most appealing and successful part of the book: lively, colourful, memorable, perhaps inspired by the very vigour of Foxe's writing, mostly free from the repetition and more technical passages of the earlier dialogues. The purpose of the dialogue

15 For an outline of the chapter themes of the dialogue, see Appendix II.

is made clear enough from the outset, as one of definition: that of the martyr, and that of what Irenaeus terms the 'pseudomartyr', who dies in imitation of the real thing but profoundly at odds with his guiding principles.

Brad Gregory's study of the whole martyrological concept in the early modern period has forcefully recreated the conditions of the age, and forms an essential foundation for any treatment of any part of it.[16] The sixteenth century was a time when the willingness to die, and to kill, for matters of religious faith went undisputed: what mattered was the definition of that death, its purpose and result. John Foxe, although more of a pacifist than many of his contemporaries in this respect, shared the fundamental convictions of the time; his attacks on Catholic cruelty should not disguise the fact.[17] Nor should modern scholarship base its methods and conclusions on an easy moralising stance which neglects the realities of an age so far removed from modern notions of pluralism, ecumenism and tolerance. The way in which such a partial understanding of the age impoverishes a proper recreation of it has already been seen with regard to the Marian period. Foxe and Harpsfield went to polemical battle not about whether it was right to punish heretics and die for Christian truth: that much, in general terms, was agreed. They fought over how to tell the one from the other.

Foxe drew for his ecclesiological model on the example of his friend and mentor John Bale. Bale's own writings on the nature and persistence of the true Church, of a gradual corruption in the institutionalised forms of Christian religion under which true faith survived through persecution and martyrdom, was encapsulated in apocalyptic terms in his *Image of Both Churches* of 1545.[18] Foxe relied on his work, claiming that 'the higher thou goest upward to the Apostles' time, the purer thou shalt find the Church: the lower thou dost descend, ever the more

---

16 Gregory 1999, esp. chapters 3 and 4.

17 The issue of Foxe's eirenicism is an interesting one. For discussions of it, see, for example, Parry 1997, pp. 298 ff., in which Foxe's desire for accommodation and an 'ecumenical' approach is lauded, and Mozley's study, which, *passim*, extols Foxe's righteous opposition to Marian cruelty. Elton, in Sheils (ed.) 1984, pp. 163–87 agreed, making the case for a mild, anti-persecution view of Foxe. Such a view, however, is treated more cautiously and nuanced more carefully by Parry himself in a later article (1999, p. 181), a view backed by Helen White, who stresses Foxe's own belief that those beyond the orthodox pale (i.e. Anabaptists) were 'justly condemned', and draws attention to his fiercely vitriolic approval of the executions of More and Fisher on the grounds of their 'treason' (White 1963, pp. 142–4, 152). See also Freeman 1998b, pp. 323–4.

18 Foxe actually made this ideological debt explicit in the new preface to the 1570 edition of his work; see also Ryrie 1999, and Fairfield 1973.

dross and dregs thou shalt perceive in the bottom, and especially within these last 500 years'.[19] To this end, Foxe had worked out carefully a historical frame of reference, tracing through the ineluctable progress of the Church to the *parousia*, and judgement, the resilient survival of orthodoxy, rigorously persecuted by the papist Antichrist. From Bale, who had commemorated figures as disparate as Oldcastle and Anne Askew, Foxe took forward the felt need of English Protestants to identify the few faithful Christians in every age, particularly in England, who had kept the truth alive. As Fairfield put it, 'the creation of a protestant saint's-life genre followed naturally upon the interpretation of history which Bale had worked out'.[20]

In the construction of this framework, and the elements within it, Foxe opened himself up to criticism of the accuracy of his scriptural interpretation, his historical understanding and the veracity of the tales he tells. In all three areas, Harpsfield takes him on. Some scholarly attention has turned to his efforts in the third area; Harpsfield's corrections and rebukes about Foxe's description of the lives of some of his saints, and his attack on Foxe's somewhat misleading attempts to claim doctrinal uniformity for them all, led to changes in subsequent editions of the book which will be examined later. But such criticisms were only the icing on the cake as far as Harpsfield was concerned; they gave easily demonstrable credibility to his more general assertions of Foxe's essential untruthfulness. More central was Harpsfield's challenge to Foxe's undergirding ecclesiology. Space (and the reader's patience) did not permit of a treatment of the historicity of each martyr in turn. Rather, Harpsfield sought to undermine the truth of Foxe's claims by finding criteria which pulled the rug from beneath them all at once. The sixth dialogue seeks to do that, and therefore responds to Foxe through two interrelated enquiries: firstly, an ecclesiological one: what is the Church? How can it be defined, and how can authenticity be guaranteed amid present uncertainty? Secondly, how can martyrs be defined: how can membership of this true Church be assessed? In these questions, of course, Harpsfield built on the investigations and arguments of the previous five dialogues; but he gave them a new dynamic too which, in denying Protestant claims to martyrdom, also rescued the concept for English Catholics unused to having to view it as an innate element of their church and a sign of their orthodoxy.

Harpsfield fairly early on in the dialogue attempts to prove his credentials by basing his appeal on scriptural grounds. The heartbeat of the dialogue is 1 Corinthians 13, St Paul's declaration that charity stands

19 Quoted in White 1963, pp. 170–1.
20 Fairfield 1973, p. 150.

at the heart of the Christian identity; it is this charity which Irenaeus calls 'what binds together and gives strength to the Christian commonwealth'. This was becoming, through Harpsfield and his contemporaries, a standard text in Catholic writings about the maintenance of unity and consensus, and the discrimination of true martyrdom, with verse 3 of the passage particularly in mind. It was a formulation they found in Augustine, Cyprian, and the thinkers of the early Church whose clothes Foxe sought to steal, and had been at the heart of the Marian appeal for the re-introduction of authentic sacraments.[21] As the dialogue unfolds, however, Harpsfield reveals his understanding of the multivalent characteristics of charity in the believer's life. When he comes later to stress the centrality of a proper understanding of Christs's strictures in Matthew 7 about the believer's life being characterised by the right kind of 'fruit', the fruit of charity is clearly the one envisaged. Charity is the charismatic quality which maintains adherence to consensus and unity from Rome, dissuades the Christian from rebellion and sedition, teaches patience and endurance in the face of persecution, and leads the believer to the channels of holiness and the divine presence which he has lengthily described already.[22] As such, it is a concept which underpins all the criticisms Harpsfield makes of Foxe's martyrs.

In common with all writers on issues of martyrdom and martyrology in this period, Harpsfield is at pains to stress the underlying Augustinian premise upon which such a discussion must proceed: that it is the cause for which a martyr dies, not the mere fact of their punishment, which determines their status.[23] He adds to this agreed basis his own interpretation concerning charity and the sanctity of the Church, based on the book's foregoing evocation of the nature of unity and the importance of unbroken consensus. So, at the beginning, he gives to Irenaeus a speech expressing amazement at the apparent fortitude of the deaths of Foxe's martyrs, but stressing that, just as one would not praise a fool, thief or adulterer for their courage in receiving punishment, neither should heretics be so honoured. Like the Spartan boy allowing himself to be devoured by the fox rather than be discovered, their actions are a matter of wonder, not praise: 'admiranda ... sed non laudanda'. He argues that it is to the patristic authors that the would-be martyrologist must look, not only for the definition that it is the cause of death which

---

21 ['vinculum & nervus reipublicae Christianae']; see for example Gregory 1999, p. 327; and above, Part Two, on the Marian material.

22 Harpsfield 1566, pp. 740, 743, 896 ff.

23 A formulation originally suggested by Augustine in Letter 89:2 and Cyprian in the *De Unitate Ecclesiae*, XIV, 12; see Dillon 1999, p. 5; Gregory 1999, pp. 87, 329 ff.; Houliston 2011, p. 43.

makes a martyr, but also for the description of that cause. Augustine, Tertullian, Epiphanius and others all agreed that those unwilling to remain peaceably within the body of Christ must be cut off from it entirely. Otherwise, even the defiant atheists executed in Hungary by the late Charles V must themselves be accorded the status of martyrs for truth.[24]

With this argument Harpsfield seeks to undermine Foxe's reliance on the Protestant notion of the 'invisible' Church, which survives despite and because of diabolical persecution. He exploits a major weakness of the *Acts and Monuments*, its essentially disparate cast of anti-Catholics, and argues that, without clearly defined boundaries of orthodoxy, any definition of the martyr becomes redundant because impossibly diverse. On the need to punish heresy and false doctrine, even Calvin and Cranmer had agreed. The former had burned Servetus in Geneva for his Trinitarian error, as had the latter an unfortunate Englishman, named only as 'George',[25] for the same reason: where and how then could appropriate, and easily discernible, demarcation lines between truth and heresy be drawn? How could a persecuting Protestant like Calvin ever, with any authority, construct the bounds of orthodoxy without being guilty of an essentially subjective, private version of revelation, which any heretic, madman or tyrant could repeat in his own city, land or kingdom at whim? In Foxe's work, Harpsfield claims, this subjective, essentially disparate quality of Protestant faith was laid bare:

> Nor is there a single one of these, however absurd his belief, who does not suppose that he professes the pure gospel, and shows himself ready to undergo all danger for the defence of his sect.

It was, for a new age of Catholic opposition in England, the Marian argument against the royal supremacy reinvented.[26]

Drawing on the previous, detailed examination of the nature of orthodoxy, Harpsfield repeats against Foxe his conclusion that the only obvious, verifiable, easily discernible, authoritative definition of the martyr must rest on their continued membership of the Church of Rome, its unity focused by the papacy and its teaching and belief received from the very apostolic times of which Foxe makes so much. Self-understanding and knowledge matter; those outside consent, those who resist the interpretation of Christian faith held by the Roman Church,

---

24 Harpsfield 1566, pp. 739, 741, 745.

25 Probably George van Parris: cf. Dickens 1967, p. 327. I am grateful to Prof. Peter Marshall for this reference.

26 ['Neque quisquam ex his omnibus [i.e. Foxe's martyrs] tam absurde sentiat, qui non putet se purum Euangelium profiteri & paratum se ostendat ad omnia pericula subeunda pro sectae illius defensione'] Harpsfield 1566, pp. 753, 755.

know of their departure from it. They have made a choice to abandon consent and are thus heretics: to claim otherwise smacks of the sick claiming to be well. Asking why heretics should be damned for rejecting one article of faith is like asking why those who respect all the laws except murder or adultery should be punished; and the result of such independent judgement in matters of faith is the very confusion and subjective muddle already seen in Protestant Europe, and especially Edwardian England, in which Protestants build their belief 'not on a proper Christian basis, but on a personal and subjective opinion', and in which the heretical government 'sets up something different than the tradition of the Church holds, about some part of faith.'[27]

It has already been observed that, just as Harpsfield drew on the notion of an apostolic succession, in the orthodoxy, orthopraxy and ongoing truth of the Catholic Church, so he recognised an equal and opposite heretical line of descent throughout the Church's long history. Here then was the outline of the rival ecclesiological interpretation he offered in the face of Foxe's work. He draws, in the sixth dialogue, a picture of a visible church, continually subject to the perpetual revelation of the Spirit, but essentially true to its origins, in constant battle, not with a single strain of opposition, but with a whole host of rival ideas which crop up at various phases in its life in a number of forms and through a number of spokespeople, always articulating one perversion or another, uttering an old heresy in a new way. Those celebrated by Foxe constitute the advocates, in their own time, of one or another of the besetting errors which Catholic Christendom has had to refute, by punishment and execution if necessary, for the common good. Harpsfield's Church is the lamp on a stand, the city on a hill, resolutely defiant against the succeeding generations of evolving heresy with which it has had to fight. Foxe's invisible church, witnessed in the deaths of the Protestant martyrs, is merely, in Harpsfield's interpretation, evidence of the way in which heresy occasionally breaks the murky waters of falsehood and shows itself in unmistakable colours before being pushed down again.

The ideas and beliefs of the martyrs celebrated by Foxe are, according to Harpsfield, merely temporary reappearances of old and hated heresies. Some, indeed most, have attacked the Mass, in imitation of their spiritual forefathers. Several have participated in rebellion and brutality, after the style of the fourth-century Donatist Circumcellions. There are men whose claims to private inspiration mirror Montanus, people whose beliefs about the nature of Christ smack of Arianism.

27 ['idonea & Christiana ratione, sed privata tantum & speciali credentis opinion' ... 'aliter de aliqua fidei parte statuit, quam habet Ecclesiastica tradition'] *Ibid.*, pp. 775, 876.

Like previous heretics, they glory in the paucity of their numbers while boasting of their growth. Luther had taken heretical views on free will from Wycliffe, who in his turn found it in the thought of Marcion and the Manicheans; he had purloined *sola fide* from Simon Magus, found opposition to prayer to the saints in Claudius and Vigilantius, and to fasting and Mass for the dead in Arius, and his rejection of those parts of scripture and conciliar definitions with which he disagreed was profoundly Marcionite. The claim to Catholic continuity with the early Church is thus made by citing the similarity between the opponents of each, as well as by that between the belief of the Church itself past and present. In all of this, Harpsfield makes plain the horror and outrage of what Foxe is asking of Christians who cherish the authority of the Church and the witness of history: that they are to see as martyrs those who die espousing the views of the great heretical movements of the past, unless it should happen that those whom the Church has always defined as heretics 'we should perhaps worship, after 1300 years or so, as the most holy Martyrs of Christ'.[28] These are words, indeed, which could have been written by Thomas More; unsurprisingly, More provides a hermeneutical key to this dialogue as to the others, the true martyr whose attack on its *ersatz* Protestant version had been so important for Harpsfield's Marian work of reconstruction, as now to his Elizabethan task of edification.

Such was the foundation of Harpsfield's ecclesiological appeal, based on the conclusions of the first five dialogues but given added colour and life through engagement with Foxe's own vigorous work. The fundamental necessity of boundaries and clear lines of permissible orthodoxy is still clear; equally central is Harpsfield's assertion that history is the only sure guide to the identification of heresy and its character. The principles of visibility, the papacy as the guarantor of authority, and continuity with the past underpin the whole. For English Catholics in the 1560s, there were challenges here, of how to react to an established Protestant church, and of how to construct their own identity, themselves now a 'persecuted' church, in a way that was faithful to their religious convictions whilst respectful to the Queen. This primary idea, of continuity, consensus and the clearly defined boundaries of orthodoxy allowed Harpsfield to play his strongest card, especially in the situation of the 1560s in England: his observation of the essentially diverse and inchoate nature of Protestantism. Such an observation, of

---

28 ['forte post mille iam & trecentos paene annos ... ut sacrosanctos Christi Martyres adorabimus'] *Ibid.*, pp. 747–53, 780ff., 862, 873–4, 885ff., 934. See above, pp. 70ff., on the earlier use of the 'heretical succession', and my suggestion that Harpsfield's portrayal of Cranmer in his work on More drew on it.

course, was meant to indicate both the heretical nature of the belief of Elizabeth's Church, and the fragmentation in belief to which a royal supremacy irresistibly led.

The Elizabethan Settlement itself rested on a diversity of Protestant views, and constantly suffered from an underlying tension about its authenticity. The Queen's own conservatism brought her into conflict with the church authorities, as she refused to alter the terms of the Settlement. Even Bishop Jewel, the main literary defender of the Elizabethan position, expressed doubts about vestments, and muttered darkly about a church 'but halfly reformed', less golden than leaden, as mediocrities go.[29] Against this background, encouraging English Catholics to remain fixed in continuity and hostile to heresy, Harpsfield in the sixth dialogue ruthlessly exposed Protestant division and disagreement in the way already described. In many cases, however, the point Harpsfield wishes to make is simply the absurdly unchristian nature of those claimed as martyrs for truth. Some have denied the incarnation, others the name of Christ. Many are Anabaptists and therefore well beyond the scope of even Protestant acceptability. Others again have denied the double procession of the Spirit, the nature of the Trinity, or the necessity and efficacy of the passion and cross of Christ.[30] When the dialogue returns to the subject later on, Critobolus's unease at Foxe's inclusion of Anabaptists as martyrs for the reformed cause is clear. The point at issue conceded, Irenaeus takes the witness of the *Apology* itself as his starting-point, and drives the message home. At the heart of the argument is Jewel's claim that the reformers are united in their cause as brothers, a claim mirrored in Foxe's rather uncritical and undifferentiated celebration of them as brother martyrs; Irenaeus tries to prove otherwise. He takes as the proof, predictably, the range of Protestant responses to the Eucharist.[31]

Harpsfield's grasp of the various issues at stake and interpretations on offer amongst the continental reformers concerning the Eucharist is impressive in its accuracy. He examines the Eucharistic theologies of several key figures, placing their nuanced understandings of Christ's words of institution against his own understanding of their plain meaning. In particular, he uses the debates amongst the Protestants over the issue, and their frequent descent into bitter exchanges and vitriolic name-calling, as an indication of the lack of the fraternal feeling which Jewel had posited. Melanchthon and Oecolampadius had quarrelled so bitterly that the former could no longer even greet his opponent; Luther

---

29 *Zurich Letters*, pp. 68, 148–9 .
30 Harpsfield 1566, pp. 754–5.
31 *Ibid.*, p. 802.

had often referred to Caspar Schwenkfelder as 'Stencfeldium', an insult which barely needs the English translation Harpsfield supplies. Calvin rejected the Consensus Tigurinus, which had in turn rejected earlier agreements. Beza affirmed the real presence but later, presumably under pressure, changed his mind. The *Apology* admits that full Eucharistic agreement has not been achieved by Lutherans and Zwinglians; but it disguises the extent to which other things also divide them, and indeed the amount of disagreement which exists even *within* the Zurich reformers. Given that:

> When there is such a great battle concerning only the Eucharist, and just between the Zwinglians, can you really expect that somehow there will be a greater peace between the Lutherans and the Zwinglians?[32]

Harpsfield appears to have to hand here some of the very books in which such attacks have been made, and quotes precise references to intra-Protestant debates on the Eucharist.[33] Mocking Critobolus's assertions of 'brotherly and friendly' relations between the reformers, Irenaeus is led to ask whether accusations that opponents are 'stubborn heretics' should be taken as the kiss of friendship. But he certainly has to hand the *Apology* itself. Drawing from it the thought that Luther is a gift of God for the illumination of the world, he adduces both Luther's attack on Zwinglian Eucharistic theology and Jewel's own denial of the Lutheran real presence doctrine before asking of the authors of the *Apology*:

> Let them think through, again and again, how, when Luther by their own admission 'was given by God to illuminate the world', can he extricate himself from this hypocrisy?

Critobolus, of course, is in real difficulties by now, floundering in his confusion, and wondering whether in fact it is only Lutherans who

---

32 ['Cum tantum itaque sit bellum de sola Eucharistia, inter ipsos Zvinglianos, exspectabis forsan maiorem inter se Lutheranorum ac Zvinglianorum pacem?'] *Ibid.*, pp. 804–12. Harding may have been indebted to Harpsfield's strong use of this kind of argument when he wrote, two years later, that Bucer was 'nor perfect Lutheran, nor perfect Zwinglian, but an uncertain, and ambiguous mongrel between both'; 1568, fol. 34.

33 Harpsfield refers, sometimes with page references, to: Brentius, *In recognitione prophetiae et Apostolicae doctrinae* 1564; Bullinger, *De Caelo et dextra Dei*; Melanchthon, *Ad Fridericum Myconium* 1558; Oecolampadius, *De Eucharistia*; Tilemanus Heshusius, *In Victoria veritatis ac ruina Saxonici Papatus* 1561, and particularly to the work of the Magdeburg Centuriators on the Mass, among others.

are the real martyrs for true Christianity.[34] Such fictional confusion is Harpsfield's method of making his central point: that, without the kind of unity and consensus experienced by Catholics, doctrinal formulations multiply, faith becomes a matter of private opinion and public confusion, authenticity is impossible to claim, and martyrdom is made a redundant and meaningless concept.

Such an ecclesiological appeal, and construction, may have said little to English Catholics at home and abroad that was new. But it was the first tailored directly against the *Acts and Monuments*, turning from this general discussion to Foxe's undiscriminating inclusion of every shade of Protestant opinion at home and abroad among his 'martyrs'.[35] Just as the first five dialogues had pointed to the Mass and to traditional devotional practice as the only sure channels of holiness in the face of Protestant attack, so the sixth dialogue covertly urges its readers to seek sanctity in the old, tried and trusted places: those who have lived and died in the unity of the Church of Rome. It was, thus, a reminder to them of a traditional understanding, both of heresy and its proper treatment, and of what constituted true martyrdom. Based on this model of the church, then, Harpsfield broadens his attack on Foxe to attempt to show the very creation of the *Acts and Monuments*, like that of Protestant theology in general, as constituting an attack on the very sense of the holy which has been at the heart of his appeal.

'Foul-mouthed': Foxe as desecrator of the holy

The English Catholic writers of the 1560s shared the understanding that Protestantism's destruction of 'superstition' and 'popery' was, in effect, an attack on holy things and the whole Catholic concept of holiness. John Martiall's claim that Protestants aimed to invade the Church and 'spoil her of her armour [and] rob her of her treasure' cut to the heart of the matter.[36] So too Harpsfield's first five dialogues should be seen, essentially, as an extended defence of Catholic notions of holiness. Yet, as they argued, history, too was a sacred treasure which underpinned Catholic life and devotion. Indeed, as Harpsfield, Stapleton and Harding set to work, they were at pains to point out that, without an adequate understanding of the course and content of Christian history, believers were prone to precisely the kind of fragmentation and bewildering

---

34 ['A qua, cum Lutherus ipsorum confessione *ad illustrandum orbem divinitus sit datus*, quo modo se extricare possit, etiam atque etiam cogitent.'] Harpsfield 1566, pp. 812–17.

35 *ibid.*, p. 820.

36 Martiall 1564, fols. 6–7.

diversity which so plagued Protestant life. It was for this reason that Harpsfield, quoting Cicero, had claimed history as the 'magistra vitae' in the preface to the book. Thomas Stapleton put it more vividly, writing against Horne, but graphically representing the Protestant use of historical sources as a violation and dismembering of a holy thing:

> Wherein even as Medea, fleeing from her natural father, and running away with a stranger, with whom she fell in love: her father pursuing her, and she fearing to be taken, slew her young brother scattering his limbs in the way, thereby to stay ... her father's journey: even so M. Horne running away from the Catholic Church, his mother, with Dame Heresy, with whose filthy love he is ravished, to stay the reader that would trace him, and his heresies, for the authors he allegeth, doth so miserably tear them in pieces, and dismember them, that it would pity any good Christian man's heart to see it.[37]

Perhaps for Catholics gradually deprived of the Mass, the observance of traditional rites and ceremonies, and the external apparatus of their faith, the concept of history as the guarantor and preserver of the holiness they sought became increasingly important. They stood in a long and distinguished line of belief, even if they lived under a regime opposed to them. And they drew comfort from the witness of their history in the face of difficulty. Such, at least, was the hope Harpsfield seems to have had for the re-telling of history and renewal of historical feeling amongst the Catholic community. The need to tell, and to renew, became paramount, of course, once Foxe had attempted to subvert the entire medieval cult of the saints by redefining martyrdom and reinventing holiness along Protestant lines. The Latin preface to the 1563 edition contained an attack on the lies of the *Golden Legend*, which Foxe thought, rather, to be leaden, a mixture of fear and flattery which threatened true historical sense. The 'monuments' of Foxe's martyrs constituted an analogy to the Catholic reliance on relics and shrines.[38] It was therefore at least part of Harpsfield's purpose in the sixth dialogue to add a different and yet parallel dimension to the defence in the third of the cult of the saints, in particular their relics and shrines. Where access to such things was denied to Catholics, he urges them to treasure, even more than Protestants, the memory of the lives which imbued material things and places with sanctity. It was, in a sense, a necessary shift from

---

37 Stapleton 1567, fol. 371; Harpsfield is credited, at least in the *Revised Short Title Catalogue*, with some responsibility for the provision of the material in the *Counterblast*.

38 Foxe 1563, *Preface to the Learned Reader* (unpaginated); King 1997, p. 22; Ryrie 1999, pp. 64ff.

devotion to the material to a more difficult, spiritual veneration of the same stories. In the sixth dialogue, Harpsfield attempts to reclaim the power for Catholics of traditional, martyrological, hagiography and to undermine its *parvenu* rival, whose aim was its destruction, by pointing to the endurance of historical memory when material devotion has been eliminated.

From the beginning, the dialogue focuses its criticism of those Foxe has celebrated on his method of doing so. At the beginning of the 1563 edition of the *Acts and Monuments*, he had included a 'Kalendar', a list assigning to many of those whose stories were contained in the book a particular date, normally that of their execution, with which they were especially connected. Their names appeared, printed in red, a compendium of Protestant heroism which covered a whole year. In the Latin preface, Foxe had defended the inclusion of such a list, not as the institution of a new, Protestant, cult of saints, but as an aide to the better remembrance of those whose allegiance to truth in the face of papist persecution had cost them their lives. In passing though, he exposed his opposition to many of those honoured by Catholics, and his hostility to English clergy allied with Rome, by claiming that Cranmer was worth six hundred Beckets.[39]

Harpsfield chose to ignore Foxe's denial of the institution of a new cult. The Kalendar offered, in an easily accessible form, a virtually complete list of those Foxe was seeking to promote as the bastions of orthodoxy throughout the history of Christianity. Not only that, but Harpsfield was able vehemently to object to the very genre which Foxe had used. Whatever he claimed, the Kalendar looked like nothing more than the institution of a new, wholly revised, cult of a very different group of saints:

> In this matter is that which I judge the thing most worthy of censure, that he assigns certain days in the Kalendar to certain Martyrs and Confessors of this new gospel, having expunged and removed from it virtually all the Saints whom the Church has up to now venerated most devoutly ... I see the old Martyrs of the Catholic Church impiously removed from the Kalendar, in order to bury their names in eternal oblivion, and the new Pseudomartyrs just as arrogantly put in their place.

In addition, the choice of those included had been all Foxe's own: he was the sole arbiter of their worthiness to be included, and their claims to martyr status and sanctity. There was no question of conciliar backing or consultation with the faithful or the demand for proof of the criteria

---

39 Foxe 1563, *Preface to the Learned Reader* (unpaginated).

of martyrdom. Harpsfield launches a devastating attack, lambasting Foxe that, though he deplores the papacy, he outdoes it, in deciding for himself whom the Church should venerate, who has earned a place in heaven with the saints. Again, the underlying argument is the critique of Protestant subjectivity which was so central earlier: that the lack of an authoritative boundary of acceptable belief leads to the replacement of it with private opinion, and to outrageous acts of arrogant sacrilege.[40] The falsification and revision of Christian history is a sacrilege, too.

Perhaps the point is made best in Harpsfield's comparison of Foxe's Kalendar with the traditional calendar of the saints. In place of the great saints, worshipped in common across Christendom, Foxe has substituted what Harpsfield portrays as a ragged collection of heretics, criminals, rebels, traitors, occultists and desecrators: 'notable henchmen of Satan'.[41] Luther displaces Saints Maximus and Claudius; Athanasius is knocked from memory by Hus; Matthew the Evangelist is made to yield to Hooper, whilst Bilney's name occupies the space traditionally taken by Jovinus and Basileus, true martyrs for Christ. Thomas Cranmer deposes the African victims of the Arians, and John Frith that of Procopius, Martin of Tours and forty-seven other martyrs.[42] Not only that, but the criteria for inclusion are hard to discern: Wycliffe is included, although he died at home of old age; Zwingli is not, despite having died in battle for the reformers' cause. Thomas Bilney is also amongst Foxe's heroes, another case in which Harpsfield quotes the work of More, in asserting his status as a repentant heretic, whose burning brought him back into the Catholic fold, and did not make of him a Protestant martyr.[43] The final area of criticism concerns the perfectly orthodox Catholics Foxe does include, neither Protestants nor martyrs, merely those of a reformist bent or with humanist credentials. The ranking of Erasmus and Pico della Mirandola (another hero and biographical subject of Thomas More) as confessors with Bucer and Fagius is, by Harpsfield's

---

40 ['In quo illud ego animadversione in primis dignum existimo, quod singulis huius novi Euangelii Martyribus & Confessoribus singulos in Calendario dies attribuerit, inductis & deletis ex eo Sanctis fere omnibus quos Ecclesia hactenus venerabunde coluit ... video veteres Catholicae Ecclesiae Martyres, ut eorum nomina perpetua oblivione sepeliantur, e Calendario impie subductos, & novos ... Pseudomartyres nimis quam arroganter suppositos.'] Harpsfield 1566, pp. 819–21.

41 ['insignes Satanae athletas'] *Ibid.*, p. 914.

42 *Ibid.*, p. 821.

43 *Ibid.*, pp. 822–3, 826; Harpsfield is even able to give a precise reference to the *Confutation of Tyndale's Answer*, and More's discussion of Bilney's death. It must have been unlikely that he possessed a copy of Rastell's 1557 edition of More, which he quotes, but the reference might have been added by an editor, presumably Cope himself.

judgement, a ludicrous and deliberately misleading attempt to ignore the vast theological gulf which separated them.[44]

Doubtless Foxe was being honest in stating his intention about the insertion of the Kalendar into the first edition of his work. Its appearance, however, certainly suggests that he was, in fact, subverting the whole framework of the medieval cult of the saints, and replacing the objects of Catholic devotion, for some of whom he expressed respect, with Protestant saints of his own choosing. In this, Harpsfield exploited a major weakness in Foxe's case, which allowed him to suggest that even those saints and martyrs of the primitive Church, by whom Foxe and Bale put so much store, had been evicted from their places of honour in favour of heretics. Mozley's attack on Harpsfield's criticisms here seems therefore unnecessarily defensive and blind to the real flaws Harpsfield is noticing. If, as he states, Foxe merely wished to provide an 'index' to the book, then he needed to do nothing, since the book has one.[45] Furthermore, Foxe's own attacks on Becket and the medieval Catholic saints, and his unfavourable comparison of them with more recent English reformers, tends rather to give the lie to his claims. The difficulty is the *apparent* arrogance of the Kalendar's inclusion, the creation of a private cult of martyrdom which disregarded centuries of consistent devotion to the saints. There is evidence, too, that Foxe recognised the force of the accusation, as will be seen.[46]

The attacks on the Kalendar, then, are used to exemplify the mangling of history which Harpsfield sees as the essence of Foxe's sacrilege. Harpsfield claims that Foxe shows himself a true Protestant in his selective approach to history; he and his kind possess, as Irenaeus puts it, 'their own Fathers, not the Church's ... their own Councils, not the Church's ... their own scriptures, not the Church's'.[47] They use scripture like history, he charges, as a wax nose or a Lesbian Rule, 'in order to reinforce their errors for them, rather than revealing them for what they are'. So it is that Protestant thought produces, on scripture and history, voluminous numbers of commentaries, interpretations, new translations and sundry personal views, 'in which sort of thing Luther is King'. They are silent, however, on subjects over which they feel weak or vulnerable to valid criticism; they resort to name-calling when argument fails them; they ignore the work of the Fathers when it is against them, and they stir up amongst the laity upheaval and discontent in religious matters. This

---

44 Ibid., p. 861.
45 Mozley 1940, pp. 133–4.
46 See below, pp. 198–9.
47 ['suas, non Ecclesiae patres ... suos, non Ecclesiae, Synhodos ... suas, non Ecclesiae, Scripturas'] Harpsfield 1566, p. 872.

undermining and distortion of sacred texts, scriptural and historical, is, in fact, the intellectual undergirding of the whole of their attack on the Catholic concept of what is holy.[48]

Building on that foundation, the dialogue explores also the tension which seems to exist in Foxe's work, as in the Protestant mind more generally, over the signs which witness to holiness. In particular, Foxe, though he had castigated the 'fables' of medieval hagiography and the cult of the saints, made use of notions of vision and even miracle in his description of his martyrs. Although his stated aim was to hold up their acts and words (the 'monuments' of the title), instead of their relics and possessions as the essence of their sanctity, his use of the supernatural indicated a difficulty here.[49] Foxe's use of miracle and vision stories perhaps indicates the persuasive power such things still exercised over English minds; but he was, having attacked the medieval inheritance, facing both ways on the issue. Sometimes, Foxe passed over a claim that one of his martyrs enjoyed the sign of miracles, citing lack of space as his reason; at other times, he claimed the gift for them and described it in detail. In such cases, Harpsfield was quick to exploit the apparent confusion and contradiction: and of course he had no qualms, either with the concept of miracle in itself, or with an alternative explanation for what looked like the miraculous in Foxe's martyrology.[50]

Foxe had reported a range of miraculous and supernatural events as having been witnessed in his martyrs' lives. As has been seen, in so doing he was treading a difficult line between his denial of the apparent excess of the medieval saints' lives and a desire to authenticate his claims for sanctity by proof of divine favour. Several of his martyrs had had visions, he claimed; Cuthbert Simpson had appeared surrounded by light whilst in prison, and Luther himself had claimed an unusual level of revelation about his theological insights, even making apocalyptic predictions about the end of the papacy and the timing of the *parousia*. To Tyndale, Middleton and Cobham also, Foxe had attributed prophetic powers of insight. Other kinds of incident had been used to show the working of divine providence, from the death of monarchs to the preservation of a fleet when one ship caught fire. The martyrs had been given miraculous powers of speech even after their tongues had been cut out; James Bainham had cried triumphantly from the

48 ['quas ad errores suos, non autem errores ad eas accomodant' ... 'in quo genere Lutherus regnat'] *Ibid.*, pp. 890–2.

49 The aim is explored by King 1997, pp. 12–18, though he does not explore the extent to which Foxe delved into the miraculous, despite his professed hatred for the excesses of Catholic devotion to the saints.

50 For an example of the former, see Wooden 1983, p. 54, on Muther, *Acts and Monuments* vol. IV, pp. 318–19.

flames that he felt no pain.⁵¹ Harpsfield did not attempt to show that the historicity of all these stories was in question, thus adopting the mantle of the sceptic of the supernatural more natural to Protestants than Catholics. Rather, as with Foxe's claims of their martyrdom, he finds criteria to challenge all the stories at once: in this case, that the one must look first to the nature of the individual's belief before being seduced by appearances of their sanctity.

In simple terms, Harpsfield argues that it is the cause in which a miracle is produced that indicates its provenance. His favoured precedent is that of Montanism, the charismatic heresy of early Christianity whose leader claimed authority because of his extraordinary spiritual experiences and inspiration. The spirits must be tested against scripture and the Church, and true miracles will not be witnessed in the lives of those who are 'enemies of God, the Sovereign and the Church'. They are given, after all, Irenaeus points out to his opponent, for human benefit, and can be expected to be clear in their witness. He finds it unlikely that speech should be given to those whose tongues have been removed, when their speech is for the destruction of the Church. For the confused onlooker, the only way of telling real spiritual activity from the false is the life and character of the recipient of miracles: 'if it is one who shapes his life and faith carefully according to the precepts of God and the Catholic Church; if he overcomes himself and his own feelings in favour of true humility: he will never be afflicted by deceptions of this sort'.⁵² In other words, he returns to the foundation of his whole argument: the need for individual believers to root themselves in the unity of the Catholic Church; the criteria for authentic miracles are the same as for authentic martyrdom.

In one sense, this argument simply restates the basic position of the speaker. Harpsfield is doing something slightly more subtle here, however, in adducing the weaknesses and vulnerability of Protestants in this kind of argument. Foxe's claims for miracle, like his claims for martyrdom, are essentially loose and lacking any boundaries. His criteria are not watertight, but depend on the subjective judgement of the reader for verification. In rejecting the medieval tradition and yet retaining some of its distinctive understandings of holiness in a partial and arbitrary way, Foxe is, in Harpsfield's view, leading his readers here into a morass, a bewildering confusion about how to tell truth from heresy. There are, in his collection of 'saints', no definite marks of

51 Harpsfield 1566, pp. 930–5, 949–62.
52 ['si quis vitam & fidem suam diligenter ad Dei & Catholicae Ecclesiae praecepta formet; si se suosque sensus ad veram humilitatem deiiciat: numquam huiusmodi captionibus circumvenietur'] *Ibid.*, pp. 956–8, 962–5.

sanctity, no easily identifiable signs of truth:

> concerning which, and all such Pseudomartyr miracles of this kind, I shall say in conclusion what Augustine once said of the Donatists: 'let no-one sell you fairy-stories'.

Against the disparate tales of miracle Foxe tells must be weighed the mass of the legends of the lives of the saints, greater in number and power, surer signs of the ongoing presence of God within Roman orthodoxy: 'thus the old is true and certain; these more recent ones are fictitious and false, and at the very least doubtful'.[53] In the radical revision of the calendar and the claiming of miracles as a Protestant preserve, Foxe has, Harpsfield suggests, attempted something as sacrilegious as the abolition of the Mass: the denial of proper notions of sanctity, and the abolition of the traditional structures within which it might be encountered.

Charity: the 'bond' and 'strength' of Christian community

In his final survey of the ideological battle over martyrdom which was waged between Catholics and Protestants in the early modern period, Brad Gregory assesses the weaknesses of what he terms 'nondoctrinal criteria'.[54] He is pointing to the sterility of many of the arguments, which were essentially circular and subjective, about how to identify the true martyr. Such marks of identification included: the morality and lifestyle of those who had died, constancy in death, the mere fact of suffering itself, examination of their social status, and evidence of their criminality in other areas. Amongst this list Gregory mentions the Catholic charge of a lack of charity amongst the Protestants, and immediately dismisses it, as an argument which 'simply re-iterated that non-Catholics could not be martyrs because they had rejected Roman Catholicism'. Yet there was slightly more weight to the charge, as Harpsfield deals with it in the *Dialogi Sex*. In the first place, the search for what Gregory calls an 'independent' criterion for identifying true martyrdom in the various partisan writings of the period seems a misguided one. In the ideological battle between Foxe and Harpsfield, one either accepted their different worldviews or rejected them: to seek,

---

53 ['De quibus, & omni hoc in Pseudomartyribus miraculorum genere, id in summa, quod olim de Donatistis Augustinus, dixerim: *nemo vobis fabulas vendat*' ... 'vetera denique illa vera sunt & certa; haec recentiora, vel conficta & falsa, vel certe dubia'] *Ibid.*, p. 965.

54 Gregory 1999, pp. 327ff.

in a twenty-first-century fashion, for independent objective criteria is a pointless and anachronistic exercise. Secondly, the inclusion of the charge of lack of charity amongst 'nondoctrinal' criteria is questionable, for clear and deliberate separation from the Roman Church was an issue of doctrine, or rather its abandonment. Defining such a separation as a lack of charity, further, was for Catholics like Harpsfield the suggestion of a multivalent concept which encompassed a range of sins. Rooted again in his Marian interpretation of the Edwardian period,[55] Harpsfield reconfigures charity as the guiding principle for beleaguered Elizabethan Catholics, a clear indicator of both the importance of doctrinal obedience and thus the proper relationship between individual, commonwealth and Christendom.

The Marian writers had pointed to the establishment of the royal supremacy as an arrogant act of schism, which led inevitably to the abolition of the Mass and the breakdown of England's social fabric and moral fibre. Within all three areas, withdrawal from consensus, sacrilege against holy things and incitement to anarchy, they pointed to the fundamental sin of the supremacy and its consequences. Harpsfield, writing against Foxe and his martyrs, uses the same three issues to point to what he sees as the real defining characteristics of the 'pseudo-martyrs'; he uses the notion of a lack of charity to encapsulate them all. Drawing heavily on Augustine, he gives voice through Irenaeus to his central idea:

> [They act] not through charity, but against that charity, with a desperate arrogance, which nevertheless seems to imitate courage ... for charity, joined with true faith alone, is the mother of the martyrs ... charity is the one thing, which, if we remain in it, we shall never leave the right path, or if perchance some human vice should surprise us, it will be overthrown by charity like water by fire.

The departure from unity and consensus is the breach which even those who crucified Christ dare not make: the rending of the fabric of Christ's clothing. In a slightly more laboured and less successful argument later on, Harpsfield attempts to prove Augustine's dictum that 'whoever does not have this charity, denies that Christ came in flesh'. In fracturing the unity of the Church and dishonouring the sacrifice of Christ in the Mass, all the Protestants have in effect committed this crime, he alleges. Whatever their professions of faith, their actions have torn apart Christ's body and set them in entrenched opposition to his

---

55 See above, pp. 41–7; 56–8, on the Marian understanding of charity, and Chapter 3 on Harpsfield's treatment of its breakdown under the royal supremacy.

purpose of the creation of unity.[56]

Harpsfield's careful exploration of the function of the Mass, discussed in the previous chapter, demonstrates that for him the Mass was the bond of the charity which Foxe's martyrs had rejected. It binds humanity to God; it binds them to one another; it is the unifier of Christendom itself, the mystical force which holds together disparate nations and people under the headship of Christ. In their attack on the Mass, Foxe's saints and the reformers generally have attacked the very fabric of the commonwealths in which they have lived. So, in this very Marian construction, he goes on in the sixth dialogue to offer evidence of the way in which the abolition of the Mass has been the mother of division and anarchy, rebellion and disloyalty to the state. In particular, Harpsfield wants to claim that a rejection of the spiritual unity of the Mass has led inescapably and irresistibly to the rise of sedition and treason against the state in the lives of those Foxe has celebrated. As Irenaeus puts it, 'sedition is not new or rare, but happens daily amongst the Protestants'.[57] For English Catholics, such an exploration was vital, as they confronted the problem of loyalty to the sovereign; Harpsfield, while stressing that loyalty to Christ is paramount, suggests that Protestants in any case are the real traitors, and have a shoddy history to prove it. In the discussion, the figure, and thought, of Thomas More is again never far away.

The most devastating attack centres on Luther, who, though not strictly a Protestant martyr, is obviously still a key figure in Foxe's work and therefore in Harpsfield's response to it. The heart of the criticism is Luther's alleged share in the ideological and theological contribution to the Peasants' Revolt, and his setting in motion irresistible forces at whose results he then expressed his horror and disgust. Using again the idea of 'fruit', the chief of which must be charity, Irenaeus describes both Luther's appeal to the people, in his doctrine of universal priesthood, and the consequent furore it produced, as new Lutheran theologies met with agrarian discontent:

> A little later the plentiful fruit of his doctrine burst forth, through the peasants and Anabaptists in Germany, with the Protestants demanding a new agrarian law, and everywhere complaining

---

56 ['Non pro caritate, sed contra ipsam caritatem, desperata quadam audacia, quae tamen fortitudinem imitari videatur ... Caritas itaque, sola cum recta fide coniuncta, mater est Martyrii ... Caritas sola est, qua manente, nusquam ab officio discedemus, aut si quid forte vitii humanitus obrepat, ab ea ut aqua ab igni obruetur.' ... 'quisquis non habet caritatem, negat Christum in carne venisse'] Harpsfield 1566, pp. 761, 766, 879.

57 ['seditionem non esse aut novam aut raram, sed quotidianam inter Evangelios'] *Ibid.*, p. 900.

that they were unjustly deprived of their fields by the nobility, no less than before they had complained that they had been kept from the chalice by the clergy.

Whilst he later wrote vehement repudiations of the peasants' actions, Luther, Irenaeus claims, did much to encourage them; in a forceful simile, he likens him to a man who climbs to the top of a high mountain and proceeds to heave great rocks off from it, whilst simultaneously shouting to those living in the villages below that they should watch out for falling rocks.[58]

From Luther to Thomas Wyatt, Hutten to Bolinbroke, Margaret Jourdemayne, Oldcastle, Acton and even Cranmer, Harpsfield is attempting to point to this common, uncharitable, fruit in the lives of Foxe's martyrs, the act of sedition and treachery. Harpsfield had used a discussion about Thomas Cranmer as the literary way into the section concerning Foxe's work, at the end of Dialogue Five. The description of his trials and final speech before execution had been one of the high points in the *Acts and Monuments*, an evocative and memorable unmasking, as Foxe wished to portray it, of the cruelty of the Marian authorities. It remains a possibility that the use made of him under Mary and particularly by Harpsfield, as the heretical opponent of the martyr More, could even have influenced the well-read Foxe in his own work. In the sixth of Harpsfield's dialogues, Cranmer is still the betrayer of his nation, the anti-Christian villain whose inconstancy, wavering theology and execution should warn Elizabethans against a royal supremacy as much as they encouraged Marians to be reconciled to Rome. His mobile and inconstant theological understanding, 'who, from Catholicism turned to Lutheranism; and soon from Lutheranism became a Zwinglian', represents for Harpsfield the ultimate proof of the jettisoning of charity, unity and agreement that is the heart of Protestantism, and he was amongst those who 'with their seditious words and books inveighed against the most devout queen, Mary'. He says of Cranmer's right hand, made by Foxe into the focus of Cranmer's heroic last stand, that now 'with the rest of his body it undergoes everlasting punishment in perpetual fire'.[59] This was the next instalment in a propaganda war over Cranmer that was far from finished.

58 ['paullo post generosus huius doctrinae fructus, per rusticos & Anabaptistas in Germania erupit, populo Evangelio novam legem Agrarian postulante, nec minus se iniuste per nobilitatem ab agris, quam prius per clerum a calice depulsum passim clamitante.'] *Ibid.*, pp. 870, 899–900.

59 ['qui ex Catholico Lutheranus; mox ex Lutherano Zwinglianus factus est' ... 'seditiosis verbis et libris religiosissimam reginam Mariam insectati sunt' ... 'cum reliquo corpore sempiternas in perpetuo igna paenas luitura est'] *Ibid.*, pp. 743 ff., 847.

Another such war, less edifying and less interesting, was that over the character of the believer's behaviour. Harpsfield constructs his treatment of this area on the same premise, of the fruit of charity, and its absence in the lives of the reformers generally and Foxe's martyrs in particular. He ranges from Luther's marriage (he rates Katherine von Bora's acceptance of his proposal as the only miracle of Luther's career), to Zwingli, the 'Evangelical warrior' to the various nefarious acts of Foxe's martyrs, libertines, schismatics, lechers and rebels amongst them. It is the doctrine of justification by faith alone which has opened this Pandora's Box, resulting in the death of good works, the rejection of discipline and a descent into debauchery and hedonism. Continuing the analogy of fruit, Harpsfield likens them to the Dead Sea fruit, which, despite its pleasant appearance, contains only ash, not unlike the way in which the cloak of *sola scriptura* covers a multitude of sins in the lives of those who have adopted it.[60] If Foxe's aim was to prove Catholic barbarity and cruelty, Harpsfield's equal and opposite aim was to suggest the moral breakdown which accompanied reformist doctrine and the breach of charity such doctrine represented.[61]

'Charity', as defined in the dialogue, is therefore a complicated nexus of concepts and behaviour the violation of which marks the Protestant from the Catholic. As such, there were clear and identifiable characteristics of its presence, and of the rejection of it by the reformers. It is a doctrinal matter, in the preservation of consensus and unity; it is a spiritual matter, through attendance at the Mass through which communal and fraternal ties are forged and strengthened; it is a behavioural matter, because charity, received through union with Christ and his one Church, is easily witnessed in obedience to state and the law of God. In all this, Harpsfield was reflecting a Marian idea of charity, and attempting to offer his audience discernible criteria for the discrimination of true martyrdom. Essentially, the appeal was for English Catholics to maintain charity through attendance (where possible) at Mass and the rejection of heretical substitutes, through their commitment to the unity of Christendom, through their communal ties of obligation and care to one another, and through respect for their Queen, even if their greater commitment to religious truth prevented them from obedience to her in every particular. By way of illustration

60 Ibid., pp. 903–6, 939–40.
61 Although primarily interested in the cruelty of their persecution of Protestants, Foxe was not averse to using evidence of Catholic debauchery, where it presented itself. His mentor, John Bale, had done so much more colourfully. A passage from the *Image of Bothe Churches* of 1545 described the 'buggery boys' of the clergy, and their 'noyful nocuments', which were the 'holy fruits of the whoredom of that holy whorish church' (unpaginated).

of the outworking of this charity, and to encourage them in the attempt, the dialogue ends with a discussion of the real thing: Catholic martyrs whose lives and deaths challenged Foxe and upheld the persecuted faithful in England.

The re-creation of a Catholic martyrological understanding

The deaths of Fisher, More and the Carthusians had become a key event in the self-understanding of English Catholics. In the hands of those who described and celebrated their deaths, they became powerful voices, calling for connection with Christendom and rejecting national separatism.[62] Cochlaeus in 1536 had set the ball rolling, closely followed by Pole in the *De Unitate*; their reflections were continued in the Edwardian period by Chauncy's *History of some martyrs of our age*, of 1550. The work of Marian writers, and chiefly Harpsfield, has already been examined. But, under Elizabeth, a new twist was needed to allow the voices of More and Fisher to speak to Catholics wrestling with their duties of obedience and conformity. Harpsfield concludes the dialogue, and the work, by offering a brief portrait of true martyrdom, its characteristics and implications. At the heart of that picture are the Henrician martyrs, but he connects them with those living and dying across the globe and in all times for the Catholic faith. In place of Foxe's very English project, he offers a glimpse of a global vista, a martyrdom that connects More with the martyrs of all times, and with the missionaries in the New World, dying in their widely separated countries for the same cause: the faith of the Roman Church. He thus connected English Catholics, in straitened circumstances, with the glories of their faith in places where its expression was more freely possible.

The importance of Thomas More particularly has already been claimed. More's work against heresy, how to describe it and discern it, provides the ideological foundation of Harpsfield's critique of Foxe's martyrs, in terms of the nature of unity, consensus and continuity. But the link is made more explicit even than that. Indeed, in the discussion of the punishment of Bilney, Harpsfield claims that the first critic of Foxe's historical reliability, even a generation before publication of the *Acts and Monuments*, was Thomas More, whose own writings already gave the lie to many of the martyrologist's assertions:

---

62 On this see Dillon 2002 and esp. chapters 1–2. Dillon's work has been fundamental in re-evaluating and interpreting this material, and points, pp. 64–6, towards Harpsfield as a key figure in its transmission.

> Thomas More throughout his work contradicted Foxe's version of events, namely that Bilney, to his last breath, had always defended his errors: More, whom all Europe upheld and admired. I do not think that any sensible person will deny that More is more trustworthy than Foxe.

So, too, further back, More's spiritual hero St Augustine had rightly asked his correspondent Parmenianus, in relation to the Donatists, what was not done justly to those who divided the unity of Christ's Church. It is the sin against the Holy Spirit, the product of an obdurate, stony heart which will not be moved by divine command or human entreaty. In dying for the survival of Catholicism in England, as well as in his writings, More was not only opposed (oppono) to the pseudomartyrs, but also took pre-eminence (praepono) over them.[63] Harpsfield thus demonstrates the extent to which not only his questioning of Foxe's historical accuracy, but also his defence of the just circumstances of the execution of Foxe's martyrs was a debt to More, and indeed of all such treatment of heretics. Mozley's comment that Harpsfield's silence on the Marian burnings indicates the level of shame Foxe has evoked in him seems misplaced on several levels therefore. Firstly, Harpsfield does lay out a justification for the punishment and even execution of heretics in any age, based on patristic precedent and continued historical practice, right up to More, and then Cranmer. Secondly, if guilt was his predominant feeling on reading the *Acts and Monuments*, writing a 250-page critique of it seems a strange response. Finally, the circumstances of his pseudonymous publication of the *Dialogi Sex*, from prison, uncertain of the consequences of his identity being revealed, do rather seem to indicate the reason why he resisted including the *apologia pro vita sua* Mozley suggests it should have contained.[64]

Thomas More's fundamental criticism of heretics and the nature of heresy is therefore the ecclesiological framework around which Harpsfield constructs his own attack on Foxe's martyrs. Holding it before the reader, Harpsfield attempts to show the comparative unity of purpose, and unity of faith, of the recent Catholic martyrs. The marks, of miracle and conversion, which should accompany true martyrdom are visible.

---

63 ['Haec quidem contra Foxi narrationem, qui eum ad extremum spiritum errores constanter defendisse ait, Thomas ille Morus, quem omnis Europa suspicit & admiratur, diserte scripsit: cui nemo, credo, prudens est, qui non maiorem, quam Foxo fidem habebit.'] See Harpsfield 1566 pp. 771–5 for this, and 'Morian' arguments about the private arrogance of heresy, and pp. 822–3, 991 ff. for the claim that More was the first anti-Foxian. The Parmenianus correspondence: pp. 915–18.

64 Mozley 1940, pp. 161, 175–86; his claim that those who allege Harpsfield's effectiveness can never have read the book is, in fact, hopelessly uncritical itself, and faintly ludicrous.

The Attack on Foxe

His sweep is broad, and he is well-informed, mentioning the work of Fazellus, the Jesuits, Alvarus, Lopez, Dominicans and others, all of whom have died for their unhesitating witness to the faith of Christ taught by the Church, so that 'I reckon that the things related by me and learned by you are most fitting to suppress the variable and arrogant Protestant boasting about the false and silly 'miracles' of the Pseudomartyrs'. He describes the conversion of foreign tribes from their idolatry as tantamount to a resurrection for them; faced with death by cannibalism, drowning, crucifixion and torture, the heroes of Counter-Reformation Roman Catholicism witness fearlessly and die bravely, the importance of their mission attested by miracle and consummated in their deaths.[65]

Thomas More, however, contributes more to this reconstruction of English Catholic martyrology than its theological character. From glorying in the deaths of the missionary martyrs abroad, Harpsfield turns to the Henrician martyrs. The link between them is the papacy, and a final appeal is made by Irenaeus for his opponent to see the pope as the guarantor of an authentic faith, the authority behind the task of the missionaries just as he was that behind the deaths of Fisher, More and the Carthusians. Both groups alike have died for the establishing and maintenance of one, true, faith, throughout the globe. Both groups alike have offered their witness and their lives for an unbroken succession of orthodoxy, handed down from the apostles and preserved by the Spirit. The papacy, in this respect, is as Gregory understood himself, the *servus servorum*, the head which enables the existence and mission of the body. The Henrician martyrs died to keep England secure in this unbroken succession, lest men, women or children decided matters of doctrine on the hoof and England's church descended into heresy, for which reason 'I reverence their innocent blood'. Though Harpsfield devotes only a few pages to the Henrician martyrs, their place at the book's conclusion is significant, as are the echoes of Marian views of More and Fisher. They were 'the lights of all Europe ... one a priest, the other a layman'. Henry VIII, Harpsfield claims, may have vacillated in his decisions about the papacy, 'but he did have More': if only he had listened. Even those true martyrs who died for the papal supremacy in England outweigh all of those falsely celebrated as such in the *Acts and Monuments*, written by an author 'who piles up, but doesn't properly weigh up, his martyrs' ('numerat ... ponderat'). John Houghton, John Stone, John Travers, Powell, Featherstone and Abell, and the rest of the Carthusians, cry out to English people to remember the sanctity of

---

65 ['quae ut a me recenseantur, & a te cognoscantur ad reprimendam varium atque arrogantem Euangelium de falsis & ridiculis Pseudomartyrum miraculis gloriationem dignissima existimo'.] Harpsfield 1566, pp. 967–76.

religious unity and the inheritance they have from the saints of previous generations. Thomas More and John Fisher do the same, the most outstanding ambassadors for their cause whom God could have chosen, against Henry's 'new-fangled, halfway-house religion'.[66]

Irenaeus's final appeal to Critobolus, which finally wins him back to orthodoxy, is based on the Augustinian plea for people to remember how little they can know, and, when troubled by doubt and scruple, to cling resolutely to things made absolutely clear by scripture and well-attested within the Church. It reveals the extent to which the book intended to give Catholics resources to help themselves feel connected to the Church in every time and place. Such a sense of connection could not have been easy to come by in early Elizabethan England, still less as time passed. In More and the Henrician martyrs, Harpsfield pointed to a spiritual connection, an example of fidelity and strength. In following the example of More, in their resistance to heresy and their ongoing intellectual and spiritual assent to the unbroken unity centred on Rome, English Catholics were connected to the glories of the Counter-Reformation, to the medieval saints and martyrs, and to the witness of the faithful in every generation. For Marian Catholics, More's martyrdom underpinned the understanding on which they built their church. For Elizabethan Catholics, he had the more direct and more painful task of identifying with and encouraging them in their spiritual isolation and principled resistance to the religion of the state.

Harpsfield's effectiveness and the changes to the 1570 *Acts and Monuments*

The evolution of Foxe's work bears witness to its popularity, effectiveness and appeal. The mere publication of the 1570 edition, greatly expanded and with new prefaces and material, indicated both the success of the first edition and its continued importance as a tool for creating a Protestant mentality in England. Betteridge, however, sees darker authorial motives at work as well. In his view, the shift from the 'prophetic' manner of the 1563 edition to the more 'apocalyptic' 1570 version shows Foxe's response to the situation in which he revised, and does not demonstrate a simple teleological accretion. There is, in the 1570 edition, a greater use of mythical and biblical comparisons, in place of the merely historical; 'the scale of his history increases; it becomes more universal and simultaneously less human and less worldly'. In Betteridge's view, such a shift is towards the apocalyptic in the sense that it reflects Foxe's despair at the lack of progress in making the Elizabe-

---

66   *Ibid.*, pp. 977 ff. and esp. p. 991.

than church more Protestant, and therefore reveals that his 'view of the possibility of continuing reform carried out by worldly human actions darkens'. The 1570 edition emphasises discontinuity, and reflects Foxe's displeasure that the predominance of Catholics at court hinders further reform through political means. What, for Foxe, were the 'defeats and disappointments' of the 1560s produce the starker, more threatening, grander scale of the 1570 book.[67]

Such a view is ingenious, but over-convoluted.[68] It also attempts to support literary-critical observations with questionable historical assertions. The presence of a large number of Catholics at court, hindering progress to a fully reformed church, is a fundamental misreading of the Elizabethan situation; however much Elizabeth herself refused to make windows onto men's souls, however mild the regime intended to be with Catholics, the settlement was definitely not Catholic, and left no room for the public expression of Catholic identity. There is, further, clear historical evidence for the motivation behind some of Foxe's alterations much nearer to hand. They revolve around Harpsfield's work in the *Dialogi Sex*; in scope and content, in argument and sweep, it is possible to see many of Foxe's revisions as responses to the work of Harpsfield. Foxe was stung, not so much by English Protestant intransigence as by English Catholic opposition, into the precise refinements of the 1570 edition of his work.

Foxe, in various places, made it clear that he felt challenged by the *Dialogi Sex* into further and carefully targeted response to the author's claims. Writing around 1569 to Matthias Flacius, another of Harpsfield's targets, he had asked what was the Centuriator's response to the arguments presented in 'those Dialogues'. Indeed, he wonders whether it is right to reply at all, and merely give the author a false authority, or whether to provide a 'brief reply' to the work, and to Harpsfield's 'slanders'. It is not clear whether Flacius replied, or whether he took the dialogues as seriously as Foxe. But such a letter indicates at least that the question of the correct method of replying to 'Cope' was in Foxe's mind as he prepared the second edition of the martyrology, and it may hint at a greater sense of unease in Foxe's mind, as he remembered the section of the book 'which attacked my book, particularly and by name'.[69]

Foxe's preface to that 1570 edition, as has been seen, suggests further that some at least of the Catholic criticism of its predecessor had stuck. Four questions were included in a separate preface aimed at 'all the

---

67 Betteridge 1997, pp. 212–31.
68 For Freeman's doubts about it, see Freeman 1998b, pp. 320–1.
69 MS Harleian 417, fol. 105 ['cum liber meus peculiariter et nominatim impetit'].

professed friends and followers of the Pope's proceedings', enquiring how they equated a claim to spiritual authority with persecuting zeal. In a clear reference to Harpsfield (Foxe knew of his authorship, although he addressed his remarks to Cope), Foxe asked after the reason for Catholic hatred of Protestants, when they themselves have been shown kindness in England 'though a few of your Archclerks (i.e. Archdeacons) be in custody'. More fundamentally, he enquires after the nature of the Christian faith, whether it is spiritual or corporal, a reinvention of Jewish ceremonial or a religion of the heart. The Catholics who attacked the first edition seem therefore to be in his sights from the beginning: and, since the *Dialogi Sex* represented the main literary contribution to the debate, it is hardly surprising that it figures large.

In several sections of the book, Foxe responds directly to Harpsfield's charges of historical inaccuracy. These had been few, and dealt with relatively minor incidents. In doing so, Harpsfield had clearly hoped simply to cast enough doubt on Foxe's trustworthiness as a historian that the whole of the work was undermined. Foxe of course drew attention to the small number of cases which Harpsfield had specifically challenged, asking how 'Cope' could withhold his pen from writing about a mountain of popish lies and 'find nothing else to set your idleness on work, but only to write against the Lord Cobham, Sir Roger Acton, Browne, Onley, Cowbridge with a few other whom with much ado at length you have sought out, not so much for any true zeal to rebuke iniquity, as craftily seeking matter by these to deface and blemish the book of Acts and Monuments, which seemeth be like to make you to scratch there where it itcheth not'.[70] Two such examples will be sufficient to show the effect which Harpsfield's criticisms had had in specific cases: the stories of John Oldcastle and Master Cowbridge.

In giving prominence to Oldcastle, otherwise known as Lord Cobham, Foxe was again following the example of his friend John Bale, who had celebrated the peer in an earlier treatise. With Anne Askew, he represented a key figure in Bale's efforts to redraw martyrology along English Protestant lines. Foxe in 1563 followed the main lines of Bale's version, dealing with Cobham as a fighter for truth against a king, Henry V, made by the bishops of a corrupt papacy 'fit for their hand'. Cobham saw his rank as placing upon him a duty to defend the gospel; he is made by Foxe to make a speech denouncing pilgrimage, penance, images, saints and all the paraphernalia of a filthy papist religion, fighting valiantly against the plot of the Archbishop of Canterbury, Thomas Arundel, to persuade the king to rid England of all remaining Wycliffites. Arundel's success brings down divine retribution in the form of a disease which

70 Foxe 1570, p. 689.

deprives him of the powers of swallowing and speech, while Cobham himself is condemned to death and executed, dragged to his death on a hurdle 'as though he had bene a most heinous traitor to the Crown'.[71]

Drawing on his evocation of charity as the mark of the true Christian, a charity which has a proper sense of its duties and responsibilities to both commonwealth and Christendom, Harpsfield in the *Dialogi Sex* set out to show that Cobham's death had been suitable for a traitor because that was in fact what he was. From the outset, he argues that Cobham not only peddled views entirely at odds with Catholic orthodoxy, but also intrigued and plotted against his king, and was therefore a heretic and a traitor, much in the style of the Circumcellions or the Arians. The historical details of Cobham's execution, which even Foxe retains, that he was both burned and hanged, indicate the double nature of his crimes, a man who was 'an enemy of God, the Sovereign and the Church'. Where Foxe had attempted to claim that the advocacy of Cobham and others of vernacular scriptures was the reason for their persecution, Harpsfield shows instead that it was a mixture of their isolationism in so doing and their nefarious activities against the king that proved their downfall.[72]

Foxe, stung by the criticism, and the potential loss of a figure central to his purpose, replied at almost extraordinary length in the second edition. He claimed that the full refutation of Cope's 'gall and choler' would require a full treatise, and did not rule out such an enterprise, further indication perhaps of the extent to which the *Dialogi Sex* had irked him. As he puts it:

> you heap up a dung hill of dirty dialogues, containing nothing in them but malicious railing, virulent slanders, manifest untruths, opprobrious contumelies and stinking blasphemies, able almost to corrupt and infect the air.[73]

The main difficulty for him is revealed in his treatment of Henry V, whom he wishes to portray as a man caught up by popish plotting against the Lollards, and thus led to open hostility with Cobham. The true traitors on this reading are the bishops and archbishop whose loyalties lead them to place their obligations to Rome above that to their own country. He bases such a version of the history on his distrust of the chroniclers upon whom Cope has relied, whose tales disagree with one another and whose own motives are in question. Aside from this, Foxe's defence consists largely in assertion rather than argument; he sidesteps the question of Cobham's treachery and concentrates on

---

71 Foxe 1563, pp. 261–81 *passim*.
72 Harpsfield 1566, pp. 747–8, 827–8, 833–4, 954.
73 Foxe 1570, p. 686.

Henry, Arundel, and the bishops, and more properly can be said to begin the kind of 'cratered wasteland' of variant historical readings for which Parry criticises Harpsfield.[74]

Such assertions aside, however, the predominant tone of these twenty pages is angry and defensive. Foxe's counter-attack is also wide-ranging: in attempting to deal with Cobham, he attacks the claims of the *Dialogi Sex* in an indiscriminate way, seeing it as further evidence of papist intransigence, malice and cruelty; Harpsfield has preferred 1000 pages of literary bile when a gentle letter of historical correction would have sufficed, if the *Acts and Monuments* was thought to contain error. He refutes the charge of overtaking even the Pope in his saint-making, accusing the papacy of being the 'God-maker of Rome', given the devotion enjoined on Catholics towards the saints. And there is a further defence of the Kalendar of the 1563 edition, denying the slander that he is attemping to deprive the Church of her early saints and role models. The different readings, Catholic and Protestant, of the life and death of Cobham cannot be resolved and reconciled; what the plethora of fierce replies Foxe includes with his defence of the Cobham material indicates is the extent to which he himself had been irked by the dialogues. But whatever the nature of the response, there is every reason to think that it indicated for Harpsfield a task successfully accomplished: defensive anger probably did as well as material change to the text of the *Acts and Monuments* as an indication of this.[75]

In the case of Master Cowbridge, however, Foxe is forced into material change, and a more serious historical climb-down. In the 1563 edition, the story occupied a brief paragraph, detailing Cowbridge's fierce treatment at the hands of the Oxford dons Drs. Smith and Cootes in 1539. Cowbridge, having inherited a sum of money from his evangelical father, had commenced an itinerant preaching ministry, intended for 'instructing the ignorant'. Arrested in Wantage, where he was ministering without ordination, he had been sent back to Oxford via Bishop Longland, and incarcerated in conditions which affected the balance of his mind. Suspicion about Cowbridge's views and the hatred of Oxford papists, who pressured Lord Chancellor Audley to issue a writ for his execution even though he was 'somewhat allied' with Cowbridge's cause, led to his inevitable execution. The unfortunate young man went to his death quietly and with grace calling on the name of Christ, his wits now restored after better treatment in jail through his eventual capitulation.[76]

74 See above, p. 167.
75 See also Aston and Ingram 1997, pp. 82ff.
76 Foxe 1563, pp. 570–1.

The Attack on Foxe

Harpsfield in the *Dialogi Sex*, in turn, challenged the historicity of the story Foxe had presented of the zealous young evangelical hounded to his death by furious papist foes. It is possible, of course, that these were events Harpsfield himself remembered, and at which he may even have been present; the trial of Cowbridge certainly occurred while he held a fellowship at New College. In the dialogue, he is portrayed as the heretic who attempts to place his hands on holy things, as impious as Foxe himself. He was a denier of episcopacy and the validity of ordination, and a disciple of Wycliffe. Most importantly, Harpsfield's legal training enabled him to pounce on Foxe's historical inaccuracy. The account of Cowbridge's trial had been in error: men could not be burned on the recommendation of academic inquisitors. Such a sentence required episcopal jurisdiction. The alleged barbarities of Drs. Smith and Cootes are therefore false. It was, in fact, his trial before Bishop Longland which eventually resulted in his condemnation, but not before Longland had tried every method of persuasion and entreaty to redeem the life of his interviewee. Harpsfield describes the gentle treatment of the young man by Longland, suffering his crazy views and attempting to point out to him the consequences of his heresy. Cowbridge rejected fasting, denied the name of Christ, believing that all who called on him would be damned, and believed that the Mass was an idolatrous deception. Even Cromwell, taking his views as a whole, declared that they fell on the wrong side of orthodoxy.[77]

In the face of this, the version of the story which Foxe re-tells in 1570 is rather different, and somewhat shorter than the first edition. Cowbridge is condemned by Longland; his academic tormentors are not mentioned. There is now no rehearsal of the charges against him. But an assertion of his madness is made, as a means by which Foxe can turn on his enemies the charge of cruelty, differently aimed. If indeed Cowbridge said the things 'Cope' has alleged, Foxe says, then he was 'a man more fit to be sent to Bethlehem (i.e. Bethlem Hospital, for the mentally ill), then to be had to the fire in Smithfield to be burned'. The point is now not that the papists punish severely those who stand in the pure faith of the reformers against their corrupt version, but that they are simply barbarous and merciless towards those, like Cowbridge, whose minds are weak: 'there is no other way: neither pity that will move, nor excuse that will serve, nor age that they will spare, nor any respect almost that they consider'.[78] Whilst Foxe has re-sharpened his blade against the Catholics, using the same figure, the details are different. A comparison of the 1570 version with that from the 1563 book indicates

---

77   Harpsfield 1566, pp. 852 ff.
78   Foxe 1570, p. 1292.

a tacit admission of historical error. And, while the story represents a tiny incidental detail in Foxe's great narrative, the necessity for such an alteration was victory enough for Harpsfield, who would have been hoping that such minor corrections would lead to a more serious seed of doubt being sown in Foxe's readers' minds.

The same was true of the evolving story of the 'mother of Lady Young', first included in the 1563 *Acts and Monuments*. There, Foxe had described her death in 1490, a woman 'who for her constancy and virtue, was greatly to be commended and praised', and who died courageously in the face of fierce papist persecution of her reformist beliefs. Harpsfield unmasked this curious figure in the *Dialogi Sex* as Margaret Jourdemayne, a woman who, far from living a saintly and heroic life, had devoted herself to bringing about the assassination of the king through her use of dark arts. In this light, Harpsfield suggested, she made a unseemly, but typically treacherous, addition to Foxe's list of martyrs. In the 1570 edition, Foxe somewhat confusedly listed several options for rescuing the situation, and asserts that he meant to honour not Margaret Jourdemayne, but the anonymous mother of Lady Young, a different figure entirely. His conclusion to the section, however, admits error in the coupling of her with Eleanor Cobham and Roger Onley, whilst grumpily charging Harpsfield with the customary failings of a nit-picking, carping and grudging approach to the essential wonder of the material of his book, 'finding quarrels, where no great cause is justly given':

> If M. Cope be so highly offended with me, and become so heavy master unto me ... let him take this for a short answer, because my leisure serveth not to make long brawls with him: that if I had thought no imperfections to have passed in my former edition before, I would never have taken in hand the recognition thereof now the second time, whereby to sponge away such motes.[79]

Other changes between the two editions at the very least suggest that Foxe's reading of the *Dialogi Sex* had alerted his mind to ways in which he could tighten up his book in order the better to meet Catholic criticisms. Perhaps the greatest concession to the strength of Harpsfield's arguments comes in omission: the Kalendar, subject of so much accusation, is left out. Its place is taken by a simple alphabetical list of those whose martyrdom Foxe commemorates within the book. Though he later defends its original inclusion, its removal indicates the power of Harpsfield's criticisms, that, in creating such a commemorative aid, Foxe was open to the charge of having displaced the great saints of the

---

79 Foxe 1563, p. 371; 1570, p. 830–2; Harpsfield 1566, pp. 830–1.

Church's past in favour of those whose status he himself had decided independently. Whatever Foxe's own motives and understandings, he understood the need to remove not only what was actually misleading, but also that which had the appearance of being so.

On other occasions, Foxe doubled down on claims justly challenged by Harpsfield. Elizabeth Evenden and Thomas Freeman note a shift in Foxe's use of illustrations in the 1570 edition in this regard. In relation to Roger Acton and his Lollard associates, for instance, Harpsfield had correctly challenged Foxe's glorification of them and their executions by pointing out that they had been rebels against the Crown. Foxe responded by including in the new edition of the book an illustration of these hangings. As Evenden and Freeman remark, 'sensational illustrations were being used to undermine valid arguments'. Again, in the celebrated and contentious case of Thomas Bilney, who was executed for heresy under King Henry but about whose constancy in his beliefs there had been great dispute, Foxe emphatically repeats his claims for Bilney's courage and resolute Evangelicalism, against Harpsfield's challenges, by including a new woodcut of him holding a finger in a candle as proof of his lack of fear about the fire of the stake. Three martyrs revealed by Harpsfield as having been misidentified in the 1563 edition were celebrated further in the 1570 version by being pictured. Similarly, a prophecy attributed to Hus about Luther, which the *Dialogi Sex* emphatically disproved, was repeated but with the attribution removed. There is a pattern here, of defending against critique by offering a trenchant repetition of the original claims, tidied up in the wake of legitimate correction.[80]

Foxe also makes changes to the 1570 edition which are a clear attempt to begin to undermine the Catholic martyrology with which the *Dialogi Sex* had ended. There is, thus, rather more material in the book than there had been in 1563 which relates to More and the Henrician martyrs.[81] The tactic is simple: to attempt to turn against Harpsfield the charges which he made against Cobham and his like: that they were traitors. In his taking of the pope's side against his own prince, Foxe alleges, More was in fact the one disloyal to his own country. But he seems to have seen his prime rhetorical weapon against More as being to enlarge upon the accusations of cruelty and fierce, unbending persecution, which had predominated in the 1563 edition, of the Lord Chancellor's 'hatred and deadly pursuit', and his nature as a 'heavy troubler of

---

80 Evenden and Freeman 2011, pp. 213–14.
81 There was also an omission of the dispute on free will among the Marian martyrs, after Harpsfield had played it up: see Freeman 1998*b*, p. 322.

Christ's people'.[82] Asserting that More, Fisher and the Carthusians may be martyrs in the pope's kingdom, but never in Christ's, Foxe goes on to attack the Carthusians' treachery in particular. And he reveals, in discussing Houghton, who had been singled out for special praise in the closing pages of Harpsfield's book, that he has a good clue as to the author's real identity. The author, through Irenaeus, had revealed a personal knowledge of him, which could not have been Cope's, since he is too young to have been acquainted with a man who died thirty years previously. The dialogue, Foxe concludes, was written by 'another "pseudocopus", whatsoever, or in what Fleet (Prison) so ever he was'.[83] In acknowledging the potency of the criticisms of the *Dialogi Sex* in the revision of his work, Foxe acknowledged also that he knew the real identity of his opponent.

Most fascinating of all, as has been indicated, the sheer historical sweep of the second edition is also greatly increased. Where the first edition had begun with a long and fierce attack on Thomas a Becket, taking him as the *terminus post quem* for the serious examination of Protestant martyrs in the middle ages and particularly after Wycliffe, the 1570 edition began with the earliest church. Though the 1563 edition claimed the martyrs died in accordance with the beliefs of the primitive church and apostolic fathers, the 1570 edition tried to prove it by beginning its survey in the apostolic age. The aim, still, was to show papal deviation from the first Christians and their belief, but Foxe assumed and asserted less and attempted to 'prove' rather more, in starting from AD 34, and not with the death of Becket.

Betteridge, already quoted, sees this as Foxe's response to the slow progress of England becoming a Protestant nation, a move to a more 'apocalyptic' frame of reference.[84] A more obvious and less fanciful suggestion might be to adduce the influence of the *Dialogi Sex*. Although Harpsfield's work was not, as Foxe's, chronologically organised, his reliance on the lives and writings of the fathers had been immense, in allusion, description and direct quotation. The battles Irenaeus and Critobolus had waged over Epiphanius, Augustine, Jerome and the rest had been a direct rebuke to the claims of Foxe, given that the 1563 *Acts and Monuments* had seemed to undermine its own claims, that the Protestants were the direct spiritual descendants of the early church believers, by its failure to deal adequately with the martyrdom of that period. It must be more likely, therefore, that the vastly different time-frame of the 1570 edition was an attempt to remedy the imbalance and

---

82 Foxe 1563, pp. 497, 508.
83 Foxe 1570, pp. 1216–17.
84 See above, p. 192.

be a riposte to Harpsfield's firm reliance on patristic sources, given that Foxe makes it clear in other ways that Harpsfield's work has been an influence on his revision.

Conclusion: new identities from old

It is the conclusion of Anne Dillon that the sixteenth-century English Catholic community, 'in constructing the martyr, constructed itself'.[85] Their debt to Nicholas Harpsfield, because of the work of Foxe, is central in this reconstruction. English Catholics had been unused to seeing themselves as potential martyrs, those who might be called to share in the glorious deaths of the martyrs celebrated in the *Golden Legend*, as well as in images, festivals and even scripture. Their faith had been the established faith of their country for centuries; resistance unto death was a remote concept. First the Henrician martyrs and then the Edwardian experience changed their identity radically; even if they were not executed, allegiance to the faith of Rome placed them in a strange, disconcerting, new world of minority and opposition. As the Elizabethan Church settled, that Edwardian Catholic self-identity began to seem rather more a permanent state of affairs. Foxe's publication of the first edition of the *Acts and Monuments* was meant to undergird the integrity of Elizabethan Protestantism by defining true martyrdom and offering the sense of a bright succession. In the *Dialogi Sex*'s repudiation of Foxe's work, Harpsfield drew out further the traditional arguments so characteristic of his hero More, arguments he had spelled out in the first five dialogues, and offered English Catholics in the sixth equal and opposite martyrological resources for their comfort and self-definition.

Drawing on themes which had been central to Marian Catholic theological writings, of the fundamental importance of a historical sense, the location and importance of holy things, the nature of charity, and the true character of loyalty to the state, Harpsfield fashioned a response to Foxe which tailored a Marian, and Morian, understanding to the situation of the 1560s. And Thomas More, the man whose life and death prophetically warned against a royal supremacy, and whose thought underpinned the Marian restoration, was a main source again of Harpsfield's resources. Through Harpsfield, More became the first proper critic of Foxe, even before Foxe wrote, through his writings against heresy; he was the figure who first pointed Englishmen to a thorough sense of history and a proper sense of sanctity; and he was the first English martyr since Becket, the prototype for an oppressed English

---

85 Dillon 1999, p. 226.

Catholicism, the supreme example of the error of Foxe's celebration of traitors, heretics and scoundrels.

The attack on Foxe, then, marks the next stage in Harpsfield's evolving attempt to define for the English the integrity and character of Catholic faith. Through his attempt to undermine Foxe's criteria for martyrdom, and the 'martyrs' themselves, he draws on themes, not just from the first five dialogues, but from his Marian writings also, to illustrate the areas in which Foxe's 'pseudomartyrs' demonstrate their true character. And he exploits the martyrological debate, which Foxe had started, to offer to his co-religionists in England a similar sense of their own membership of a glorious line of martyrs, those whose faith, rooted in continuity and consensus, stands firm against the breach of unity and the rejection of Christendom. In so doing, he made clear the difficulty of the ecclesiological questions which English Protestants were facing, and the individual subjectivity to which their doctrines were prone. But he also prepared the hearts and minds of his fellow Catholics for the re-emergence of martyrdom which was waiting in the 1570s and 1580s, and encouraged them to trace their own membership of a line of witness more glorious and more easily discernible than Foxe's. In the process, he wrung from the martyrologist concessions and changes to the structure, scope and content of his work which deserve far greater attention than they have received. Far from being comprehensively outmanoeuvred and worsted in debate, Harpsfield demonstrated that English Catholics in the 1560s had a strong challenge to make to the Protestant assimilation of Christian martyrdom.

☩ 7 ☩

Afterlives
Harpsfield, More and English Catholic Identity

Nicholas Harpsfield's death in 1575 in many ways represented the loss of a vital link with England's Catholic past, his career having spanned the period of religious change in England. Harpsfield's final years in confinement had been spent working on two great works of polemical historiography; the *Dialogi Sex* achieved publication and importance in his own lifetime, while the *Historia Anglicana Ecclesiastica* was not destined to do so for another fifty years. Both works aimed to make the importance of that connection and unity apparent to a generation of English Catholics struggling with the radically new situation of minority and state oppression; they attempted, in the process, to say something to Protestants too. In them, Harpsfield was attempting to transmit to the beleaguered Catholic community of his own day the confidence of the succession in which they stood, and to offer them connections with the past, especially English connections, which might offer hope. In so doing, he built upon the basic convictions of his life and work, and of his generation: an adherence to Thomas More's hard-won defence of papal supremacy, and a passionately felt commitment to the continuity of Catholic faith in England. Both convictions under-girded also his attack on Foxe and his part in the re-creation of an English Catholic martyrology.

Scholarly examination of English Catholicism after the accession of Elizabeth has taken a particular interest in the way in which the English Catholic character changed and evolved, as the hope of an early return to the old faith receded and the Elizabethan Protestant regime became more firmly rooted. The arrival of seminary priests in the 1570s and 1580s, trained in the various foundations in Europe, marks for some a point of profound historical discontinuity, a moment in which the late medieval inheritance is comprehensively rejected in favour of a more militant Counter-Reformation spirit. It was on this premise, most notably, that John Bossy based his own study of post-Reformation English Catholicism, choosing 1570 and the foundation of the Douai seminary as his starting-point, and claiming that figures such as Thomas More, Reginald Pole and Queen Mary belonged to the 'posthumous history ... of 'mediaeval' or 'pre-Reformation' Christendom in England', and that English Catholicism after 1570 was 'a body which had some right to claim continuity with the past but was nevertheless in most respects a new creation'. Bossy's thesis contended that the leaders of Elizabethan Catholicism were men largely unconnected with the Marian establishment whose outlook had more in common with humanists still in England than with the exiles in Louvain, and who rejected the royal supremacy, not because it was hostile to tradition, but rather because of their high sense of clerical vocation.[1]

Bossy's version of Elizabethan Catholicism has won wide support, and has been reinterpreted and reworked by several others. Morey agreed that the first twenty years of Elizabeth's reign were characterised by what Dickens called Catholic 'survivalism', in which a Marian Catholicism of social practices which downplayed internal conviction struggled to keep itself alive, before the seminarists brought across a faith more committed to the interior life.[2] In effect, Bossy and Morey were reiterating an earlier view about the importance of the mission, put at its simplest in the statement that 'the decline of Catholicism ceases with the establishment of the 'mission''.[3] While they relied on primary sources in reaching such a conclusion, though, Bossy, Aveling and others were not primarily concerned with literary activity in these descriptions, but rather with the character of Catholicism as it was lived and believed in Elizabethan England. That reality was certainly shaped, however, by the books which were smuggled into England at the time, and which gave their readers resources for the ongoing struggle for definition and purpose. Morey acknowledges the importance of printed works in the forming of Elizabethan Catholicism, an importance noted by figures as disparate as William Allen and Bishop Pilkington.[4] But it is in the work of Lucy Wooding that the most sustained attempt has been made to associate Bossy's thesis with the evidence of published works.

The outline of Wooding's thesis, of a return to a form of scholasticism in the 1560s and 1570s, as English Catholics were pushed

---

1 Bossy 1975, pp. 4, 11, 15–16.
2 Morey 1978, p. 148.
3 Meyer 1967 (1915), p. 92.
4 Morey 1978, p. 103.

into a papal corner by their opponents Jewel and Foxe, has already been described. In adopting Bossy's discontinuity theory, she claims that 'the evidence of the published works supports Bossy's interpretation, at least in terms of Catholicism among the intellectual elite'. She describes the use of tradition by the Elizabethan Catholic writers as 'doctrinaire', as the importance of scripture was downgraded in favour of an all-consuming obsession with history, history used no longer to support the authority of scripture, but of the Church itself, and more particularly of the papacy. She links the increased recusant championing and use of the lives of English saints and martyrs as a corollary to this, adding that later Elizabethan and Jacobean attempts to claim unbroken links with the medieval church were spurious, and 'managed to caricature the fifteenth century and ignore much of the sixteenth'.[5] Subsequent Catholic claims to continuity with their past were therefore false, and belied the paradigm shift which had actually taken place in their life and thought.

A very different explanation has been offered in challenge to Bossy's version of events. Christopher Haigh's article on Catholic continuity makes a number of related points about the transmission of Catholicism to the later Elizabethan period: the most important is his contention that 'it was the Marian clergy who initiated lay recusant Catholicism, which was already well-established before the mission from the continent could have had any real effect'. He goes on to point out that the missionary priests themselves were recruited from existing English Catholics, and sent to be pastors for existing English Catholics, not to create new forms of belief. The essential tenets of his article, therefore, are the Marian foundations upon which recusant Catholicism was built, the essentially medieval piety and structure of post-Reformation English Catholicism, and the dangers of seeing 'survivalism' as 'an unfortunate gap in the history of English Catholicism'. In this he was supported by McGrath's challenge to the idea of 'survivialism' as something 'out of date, passive, inert and geriatric'. Indeed, Haigh went so far as to see even the test of unity with and obedience to Rome as one in which English Catholicism found its continuity 'fractured only briefly'. It was through the work of the exiles in Louvain as much as anywhere, he claims, that the catholicity of the Church was emphasised, a catholicity to which the English opposition claimed to belong.[6]

The legacy of Nicholas Harpsfield, the works he wrote during his imprisonment and the importance attached to them by subsequent English Catholics, have something to contribute to this debate. They

---

5 Wooding 2000, pp. 225n, 237–8, 246, 269.
6 Haigh (ed.) 1987, pp. 176–208; McGrath 1984, pp. 414–28.

do not, of course, challenge the basic truth of some of the changes which necessarily took place in English Catholicism in the late sixteenth century. The move from state religion to minority status entailed huge sociological and practical shifts in attitude and behaviour, as Catholicism increasingly found itself forced into a range of new expressions, from 'church papism' to determined recusancy: Bossy is right to see in this challenge a break with the past. But the ecclesiological and theological underpinnings of that shift were familiar. The thought of Harpsfield and his successors seems to bear out Haigh's description of the evolution of Catholicism; historical resources were offered by which English Catholics could still recognise their circumscribed and pressured religious expression as authentic and in direct continuity with the Church in every previous age and place and time. Harpsfield clearly believed that Elizabethan Catholics needed the comfort of knowing that their faith and its outworking was directly connected to that of their pre-Reformation ancestors; later Catholics, in editing and publishing his works, shared his convictions and used the resources he had crafted.

Fundamental to this argument lies the preceding one about the English Catholic mindset in the previous fifty years. Bossy, Wooding and others have either missed or downplayed the importance of the experience of Catholics under Edward, and have similarly misread the Marian period, so that they see commitment to the papacy, and to More's consuming interests of consensus and continuity, as a strange revival of the recusant age. Harpsfield and the Marian establishment actually show that the shift took place rather earlier, in the years around 1550. What they were offering in the early Elizabethan period, therefore, were the same historical insights and theological resources which had underpinned the Marian restoration, but retuned for a new and, apart from a few years under Edward, unprecedented age of Catholic minority. Harpsfield's own contribution to the shaping of a recusant mindset, and his importance to his successors, is seen in three main areas of writing and thought: his championing of the figure of Thomas More as the martyr for unity and consensus; his work against Foxe and in creation of a renewed English Catholic martyrology; and his painstaking historical survey of English religion, by which he aimed to demonstrate Catholic continuity in England. When these legacies are traced through the later sixteenth and early seventeenth centuries, they suggest a good deal of continuity within Catholicism, and a much more unbroken transmission of thought than has often been assumed.

Thomas Stapleton, Nicholas Sander, Thomas More and Catholic unity

The immediate influence of the Marian clergy on Elizabethan recusancy, as Haigh has pointed out, is likely to have been greater than Bossy has acknowledged. From writers to the personnel of the missions, there are many levels of continuity. Thomas Stapleton is a clear case of such continuity, a priest formed and coming to ecclesiastical notice under Mary, and then playing a leading role from the continent in the encouragement and resourcing of his fellow Catholics under Elizabeth. Stapleton, like Harpsfield, was the product of Winchester School, and entered New College Oxford in the year before Mary's accession. In her reign, he seems to have attracted attention, and was given a prebend at Chichester by Bishop Christopherson in the year of her death. Stapleton spent time at Louvain and, at William Allen's invitation, at Douai, and eventually took the chair of Divinity there, before returning to Louvain after a brief immersion in the Jesuit novitiate. His fame as a writer under Elizabeth became great, and he was honoured by popes and fellow Englishmen alike. Despite his production of a large body of work, it is for his work on Sir Thomas More that he has, in the words of his biographer, 'gained ... the slight attention posterity has chosen to pay him'.[7] In this work, there is every reason to think that he owed a great debt to Harpsfield.

Stapleton's work of the 1560s, twenty years and more before his biography of More, mirrored the concerns of Harpsfield and seems to have involved collaboration with him. His translation of the history of Bede in 1565 had about it precisely the same preoccupation with demonstrating the continuity of English religion which lay at the heart of Harpsfield's life's work, and which constituted the importance of that work to the generation after him.[8] The Louvain exiles were responsible for the publication of More's Latin Works in the mid 1560s. But it was with the publication of his *Counterblast* in 1567, part of the long-running literary battle over the bitter arguments between Bishop Horne[9] and his prisoner Abbot Feckenham, that Stapleton relied most on the work and insights of Harpsfield. The extent of the debt is unclear; there is little internal evidence in the *Counterblast* itself, except for an acknowledgement in the preface of the 'helps' which Stapleton has received, and a thoroughgoing commitment to establishing the papal supremacy and

---

7 O'Connell 1964, p. 68.
8 Stapleton 1565b.
9 There may have been a Wykehamist agenda, given that Horne was Bishop of Winchester.

its importance to English Catholics throughout their history. The editors of the *Short Title Catalogue*, backed by Milward, claim that the work is Stapleton's, but relied on historical material researched and provided by Harpsfield. The *Dictionary of National Biography* has gone so far as to claim the work as being entirely Harpsfield's, and merely published under Stapleton's name. Southern, basing his view on the subject matter in the *Counterblast*, including the story of Cranmer's wife and the box, thought the notes had all come from Harpsfield; O'Connell subsequently felt that Southern stated his case, given the paucity of evidence, 'rather too strongly'.[10] Whatever the extent of Harpsfield's collaboration with the exile Stapleton on the book, his hand can be seen nowhere more clearly than in the book's discussion of Thomas More.

The aim of the *Counterblast* was to reply to Horne's *Answeare* specifically on the issue of the royal supremacy, by demonstrating England's adherence, throughout its Christian history, to the papacy. The events of the reign of Henry VIII, and the stance of More, therefore became key elements of the book, in describing both the breach with history which Henry's behaviour constituted, and also the continuity with that history which More claimed in his martyrdom. Clearly, these had also been the main preoccupations of Harpsfield's Marian works on the Henrician church. Like Harpsfield in those works, though, Stapleton seems to have been keen to indicate to his readers the extent to which More had had to wrestle with his own conscience and understanding before reaching his conclusion. Taking his narrative almost directly from Harpsfield's summary of events, he indicates More's doubt, and in so doing, perhaps hoped to encourage Elizabethan Catholics in their own indecision about whether and how to maintain their opposition to the Queen:

> Sir Thomas More, whose incomparable virtue and learning, all the Christian world hath in high estimation, and whose wit Erasmus judged to have been such as England nor had, neither shall have, the like: and who for this quarrel which we now have in hand suffered death, for the preservation of the unity of Christ's Church, which was never, nor shall be preserved, but under this one head: as good a man, and as great a clerk, and as blessed a Martyr as he was, albeit he ever well thought of this Primacy, and that it was at the least wise instituted by the corps of Christendom for great urgent causes for avoiding of schisms: yet that this primacy was immediately institute of God [which we all believe now] … he did not many years believe, until … he read in the matter those things that the King's highness had

---

10 Southern 1950, pp. 125–6; O'Connell 1964, p. 60.

written in his most famous book against the heresies of Martin Luther.[11]

There are other echoes of Harpsfield's Marian preoccupations too: attacks on the Centuriators, side swipes at Foxe, praise for Thomas Becket, defence of Gardiner and others for their initial support for a royal supremacy, the connection of heresy with sedition, and an emphasis on the importance of miracle.[12] In all of these areas, Stapleton, drawing on Harpsfield, laid the ground for his later work.

Stapleton's *Tres Thomae* was published in 1588 at Douai. In it, he celebrated the lives of Thomas the Apostle, St Thomas Becket and, at greater length, Sir Thomas More. In the preface to the More section, he remarked that many in exile had been desiring a published biography of More, and been prevented from producing one through death or the pressure of other duties. He stated his aim of producing an accurate biography based on More's own works and letters, and drawing on his own memory of discussions with members of the More circle. Rather like Harpsfield in exile under Edward, Stapleton had enjoyed close acquaintance with members of More's family and household, including Dorothy Colly Harris, the widow of More's secretary John Harris, who entrusted to Stapleton manuscripts, papers, and letters in More's own hand, as the basis for his biography. Though he makes no specific mention of Harpsfield's work, his own experience of the Marian years and previous work with Harpsfield ought to indicate that he was well aware of the biographical tradition surrounding More which Harpsfield had created.[13]

Indeed, the book itself bears witness to Stapleton's own concern for the elements of More's life and death which had so fired Harpsfield. He draws attention to the prodigies and portents surrounding More's birth, miraculous signs of the child's future importance. He pays tribute to the Marian project surrounding More, making reference to Rastell's edition, which he read thirty years ago, and saying of the reprinting of More's works under Mary that they 'were of the greatest use during the restoration of Catholicism that then took place'. He emphasises, like Harpsfield before, More's monastic inclinations and pattern of life, his remarkable insight and foresight, and the loathsome character of Thomas Cranmer, 'a man after the King's own heart, ready to curry favour at any cost'.[14] Most of all, of course, it is for More's unique status in his day that Stapleton celebrates him, 'the only lay-

11   Stapleton 1567, fols. 37–8.
12   *Ibid.*, fols. 16, 22, 81, 308–9, 368, 477–8.
13   Stapleton (ed. Hallett) 1928, pp. xiii–xiv; O'Connell 1964, p. 69n.
14   *Ibid.*, pp. 1–2, 32ff., 39, 66, 70, 80–1, 152.

man in the kingdom who refused to approve of the divorce and the royal supremacy'. As in the *Counterblast*, also, he faithfully records More's seven-year search for evidence of patristic support for an alternative to the papal supremacy.[15]

Stapleton's version of More's imprisonment, trial and execution is even more full of touching human incident and claims to his sanctity than Harpsfield's; but, again, such a treatment does not lessen the fact that Stapleton's use of More's *ipsissima verba*, from his letters and papers, lends a fair claim to accuracy to his retelling of the events. Stapleton is at pains to connect More to other English saints, and especially to his previous subject, Thomas Becket, in his desire to die on the day actually chosen for his execution: the octavas of Peter, who founded the papacy for which More dies, and the eve of the feast of Becket. Like Harpsfield, and echoing other Marian authorities, Stapleton stresses More's preeminence as the first lay martyr for religion in England, a man whose stand was not simply in the interests of clerical privilege, and whose martyrdom and courage still has the ability to impress men of all ranks. In a final editorial comment, Stapleton reveals his own indebtedness to the memory of More, and his own upbringing in a pre-Marian tradition surrounding the martyr:

> I can remember quite well, and many others will bear me out, that when we were boys, More's fame and his illustrious martyrdom were constantly the subject of our talk and fired our zeal for the Catholic faith.[16]

Stapleton's childhood zeal took deeper root, was fostered by the Marian tradition surrounding More, and persisted, in the Elizabethan period, as a clear and important element in Catholic writing. In particular, works like Stapleton's *Tres Thomae* reflected a growing concern to chronicle the events of the English reformation. As the Elizabethan Settlement became ever more established, and as Catholics adjusted to minority status and the restrictions imposed on the expression of their faith, their intellectual leaders abroad felt it important to remind them of the process by which they had got to this point. Stapleton himself referred in his work on More to the work of Nicholas Sander, whose *De Origine ac Progressu Schismatis Anglicani* had been published in 1585, four years after Sander's death. Like Harpsfield and Stapleton, Sander was a product of Winchester and New College, noted as a writer, scholar and controversialist, and somewhat notorious after his death for his

---

15 Ibid., pp. 38, 196; see above, pp. 105–7, for Harpsfield's and Pole's declaration of the same view of More.

16 Ibid., p. 215.

involvement in plots to defeat Elizabeth and as a papal agent in Ireland. Early in Elizabeth's reign, Sander had written to Cardinal Morone of the situation in England, singling out Harpsfield, imprisoned and yet indefatigable in his defence of the faith, for particular praise.[17] Though his convictions took him in a direction which many see as the extreme end of the scale of opposition to Elizabeth and the English Church, his historiographical work on the English Reformation displays many of the same traits – and a similar debt to Harpsfield's earlier treatises – as his other coreligionists.

Sander divided his work into three books, dealing in turn with the reigns of Henry and Edward in Books One and Two and with Mary and Elizabeth in the third. The book's nineteenth-century editor and translator noticed its close affinity with Harpsfield's *Treatise*, in tone and subject matter. At the heart of Book One is Queen Katherine herself, who 'was older than her husband in years ... but more than a thousand in character'. The picture Sander draws of her is of a woman steeped in a very medieval piety, praying, fasting, duly doing penance and rooting her spiritual life in her membership of the Franciscan third order. Sander, as Harpsfield had done, draws attention to the propaganda drive Henry launched in the realm to lend the divorce credibility, despite the fact that 'there was not a more saintly woman, or one of nobler birth than his wife, and he had no fault to find with her but that of having been his brother's wife'.[18] Sander, further, describes the touching scene which took place between Cardinal Campeggio and Katherine, after his arrival in 1528 as papal legate in the case, and the Queen's refusal to give up her case or take the path, of becoming a religious, offered her. He states simply that 'Campeggio understood her': the weight of the judgement of the Church was to be on her side, as her husband the King drew England into heresy.[19]

The portrayal of the enemies of the case, equally, demonstrate a great similarity with Harpsfield's history of the same events. Wolsey, 'domineered by his lust of power, forced himself to satisfy the desires of the king'; it was to him that the Queen attributed her pain. Thomas Cranmer was urged on the King as a candidate for Archbishop by Thomas Boleyn, as a man malleable to the King's wishes. Sander uses the same phrase as had Harpsfield in the *Treatise*, claiming, of Henry's choice of Cranmer as the Archbishop who would carry out his wishes, 'it might have been said that the cover was really meet for the cup'.

---

17 Sander to Morone 1561, in Pollen (ed.) 1905, p. 41.
18 Sander (ed. Lewis) 1877, pp. 7, 44–5; Lewis annotated his edition by cross-referencing Sander's account with the same details in Harpsfield's *Treatise*.
19 *Ibid.*, p. 43.

Cranmer was 'the minister of [Henry's] lust', a fair-weather Catholic whose religion moved under Edward to Lutheranism and Calvinism as others influenced his thought. His final vacillating demise under Mary, and the seventeen recantations signed and then foresworn, indicate his character.[20] In all of this, Sander echoes the main elements of Harpsfield's earlier histories.

He mirrors Harpsfield also in his presentation of Thomas More, who plays a predictably important role in Sander's history, as the conscience of the nation and the martyr for unity. From the moment of his first appearance in the history, More counsels the King against the divorce, and Henry realises the importance of More's opinion: 'the King used to say that if Sir Thomas More were won over to his side, it would do more for him than the assent of half his kingdom'.[21] The details of More's careful search for authority for the royal supremacy over seven years are preserved in Sander's account, and he emphasises More's lay status, his 'natural gifts, his piety and learning', and his wit and composure in the face of death. As with Harpsfield and Stapleton, too, Sander attempts to associate More and his memory with miracles, such as that of Margaret's empty purse being miraculously provided with money for the purchase of burial linen. Like Queen Katherine, More lives and dies in the spirit of traditional religion, nurtured by its life and aspiring to achieve communion with its saints without courting death: 'for though he had a great longing for martyrdom, he never forgot that it was a grace from God'.[22] Sander's *coup de grace* is to observe that Edward died on the eighteenth anniversary of More's death, 'and so it came to pass that all might see, who rightly consider the course of this world, that Henry paid in the death of his eldest son the penalty of the death of that great man'.[23]

Sander reserves most of his fire for Henry himself, however, and it is in the attack on the King's actions that he comes to the heart of his purpose, in spelling out for his readers the catastrophe for his country which the King's Great Matter unleashed. Sander has described the King's previous sexual liaisons with other Boleyn women, and his lies to Rowland Lee at the marriage to Anne about the whereabouts of the papal brief permitting it to take place. The real thrust of the attack, though, is against the royal supremacy, and Sander reveals the same anger at the fracturing of Christian unity which had inspired the work of Harpsfield under Mary:

20 Ibid., pp. 11, 34, 87–90, 161, 180–2, 222–3.
21 Ibid., pp. 31–2.
22 Ibid., pp. 72, 120–1, 124–5, 127.
23 Ibid., pp. 216–17.

> Thus Henry cut off and severed both himself and his people from the fellowship and communion of the Roman Church, in which ever since the days of Joseph of Arimathea all those kings and people had lived, who in these islands, each in his own generation, followed the Catholic faith of Christ ... we all know, O King, that thriving and glorious Church which you have abandoned and left: the Church founded by the great apostles Peter and Paul, which has prospered and endured under 230 successors of St Peter, which the bishops, the kings, and people of all Catholic nations have confessed and honoured, which shuns and condemns the impious teachings of all heresies and all heretics.[24]

Demanding to know to which church Henry went after rejecting Rome, Sander can reach only the conclusion that 'it was to yourself'. Echoing the kind of Marian writings examined earlier, also, Sander identifies the Dissolution under Henry as a sacrilegious act which led to poverty in England as old patterns of charity were destroyed in the King's wanton actions. He charts in the second book, too, the very understanding which underpinned the Marian restoration, of the return to Roman obedience of those who realised under Edward the extent of their error in accepting a royal supremacy, that in time 'altars are thrown down and destroyed ... the ruin of the altars must be a sign of antichristian unbelief'. There is mention too of the More circle 'in exile for the faith' under Edward; interestingly, he gives pride of place among their number to 'that great light of all England, Nicholas Harpsfield, who afterwards in the reign of Elizabeth suffered a lengthened imprisonment': a tantalising suggestion of the extent to which Sander felt himself to be standing in a noble line of life and writing.[25]

The reputation of Thomas More had continued and growing significance through the late sixteenth and early seventeenth centuries, not just in the biographical work of 'Ro.Ba.' and Cresacre More, but in drama also. Alison Shell has written of the plays written to be performed in the seminary colleges on the continent, and at the school in St Omer for the sons of Catholic recusants. She claims that 'most English Jesuit dramas ... are preoccupied with exploring the didactic import of history', as seen for example in the *S. Thomas Morus*, a survival from Rome, in which again a link is made between More and Thomas Becket, saints whose friendship with a King Henry was tested and eventually destroyed by the king's anger at their integrity in the face of aggression. Shell notes that the performance of such plays, for seminarians and gentry sons

24 Ibid., pp. 104–5.
25 Ibid., pp. 157, 178, 201–2.

alike, inculcated a sense that English Catholics were 'historical exiles from the time when England belonged to the true faith'. Even Anthony Munday's anti-Catholic play *Sir Thomas More* presents what Questier calls 'an extraordinarily positive view of More', and reinforces Questier's claim that not all Elizabethan Protestants followed John Foxe in their view of him. Shell notes that Munday possessed a copy of Harpsfield's *Life of More*, a work which, although in manuscript, enjoyed 'international circulation' at this time.[26]

Questier has remarked of Sander's history of the English Reformation that 'it helped to fashion More as the leading opponent of the ecclesiastical supremacy claimed by Henry VIII'. That is certainly true, but it obscures the extent to which Sander himself was drawing on a pre-established tradition, and in particular the Marian project to undergird the restoration with an examination of Henry's divorce and its consequences. Questier's assertion that, before Sander, More had cult status in the main only among his relations thus misses the mark. He is certainly right, however, to point to More, as did Aveling, as 'the founder and archetype of English Catholic recusancy'; from Harpsfield to Sander to Stapleton, and beyond, More was drawn and re-drawn as the fountain-head of English Catholic resistance, particularly amongst the laity, to the royal supremacy. Ironically, Questier's article in part criticises Haigh for his treatment of the continuity question, and claims that defining the continuity to which Catholics laid claim under Elizabeth is a difficult task. The work on More suggests one solution: Harpsfield and the Elizabethan writers who followed him pointed to More's commitment to the unity and consensus of all Christians, symbolised in the papacy, as the feature which guaranteed authenticity and offered security. Intellectual assent to such unity was the bond that would hold Elizabethan Catholics within the Church and the communion of saints, despite the restrictions placed upon their religious expression. As Questier says, 'the narratives woven around Sir Thomas More comprise one of the great Catholic stories of the English Reformation, the telling and retelling of which generated a particular view of what Catholicism in England was and should be like'.[27] Harpsfield and his successors were quite clear, that in understanding the importance of the papacy for stability, continuity and the maintenance of orthodoxy, English Catholics would find their identity and their connection with the past. Other Catholic writers found in Harpsfield's life's work other resources for making this very point in other ways.

26 Shell 1999, pp. 195, 210, 218ff, 294; Questier 2002, pp. 489–90.
27 Questier 2002, pp. 476–509.

Robert Persons and the continuation of the attack on Foxe

Robert Persons' own spiritual journey was completed in the year of Harpsfield's death. After holding a fellowship at Balliol College, he fled to the continent in 1574, and was received into the Catholic Church in Louvain. In 1575, he entered the Society of Jesus at Rome. He won fame amongst English Catholics as Campion's partner in the mission of 1580–1, and some notoriety subsequently for his fierce opposition to the Elizabethan regime and his activity to bring it down. He lived at the centre of English Catholic life in Europe, working tirelessly for the Jesuits, particularly in the controversies which broke out amongst English Catholic clergy at the end of the sixteenth century. Persons was also a prolific writer; works such as his *Brief Discours* and the *Conference about the Next Succession to the Crowne of Ingland* aroused interest and controversy, as he outlined his views on the best means by which to secure for England a Catholic monarch and reconnection to Christendom. Like Sander and Stapleton, though, Persons built on the literary legacy he received from earlier English Catholics. In particular, he played a formative role in the ongoing Catholic response to John Foxe's martyrology; the *Treatise on the Three Conversions of England* of 1603–4 aimed to undermine Foxe's intellectual foundations by demonstrating the continuity both of Catholic belief and of elements of its heretical opposition. It has rightly therefore been seen as an important work; but what has been less noticed is the extent to which Persons drew, directly and openly, from Harpsfield's work in the *Dialogi Sex*, to find the basis of his arguments.

Persons' *Treatise* is a large and comprehensive work. It is separated into three books; the first deals with the continuity of Catholicism and Catholic belief in England, the second with the continuity of heresy, and the third, which itself takes up two volumes and is the largest by far, with a month by month refutation of Foxe's martyrs as they were listed in the Kalendar. It becomes immediately apparent, therefore, that Harpsfield's concentration of much of his criticism of Foxe on the Kalendar is mirrored in Persons' work also. Persons dedicated the work to English Catholics, hoping that it would present to them 'the history of your own house, the records & chronicles of your own family, the pedigree and genealogy of your own forefathers, the antiquity and nobility of your own progenitors, together with your just title & claim to their inheritance'. The aim of the work, he says towards the end, is to demonstrate the same essential truth as writers about More had hoped to communicate, namely that 'if there be any certainty or ground in Christian Religion at all, it must needs be in these [he has just presented 100 pages of patristic and conciliar testimony], wherein authority, universality, miracles and all other sorts of theological argument, both divine and human, do concur'.[28]

The first two parts of Persons' work make clear his debt to the previous writing of Harpsfield, but it is only in the third part that he openly confesses it. His treatment of the English Reformation in Part One is loaded with the kinds of views both of Henry's arrogance and More's integrity by now familiar. Fisher and More were 'content to give their blood in defence of Cath. Unity against this schism'; the royal supremacy was for More a 'new and strange thing unto him, & contrary to the belief of all his forefathers', and he was therefore executed 'not for that he had attempted, altered or innovated any thing as you see, but for that he would not alter & make innovation'.[29] This, he adds, was the difference between Thomas More and the heretics he so justly punished, for beliefs 'different from that which they had received, and contrary to the belief of all their forefathers ancient Christians'. And he makes special mention of those under Elizabeth who had sought to keep articulating the same keen sense of connectedness with the past, the exiles and prisoners (Harpsfield mentioned among them) who resist the Queen's 'mutation' of religion, and who 'did well shew by their constant profession unto their dying days, what root and foundation Cath. Religion had in England'.[30]

Apart from such praise of martyrs and confessors of Catholic unity, though, Persons deploys against Foxe historiographical and theological weapons immediately familiar to a reader of the *Dialogi Sex*. In several places, he makes the extent to which he is drawing on Harpsfield clear. At the heart of his detailed examination of Foxe's work is the Kalendar. As Harpsfield did in the *Dialogi Sex*, Persons examines Foxe's martyrs in turn by month, mocking Foxe for his 'replacement' of the Church's saints with his own 'dunghill clouts', and detailing their very anti-Christian activities. In particular, the figures over whom Harpsfield had spent so much time appear again, Oldcastle, Onley and Acton the traitors, Cowbridge the madman, members of old heretical sects, Cranmer the opportunist. Foxe, Persons claims, has celebrated heretics, atheists, lunatics, renegades, thieves, murderers, sorcerers, witches, rebels and traitors, replacing the saints venerated for centuries with worthless wretches. When challenged, though, by writers like Harpsfield, he

---

28 Persons 1603, unpaginated Epistle; vol. III, *Review of Ten Publike Disputations*, p. 148.

29 *Ibid.*, vol. III, pp. 240–1, 246.

30 *Ibid.*, vol. III, pp. 264–5.

has turned tail and denied the obvious implications of the Kalendar's construction:

> I thought good to advertise you by the way, before we enter into the examination of the Martyrology & Calendar following, that as John Foxe doth not presume to think his Martyrs worthy of any such honour, as here hath been shewed, to have been exhibited to true Martyrs by the ancient Catholic Church, and afterward ... so he many times being pressed with the indignity of their faith, life, or actions, urged and returned upon him by Alanus Copus & others, the poor man, when he is not able to defend himself otherwise, denieth flatly that he hath put any down here for Martyrs, as presently you shall hear out of his own words.[31]

Just as Harpsfield had done, also, Persons charges Foxe with having taken to himself in the construction of the Kalendar the arbitrary authority to canonise saints without regard to their proven holiness, a power no pope ever held, and which reveals the fundamental arrogance of his approach. Speaking of Nicholas Ridley, he says:

> by nowaies (under no circumstances) do I see how he can come to be so *enthroned and gloriously crowned a saint*, but only by the absolute pontifical power, and privilege of John Fox, who without proof of merits may canonize whom he listeth: which is a point, that no Pope hitherto among us, hath ever taken upon him to do, or ever will.[32]

Persons is working from the fifth edition of the *Actes and Monuments*, and confesses that he does not have access to a copy of Foxe's first edition of the work: 'for I have not the said edition by me'. Instead, Persons draws on the criticisms made of it in the *Dialogi Sex* in order to reconstruct its arguments. Most particularly, he cites Harpsfield's criticisms of Foxe's stories of Collins and Cowbridge, criticisms which changed subsequent versions of the work:

> Since that time his false and deceitful narration being discovered, & laid open by the said *Alanus Copus*, or rather *Doctor Harpsfield*, the true author of those learned dialogues, and the original records being cited for the wicked opinions of both these Foxian Martyrs.[33]

In another similar case, Persons points out that 'Peter the German' is

---

31 Ibid., vol. II, pp. 76–7.
32 Ibid., vol. III, pp. 207–8.
33 Ibid., vol. III, pp. 195–6.

listed amongst the martyrs in the current edition, but a description of him appears nowhere in the text. The *Dialogi Sex* reveals that he had denied Christ to have taken flesh from Mary; Foxe has therefore quietly removed him from the body of the text whilst still including him among the Kalendar of Foxian martyrs. Consistently, and even providing page references, Persons reveals to what extent he is building on the *Dialogi Sex*, not just for his basic arguments against Foxe, but also for his knowledge of the evolution of Foxe's work.

It is, though, in the very Marian area of the connection between heresy and sedition that Persons places most emphasis, and in which he most reveals his following of Harpsfield. Indeed, it appears that a major reason for his writing of the book is his anger that Foxe has persisted with the glorification of traitors as saints, despite the clear rebuke of Harpsfield nearly forty years previously. Speaking of Onley, Eleanor Cobham and the infamous Margaret 'Gourdmayn' Persons says:

> Whereof I find in their condemnations no least mention. And is there any just reply or probable excuse, for this so great folly and impudency? No truly. For though he were warned and reprehended for the same by Alanus Copus (or Doctor Harpsfield) in his Dialogues, and his madness therein shewed most evidently: yet is he not ashamed to come with it again in this his fifth edition.[34]

Harpsfield is praised for his unmasking of Foxe's elusive 'Lady Young's mother', who turned out to be a sorceress who attempted to poison the king, and for his pressing of Foxe over Roger Acton's treachery, to which Foxe replied with 'much caviling' and an eventual withdrawal of Acton from the work. In cases of factual error or inconsistency, too, Persons reinforces the points made by Harpsfield, that Wycliffe died in bed and was not therefore martyred, that John Marbeck was alive and well years after the date Foxe claims for his execution, that Bilney recanted before death, that the evidence which Harpsfield cited from More concerning the death of Richard Hunne is sounder than Foxe's, and that key protestants like Karlstadt, Oecolampadius and especially Zwingli are omitted from the Kalendar.[35]

Persons' *Treatise* has been seen by many scholars as the first effective Catholic attack on Foxe's *Acts and Monuments*. Townsend in the nineteenth century first expressed the view that his work formed the source of all subsequent attacks on the martyrology, and he has been supported by more recent work. Holmes has said that the 'most origi-

---

34 *Ibid.*, vol. II, pp. 267–8.
35 *Ibid.*, vol. II, pp. 184–5, 196–7, 199, 245 ff., 267–8, 272–8, 354; vol. III, pp. 62, 279–84, 362 ff.

nal contribution to the Catholic attack on Foxe' lay in Persons' critique of Foxe's historical analysis – in other words, his attempt to show that the 'true Church was Roman Catholic' – and his very effective attack on the Kalendar, with its implications for traditional devotion to the saints. Sullivan too has noted Persons' concern with what she calls the 'protean character' of Foxe's martyrs' theology, and the effectiveness of his attack on the Kalendar.[36] Perhaps such praise for Persons originates in his understanding of the need for a work of criticism of Foxe to be produced in English. Indeed, the real difference of approach was Persons' use of English to make the appeal; he clearly felt that Harpsfield's Latin work, designed for a wide, learned readership and intended to be a long-lasting resource, needed some translation in order to make an immediate and powerful impact on an English audience. In focusing on Persons' English work, however, scholars have overlooked the earlier, Latin, work of Harpsfield on which Persons acknowledged he built. Anne Dillon has acknowledged that the *Dialogi Sex* was the 'prototype' for subsequent attacks on Foxe, and has recognised some of the debt Persons owed to Harpsfield in writing the *Treatise*; but the extent of the debt is greater than she suggests.[37] Indeed, the *Treatise*, in its main arguments, offers little that is new or different from the basic approach of Harpsfield forty years earlier. Persons' three main approaches are exactly as were Harpsfield's: to establish the continuity of a Catholicism united to the papacy in England; to trace the similar continuity of heresy in England; and to use the Kalendar to point both to Foxe's sacrilege in overturning the devotion of centuries and to demonstrate the unworthy character of his martyrs.

Persons' work, finally, is an indication also of the ongoing and evolving concept during the Elizabethan period of a Catholic martyrology. As previously seen, this was a renewed tradition made necessary by the new circumstances of minority, for which the work on Thomas More can be seen as both the initial impetus and an ongoing central theme. As the seminary priests came to England in obedience to their calling, and as they began to be apprehended, questioned and executed by the regime, the scope for the continued renewal of a martyrological tradition amongst Catholics grew. Campion, Sherwin, Bryan and the others gave to struggling English Catholics by their deaths the sense of a connection with the saints and martyrs of the Church in all generations, a noble tradition traceable through Becket and to More, and one in which they

---

36 Sullivan 1999, pp. 154–6; Holmes 1982, pp. 50–1.

37 Dillon 2002, pp. 66, 338; she discusses Persons' treatment of the Kalendar, pp. 345 ff., without any mention of Harpsfield's focus in the *Dialogi Sex* on it, using the same arguments.

were encouraged to see themselves as sharing even by their commitment to recusancy and marginalisation. Yet this renewal of tradition was not begun in the work written about their deaths. Rather, as with the historiographical method of Persons in the *Treatise*, it built, self-consciously, on the renewed martyrological understanding of the Catholic community under Henry and Edward, an understanding fostered and celebrated under Mary and increasingly important under Elizabeth.

The work of Cardinal William Allen in the 1580s focused in large measure on the martyrdom of the seminary priests as a means of offering spiritual comfort and consolation to English Catholics. Allen's was not, though, the creation of a martyrological tradition *ex nihilo*, but a pointing towards a pre-existent idea of a line of succession, as he made clear:

> what esteem so ever the Princess present and her greatest ministers have now, by the height of their room and fortune in this life; it is but a very dream, shadow or phantasy, to the glory of Thomas of Canterbury, John of Rochester, Chancellor More, Father Campion and the rest ... the persecutors glory dieth with their authority, if not before: and they are commonly better known to posterity by the executing of such men (though to their shame) then by other their facts in their life whatsoever.[38]

Not only that, but Allen was equally clear that he and those being trained and sent over from Douai and Rome were coming to replace and carry on the work of the Marian clergy, the natural successors of those like Harpsfield who had continued their passionate advocacy of the Catholic faith under the most trying of conditions imposed by a heretical government:

> in our country at the first entrance of Heresy they had all the principal Clergy, and divers chief Catholics in prisons or places at commandment, where they could not exercise their functions; and being ancient men most of them, they knew they could not live long ... they little thought that these old holy Confessors, being worn out by years and imprisonment, a new generation would rise to defend their old Bishops and Fathers faith.[39]

Allen very clearly offers a Marian view of the English Reformation, of the progressive sacrileges of Henry and, under Edward, the 'whole Realm altered into Zwinglianism'; and he preaches the need for the English to reacquaint themselves with their own Christian history, and to acknowledge that they owe their 'first faith and Christianity' to Rome.[40]

38 Allen 1584, p. 33.
39 *Ibid.*, p. 43.
40 On Allen, see Duffy 1995, and particularly pp. 269, 273–8; he claims that

Harpsfield, More and English Catholic Identity

The work of Allen and others on the events of the deaths of the new martyrs, alongside the publication of the martyrs' writings themselves, reinforced this mindset, and gave opportunity for the dissemination of new martyr accounts for Catholic edification. Always, the martyrs and their biographers took care to link their actions to the practice and devotion of the Church in previous generations. Alfield celebrated Campion as 'our new Apostle coming to restore the faith which Augustine planted here before'; Campion himself, his words preserved by Hanmer, the vitriolic enemy of the Jesuits, had stated his life's purpose as being summarised in the statement 'so the faith was planted so it must be restored'.[41] Campion's *Rationes Decem* was a work steeped in the tradition of More and Harpsfield, tracing the continuity of the Spirit's work throughout history,

> The Church indeed is given as its (the Spirit's) guardian, not its teacher, as the heretics quibble. This universal treasure which now the Council of Trent has embraced, was commended to us for our good by the oldest Councils.[42]

He went on to stress the consistent exposition of this faith by the Fathers in all times, and by English Catholicism's most recent defenders:

> I do not have enough time to recount the letters, the disputes, the sermons, the speeches, the little literary works, and the discussions of the Fathers, in which with style, they confirmed the doctrines of our Catholic faith with weight and elegance ... for Harding and Sander, and Allen, and Stapleton ... have not railed against this new heresy more fiercely than did those Fathers, whom I have recounted.[43]

It was for this faith, in all its continuity and consistency, that the martyrs died; Allen and others, in their martyrological writings, linked the outplaying of their executions with their stand for England's need to be reunited in faith with the rest of Christendom.

Allen, like all major English Catholic authors in the 1560s, handed a Marian legacy onto the Elizabethan Mission, their work the 'late-gathered first-fruits of Marian Oxford'.

41 Alfield 1582, unpaginated; Hanmer 1581, fol. 24.

42 ['quae quidem Ecclesia custos huius depositi, non magistra, quod haeretici cavillantur. thesaurum hunc universum quem Tridentina synodus est amplexa, vetustissimis olim Conciliis publicitus vendicavit'] Campion 1581, fol. 2.

43 ['Dies me deficeret numeranem epistolas, conciones, homilias, orationes, opuscula, disceptationes Patrum, in quibus ex apparato, graviter & ornate nostra catholicorum dogmata roborarunt ... Nullus enim Hardingus, nec Sanderus, nec Alanus, nec Stapletonius ... haec nova somnia vehementius, quam hi quos recensui Patres, insectantur'] *Ibid.*, fol. 17.

Nicholas Harpsfield

Persons carried such an understanding of the importance of martyrdom within the English Catholic witness on into the *Treatise*. It had been, in works like the *De Persecutione Anglicana*, a concern of his own in the 1580s. By the early seventeenth century, he was still celebrating the martyrdom of More and Fisher as particularly important, and linked them repeatedly with Becket as those whose stand was genuine because united in belief with the universal Church.[44] Persons undertook, in the third part, to chart the succession of Catholic martyrs, month by month, to demonstrate their commitment to consensus and unity, alongside his critique of the sheer diversity of Foxe's heroes' faith. This was an exercise, however, which he stopped after March, probably through fear of over-enlarging an already burgeoning book. As Anne Dillon has found, though, Persons' debt to More, via Harpsfield, was great[45]; the Henrician martyrs and More most of all continued to offer English Catholics the hope that, in their persecuted and minority state, they were connected with Catholic saints of their own and previous generations, in resistance to the kind of error demonstrated by Foxe's martyrs and in an unbroken consensus about the nature of true faith.

Holmes thought that martyrdom in late Elizabethan Catholicism was 'one of the most important aspects of Catholic thought', citing Persons' *De Persecutione Anglicana* of 1581 as the 'first martyrological work produced by an Elizabethan Catholic'.[46] He sees also that the work of Foxe and the Catholic attack upon it, again initiated by Persons, was central to the evolution of this kind of material. A survey of the martyrological work of Persons, however, shows the extent to which it built on earlier Catholic writings, and especially Harpsfield's Marian work on More and his Elizabethan writing against Foxe. This is crucial: for Elizabethan writers were not creating new works in new genres for a new Catholic mindset which bore little resemblance to what had gone before. They were, rather, using the resources of previous Catholic writers to offer hope to Catholics under Elizabeth. That hope was based not on new theological responses, but old ones, to do with continuity, consensus, unity and the bond of the papacy. Anne Dillon's tracing of the development of martyrology in English Catholicism makes the point for that genre. As Walsham put it, English Catholic writers 'claimed that an activity traditionally regarded as the sole responsibility of martyrs was now the foremost duty of every layperson'.[47] But it is instructive also to see the extent to which the work of Harpsfield was the basis for other later

---

44 Persons 1603, vol. I, pp. 240–1, 246, 255; vol. II, p. 66.
45 Dillon 2002, p. 343.
46 Holmes 1982, pp. 48, 50.
47 Walsham 1993, p. 31.

work, on More, in attacking Protestant martyrology, and on the continuity of English Catholic faith through history. In the last respect, his influence extended well into the seventeenth century, and culminated in the publication of the *Historia Anglicana Ecclesiastica* in 1622.

Harpsfield's *Historia* and the witness of history

Harpsfield's *Historia* is a work, in one sense, of a quite different character than his *Dialogi Sex*. Whilst tracing the same continuity of faith in England as the dialogues had sought to do, it lacks their polemical fire and controversial zeal. It perhaps represents the final compilation of Harpsfield's historical research, a work of his last years: the preface certainly seems concerned with leaving a witness for posterity to England's religious past, another manifestation of Harpsfield's concern to appeal to the learned. The work seems to have been important for English Catholics, particularly abroad, after Harpsfield's death, and to have provided resources for their thinking and work even in its manuscript form. Anne Dillon has noted that copies of it were available to those creating the murals in the English College at Rome in the 1580s, as they sought to make visual the continuity of faith which had been Harpsfield's consuming passion.[48] It is mentioned in correspondence between leading English Catholics abroad: the anti-Jesuit priest Anthony Champney wrote to Thomas More, George Birkhead's archipresbyteral agent in Rome, in August 1613, chasing up a previous request for a manuscript copy of the work:

> I wrote unto you for a copy of Harpsfield his history which we desire may be copied in a legible hand ... see if you can get Wycliffe's history out of the Vatican. ... we will entreat to undertake besides the setting forth of Harpsfield a continuation of Sanders which I have long desired as a thing very grateful to posterity.[49]

Questier adds that Champney had written in May, asking for the work, and that Cardinal Allen had left a copy of it to the college at Douai; the main obstacle to its publication seems to have been the cost. Catholics of all kinds sought such a publication, however; there was even something of a competition between secular priests and Jesuits to produce the published version.[50]

---

48 Dillon 2002, p. 179.
49 Questier (ed.) 1998, p. 233.
50 Questier 2002; Questier suggests that various aspects of Harpsfield's thought bolstered the emphases of different Catholic groups. However, his observation that Harpsfield was not firmly devoted to the papacy, a feature which might recommend

The *Historia* finally found its publication under Jesuit auspices, in 1622. In that edition, it was coupled with his *Historia Wicleffiana* as Champney had intended, and Campion's brief account of the Henrician divorce. The Jesuit responsible was Richard Gibbons, born at the end of Edward's reign, whose career consisted mainly in teaching activity among the English Catholic exiles in Europe. Gibbons introduced his project with vivid praise of its author and an indication of the job of historical perspective which he hoped it would achieve:

> The author and creator of this book, Nicholas (Harpsfield), who for the defence of the faith suffered many dangers, was thrown out of the Archdeaconry of Canterbury and stripped of his possessions, condemned to prison and chains, now rejoices after his death at his labours and prayers, that he served the Church, for which he nobly fought while alive and well with his endless toil and his worthy deeds.[51]

Harpsfield's own preface to the work was further evidence of the unbroken purpose which he shared with his posthumous publisher: that of delineating the line of continuity of the Catholic faith in England. He laments England's obsession with argument and controversy, longing for Englishmen to hear the voices of the fathers of faith, and rediscover the true path to heaven. In describing Wycliffe's heresy as like the phoenix, rising from the ashes each time it is defeated to undermine orthodoxy once more, he sets the scene for his own purpose: a simple chronological retelling of England's religious history, which places its appeal only in its witness to the continuity and stability of the faith of the Roman faith in the land. Such a pure and plain approach is needed 'especially for our own times, in which all arts and types of learning, and histories, both civil and political, of our own and other races, are completed simply and neatly, refined and polished': this is a 'no frills' history of faith in England.[52]

Given its format and purpose, the *Historia* unapologetically lacks the sparkle and imaginative approach of the *Dialogi Sex*; Harpsfield in

---

him to secular clergy, is wrong, and casts doubt on his thesis.

51 ['Habebit & huius libri auctor & parens NICOLAUS, qui pro fidei defensione magnis perfunctus periculis, & Cantuariensi Archidiaconatu deiectus bonis eversus, carceri vinculisque damnatus, nunc gaudet post mortem suis laboribus atque vigiliis, ei prodesse ecclesiae, quam vivus & valens suis aliquando lucubrationibus, & insignium facinorum laude propugnavit.'] Harpsfield 1622, Editor's Preface (unpaginated).

52 ['nostris praesertim temporibus, quibus omnes artes & studiorum genera, & civiles atque politicae tum aliarum, tum etiam nostrae Gentis historiae pure & terse expoliuntur, excultam atque ornatam.'] *Ibid.*, Author's Preface (unpaginated).

the preface expressed unease at the amount of polemic coming from Protestant pens, and seems to have seen the *Historia*'s strength in the sheer weight of the evidence it offered of a continuous descent of belief in England. So, after early chapters which detail England's monastic life and the saints associated with it, the book settles into a regular pattern, of each chapter describing one century, outlining the succession of popes and monarchs, and then of the archbishops and bishops pertaining to that century. He finishes his historical survey at the end of the fifteenth century, just a few years before the beginning of the King's 'great matter' and the chain of events which was to plunge England into the cataclysm which was already well-documented, not least by Harpsfield himself.

Several features of the way in which Harpsfield undertakes his historical survey are typical both of his preoccupations, and of those of the generation which followed him. For all its lack of a polemical edge, the *Historia* is a book which very clearly indicates the nature of the continuity to which English Catholics under Elizabeth laid claim. In the first place, his tracing of the pontifical line of succession, and his careful examination of instances of dispute between papacy and monarchy, show his commitment to the papacy as the guarantor of orthodoxy and connection to Christendom. His honest description of the failings of Archbishop Stigand is used to point to a greater truth, namely the reliability of the papacy, and the dangers of subverting its proper election, Stigand having received the pallium 'ab Honorio Pseudopontifice'.[53] There is, naturally enough, particular praise for the popes whose missions to England ensured the continued existence of orthodoxy in the land. Augustine's mission as described by Harpsfield becomes nothing so much as an exercise in the banishment of pagan heresy and the material establishment of the apparatus for Catholic worship, and therefore points to the kind of reconversion he saw England under Elizabeth as needing:

> that, having thrown out the idols, as if having despoiled Egypt, he might honour Christ, and having sprinkled the church with blessed and holy water, built altars, and brought in the relics of the saints, he might bring them back from profane and sacreligious customs, to holy Christian rites and the worship of God.[54]

Good relations between kings and archbishops are celebrated, as are monarchs like Edgar and Edward the Confessor, whose faith spurred

---

53 *Ibid.*, pp. 233–5.

54 ['ut eiectis Idolis, quasi spoliato Aegypto, Christum ditaret, templumque benedicta atque sacra aqua aspersum, Altaribus constructis, divorumque reliquiis illatis, a profanis atque execrandis usibus, ad ritus sacros & Christianos, cultumque divinum traduceret'] *Ibid.*, p. 59.

them to the foundation of monastic institutions and the encouragement of Catholic faith in England. Harpsfield similarly spares nothing in his attacks on the folly of kings whose arrogance led them to place themselves above the Church. Thomas Becket, as usual, is made to mirror Thomas More, not least in his distrust of the king's affection for him:

> 'I am afraid, lest this great favour, and the remarkable affection of your heart, in which you now blaze up completely towards me, should not only chill and vanish away, but also should turn into a very serious kind of hatred'... and in this Thomas showed himself a wise man, or, rather, a prophet.[55]

Thomas is the guardian of the unity of the English church with the rest of Christendom, making his case firmly to his king, that he should not succumb to the hubris which would lead him to add to his other sins that of 'schism from the unity of the Church'.[56] It was to this firm adherence to unity with Rome and all the Church as the guarantee of authenticity that English Catholics were being called in the work. In doing so, they were encouraged to think, they were joining themselves to saints of the past, with men like Becket, to a share of their glory, especially if, like Becket, they suffered for it.

Perhaps the most successful part of the *Historia* is its vivid celebration of the lives of the English saints. Again, Harpsfield's clear aim is to trace a line of succession of those whose lives have been committed to God through the true faith of Rome, from the earliest days of the Christian faith right up to the time immediately before the Reformation: he begins with Joseph of Arimathea and ends with Thomas More. The characteristics of such saints which he draws out are just the same as those of a more international nature he had written of in the *Dialogi Sex*: their complete commitment to serving God, their absolute obedience to Rome, and the fruit, of miracle and evident holiness, which such qualities had borne in their life and death. The description of St Cuthbert, for instance, drawing on Bede, yet strikes a very Marian note in its emphasis on Cuthbert's desire for unity over the issue of Easter and his teaching ministry:

> amongst his last words about peace and mutual love, and the care of strangers, it is said that he emphasised the unity of the Catholic Church, to be preserved by the brothers, and that they

---

55 ['vereor, ne haec tanta gratia, mirusque ille animi tui ardor, quo totus in me iam exardescis, non solum refrigescat & dissiliat, sed & in grave quoddam tandem odium convertatur'... 'atque hic se virum prudentem aut Prophetam potius Thomas exhibuit'] *Ibid.*, p. 330.

56 ['a breach from the unity of the Church'] *Ibid.*, pp. 356–7.

should have absolutely nothing to do with those who observed Easter in a way at odds with the agreed rites of the Church.[57]

There is Anselm, the 'strict and firm observer of the unity and discipline of the Church', and Wulfric, noted especially for his firm avowal of transubstantiation and the wonder of the Mass. Hugh of Lincoln affirms for English Catholics the whole gamut of the church's spiritual practice, 'vigils, fasts, whippings, hair shirts, denial of food and bread, and even of water to drink', whilst Godric offers the pattern to follow, inspired by a visit to Lindisfarne to emulate the piety of Cuthbert and Aidan: 'the next day he began the emulation of the perfect solitary life, his mind a stranger to earthly things, and moved to the heavenly, stronger than iron.' Here perhaps was a more obvious inspiration for Elizabethan recusancy than appears at first glance, the possibility of being, like Godric, a new Cuthbert or Anthony 'reborn ... in England'.[58]

Harpsfield evokes the brave martyrdom of Alban under the Emperor Diocletian, the virginity of Etheldreda and her passion for the monastic life in Ely, Oswald's bias to the poor, the remote contemplation of Guthlac and the burial of East Anglia's first bishop, Felix, in Soham. He emphasises the importance of mission, citing Boniface as England's greatest export, in his work in Germany. In a clear reference to the admiration for the Jesuits which ran through the *Dialogi Sex*, Harpsfield talks of Brendan's missionary journeys too, travelling to islands he had never seen before, not unlike the missionaries in Harpsfield's own day and their destinations: 'there are found many islands beyond human knowledge, entirely cut off from our previous talk and exploration; and which are so alien and remote from our customs and way of life and lands that, also because of their great number, they are referred to as a kind of New World; and because of wonderful things which have happened, they seem to outshine all other faith'. And Harpsfield reveals his own veneration for relics and his respect for the holy, in his description of the ring found on the finger of Cuthbert's body, found in perfect condition at the dissolution, which he himself had venerated. His own sense of awe at the event is attractively apparent:

---

57 ['inter extrema verba de pace & charitate mutua, curaque hospitii, & cum primis catholicae ecclesiae unitate, a fratribus conservanda, loquutus est, utque nihil omnino commune cum his haberent, qui praeter consuetum ecclesiae ritum Pascha observarent.']; *Ibid.*, p. 100.

58 ['Ecclesiasticae unitatis, & disciplinae accuratus & rigidus observator' ... 'vigiliis, ieiuniis, flageliis, cililcio, sicci atque panis esu, aquaeque potu' ... 'coepit indies postea, a terrenis rebus animo esse alienore, & arcanoro quodam animi motu, ad perfectoris solitariae vitae aemulationem, vehementius ferri'] *Ibid.*, pp. 98–100, 324, 370, 382, 407–9.

> He had indeed a golden ring, decorated with sapphire, on his finger, which I saw and touched once, and which, wonderingly, I held and kissed as though it were a kind of memorial of God himself, and more precious than any treasure.[59]

In these attractive and colourful vignettes, Englishmen were being asked, covertly and unpolemically, to ally their own lives and allegiances with the long line of such holiness, to place themselves in the same line of commitment as the great saints of their country's history. The sense of historical continuity which undergirded Elizabethan and Jacobean Catholicism was writ large in Harpsfield's carefully researched pages, and indicates the reason for their importance to such subsequent generations. There is an unshakeable belief in divine providence through history in the work, a firm sense that, despite turmoil and political upheaval, the purpose of the Church is not thwarted, and a greater power is still at work. Writing of the Norman Conquest, Harpsfield described its profound disturbance of the religious life of England, yet declares a deeply hopeful outlook, a prophetic conviction that even setback can represent the purpose of God:

> Thus God governs human affairs, and even presses back distinguished empires, lest we should set up anything fixed or stable in human affairs, led on by an error of judgement, and rather that, from further reflection on this sort of change, we should depend on God alone. Although God has other reasons for his providence (which might seem remote to us), we should not doubt ... so for sure the Prophets everywhere proclaimed and openly witnessed to the people of Israel that changes of this kind occurred to punish and correct the sins of the people, and came from the will of an angry God.[60]

---

59 ['intra hominum memoriam insulae plurimae, a nostra prius conversatione cognitioneque penitus seiunctae, inventae sunt: & tam a nostris moribus, conditione, terrisque alienae & remotae, ut & propter earum multitudinem, novi cuiusdam orbis figuram referant; & propter rerum admirabilitatem omnem fidem superare videantur' ... 'Habuit vero in digito annulum aureum sapphiro ornatum, quem ego aliquando vidi atque contrectavi, & tanquam divinum quoddam monumentum, omnique thesauro preciosius, mirifice amplexus atque osculatus sum'] *Ibid.*, pp. 39–40, 105.

60 ['Sic Deus res humanas temperat, & sublimia etiam imperia deprimit, ne quid forte fixum, aut stabile in rebus humanis falso errore ducti constituamus, magisque ex huiusmodi conversionum accurata consideratione, a solo Deo pendeamus. Quamquam alias (licet nobis arcanas) providentiae suae Deo causas subesse, nihil dubitemus ... ita certe huiusmodi immutationes, propter castiganda & reprimenda populi peccata, ex irata Dei voluntate promanere, Prophetae passim denuntiant, idque palam *Israelitico* populo testabantur'] *Ibid.*, p. 222 .

In tracing such a providential view of England's religious history, Harpsfield is at pains, as has been seen, to ensure that he traces the features and characteristics of true faith right up to the time immediately preceding the Reformation, and the shocks and disturbances which have engulfed Tudor England. To that end, his vivid and colourful description of saints' lives and the effect of their holiness persist to the book's end. Just as he has portrayed Wulfric, Guthlac and Godric as the English successors of Anthony and Hilarion, and Cuthbert as the English Benedict, so he charts the line of descent of these English saints into the fourteenth-century lives of John of Bridlington and William of Wykeham, the latter described by Harpsfield, who had studied in the bishop's educational foundations, as 'the best father ... from whom, if I have any doctrine, virtue, piety and Catholic religion, I say I assuredly received it'.[61] John's story is cast directly from the mould of the earlier saints' life stories, with a particular relish shown for the miracles associated with his life and the place of his burial:

> The deaf, the blind, the maimed, the leprous, those possessed by demons, and those who had given up their life, were restored to wholeness; and others in their troubles and miseries felt this blessing, wonderfully and increasingly, through the aid and help of John, whom they had implored with their prayers.[62]

The century offers also a shining example of the godly king, Henry V, whose prowess in battle was eclipsed by his strengthening of monastic life and his fight against those 'who shamefully schemed against God, the Christian faith, the king, and his authority'. We are back to the stories of Wycliffite belief, and the treachery of Cobham so beloved of Foxe, and Harpsfield promises a fuller treatment later, pointing forward to the *Historia Wicleffiana*.[63]

The *Historia* ends by charting the persistence of both Catholic faith under the papacy and the lives of the saints up to the end of the fifteenth century. Using his framework, of following the succession of popes, archbishops and bishops by diocese, Harpsfield ends up with Archbishop John Morton, a man notable in his own right for his piety, learning and virtue, but also for his having noticed and nurtured the man destined

---

61 ['optimum parentem ... cui, si quid in me doctrinae, virtutis, pietatis, & catholicae religionis, maxime acceptum refero'] *Ibid.*, p. 552.
62 ['Claudi, caeci, mutilati, leprosi, a daemonibus obsessi, imo, & qui iam humanam vitam exuerant, vitae redditi; & alii in suis angustiis & miseriis, haec beneficia ope & auxilio Ioannis, quem suis precibus interpellabant, admirabiliter & cumulate sentibant.']; *Ibid.*, p. 579.
63 ['qui adversus Dei, fidei Christianae, Regis and regni maiestatem nefarie coierant']; *Ibid.*, p. 588.

to be numbered amongst England's greatest Catholics and saints:

> I do not know whether he was greatest in memory, in genius or in wisdom, and England in those days never saw his equal or his superior, unless perhaps we include Thomas More. But More at that time was a boy, and in his early boyhood, as he himself said, he learned the basics above all in the house of Morton himself. Morton used to delight wonderfully in his genius (he was the best observer of genius), and when he used to serve at the Cardinal's table, Morton used often to say to the exalted diners near him, as I understand from those who heard it from them and remembered the matter correctly: 'this boy, if he grows to adulthood, will emerge as a gifted and famous man'. And it soon turned out accurately, when More was sent by his father to Oxford to gain a greater education. Nor did More fail to fulfil the prediction of Morton, as the whole world knows.[64]

As if to remind his readers of the nature of the future martyrdom of More, Harpsfield slightly oversteps his historical *terminus* by mentioning Morton's successor Warham, who knew that he would be succeeded in his turn by another Thomas, a man who 'through ... corrupt doctrines would greatly disfigure Canterbury, and all the rest of the English church'.[65] More's stand against that doctrine, and the deformation of the English Church and her proud history of sanctity and unity with Christendom reminded the Elizabethan Catholic reader of their own share in the work of such a continuous line of saints, in whose steps they trod.

The *Historia*, then, offered compelling historical evidence to Elizabethan Catholics that, in holding to the primacy of Rome, rejecting heresy and resisting the commands of a schismatic monarch, they were stand-

---

64 ['vir fuit, cui nescio an memoriae, ingenii, prudentiaeque praestantia, quenquam illis temporibus Anglia parem ne dum superiorem, nisi forte Thomam Morum, viderit. Sed Morus admodum puer tum erat, primaque pueritiae suae, ut ipse ait, rudimenta, in ipsius potissimum Mortoni aula deposuit. Cuius ingenio (ingeniorum ipse optimus spectator) mirifice delectabatur, cumque mensae Cardinalis ministraret, assidentibus Proceribus saepe, ut intelligo ab his, qui ab eis audierant, qui recte rem noverant, dicere solitus est. Hic puer, si ad iustam aetatem maturuerit, in eximium & singularem virum evadet. Egitque mox accurate cum patre Mori ut Oxonium ad maiorem literarum cultum capessendum mitteretur. Nec fefellit Mortoni expectationem, ut totus orbis novit, Morus.']; *Ibid.*, p. 625; the account is based in part on More's own description of Morton in the *Utopia*.

65 ['per ... prava dogmata, magis Cantuariensem, omenmque reliquam Angliae ecclesiam deformaret']; *Ibid.*, p. 633; it was a prophecy which Harpsfield had previously narrated in the *Treatise*, p. 178, in which he claimed that the story had been told to him by Warham's nephew. The passage may indicate a sharpening of Harpsfield's placing of the two Thomases in apposition, arguably begun in the *Recantacyons*.

ing in a glorious line of saints, and holding true to their country's noble religious heritage. They were to be inspired by the knowledge that their faith placed them in a direct line, of being the inheritors of the grace of Alban, Cuthbert, Augustine, Becket, Morton and More. The second, much shorter, part of the book, more polemically, put the case against their opposition: the by now familiar but still necessary historical task of tracing the continuity of the heresy which they resisted, back to its fountain-head and source. In so doing, it was to give Catholics courage that they stood in the true path, and to unmask their opponents as the descendants of a heresiarch. Such was the aim of the appended *Historia Wicleffiana*.

The preface to the *Historia Wicleffiana* elucidates both the purpose of the previous 660 pages, and Harpsfield's intent to lay bare the nature of the heresy which has overrun Europe. Indeed, the purposes are interlinked; Harpsfield declares his hope that, in seeing the continuance of the heresy which opposes them, 'at last the members of the Catholic Church, who up to now have remained in the lap of the Church, might be more confirmed in this': this is a book primarily for Catholics.[66] But it has a message for Protestants too: building on the historical foundation of the *Historia*, Harpsfield reminds his readers that England has previously been largely kept safe from heresy because of a strong partnership between clergy and monarchy; now, it has spread almost from nothing to a national disease. God has offered revelations in the present age, 'plain and celebrated (miracles) in England, even if I ignore all other nations, for the confirming of the Catholic faith against the heretics', and the witness of history itself should call the right-minded back to the integrity of the English Church under Rome, 'which, right up to our times, has remained in the faith, whole and unperturbed by all heresies, from Augustine, the man who planted our faith here'. The choice is between a faith which is 'unchanging and sure, and therefore fortunate and a source of blessing in all these centuries' and a heresy which is 'protean and inconstant'.[67] His tenacious faith in divine providence seems almost to desert him for a moment as he describes England under Elizabeth, pounded by wave upon wave of relentless heresy, against which Catholic faith is the only bulwark. Written in his final

---

66 ['denique catholicae ecclesiae alumni, qui hactenus in ecclesiae se gremio continuere, magis hinc confirmentur']; *Ibid.*, pp. 663–4.

67 ['clara atque illustria in Anglia (ut ceteras nationes omittam) ad catholicae fidei contra haereticos confirmationem' ... 'quae, ad nostra usque tempora, integra & illibata ab omni haeresi, ab Augustino usque fidei nostrae initiatore ... in fide permansit' ... 'constans atque firma, atque ideo felix & beata tot illis saeculis' ... 'lubrica & inconstans'.] *Ibid.*, p. 665.

years[68] from a prison cell, it is the most moving piece of prose from a normally unemotional writer, which found new poignancy when first published nearly fifty years after his death:

> A huge ocean of infinite heresies has poured on England, having burst over our shores, and does not cease daily to pour in; and it pushes forwards, wave on wave, one after another: for sure, it will not cease to pour in, until the shores of the old and Catholic Church, having been broken and torn down by it ... are repaired and restored. Only the Catholic Church is tenacious in its beliefs.[69]

Harpsfield made it clear all through the *Historia* that the *Historia Wicleffiana* was an integral part of the writing project, even if a separate book attached at the end. Having charted the course of the English Church and its maintenance of faith through fifteen centuries, he does the same for the Wycliffite heresy through the shorter time of its existence. It was a historiographical template later used by Persons in his *Treatise*, as has been seen. The reason for the emphasis given to Wycliffe is clear, even from the preface: though not the first English heretic, he was the worst, the figure who most fired the misguided zeal which eventually broke England's unity with Christendom. As the preface has made clear, too, Wycliffe is chosen because of his importance to many of the martyrs celebrated by John Foxe, and to Foxe himself. The *Historia Wicleffiana*, then, was Harpsfield's final attack on Foxe, a final attempt to clear up what Harpsfield saw as the historical fog which the Protestant martyrologist had created. Three main threads of argument emerge over its 60 pages: tracing the line of descent connecting Wycliffe and all previous and subsequent heretics, proving the continuity of Catholic resistance to its opposite but not equal force of heresy, and making a final challenge to the historical account of Foxe.

Much of this represents nothing new in the arguments deployed by Harpsfield in other works. The *Historia Wicleffiana*, like the rest of the work, is, in effect, doing the same ecclesiological and historiographical task as the *Dialogi Sex*, except that its focus is much more Anglocentric.

---

68 The discussion of Cowbridge on pp. 679–80 cites his trial as having happened 36 years previously; this would date the book to 1575, the year of Harpsfield's death. Kenny's article becomes muddled here, one the one hand correctly citing Harpsfield's death in 1575 and on the other suggesting 1590 as a date for the *Historia Wicleffiana*'s composition; Kenny (ed.) 1986, pp. 163–4.

69 ['Vastus, quasi perruptis littoribus, infinitarum haereseon ... oceanus in Angliam inundavit, nec cessat quotidie inundare; atque ut fluctus fluctum, alia aliam trudit: nec certe inundare desinet, donec veteris atque catholicae ecclesiae convulsa illa, atque dissipata ... littora resarciantur atque reficiantur. Sola catholica ecclesia suorum dogmatum tenax est.'] *Ibid.*, p. 665.

Harpsfield, More and English Catholic Identity

Wycliffe becomes the focal point for the entry and growth of heresy in England, and Harpsfield uses him to show how English heresy derives from and depends upon earlier forms of heresy. His Eucharistic theology bears the imprint of Berengar; his misuse of scripture is like that of the Manichees; his views on human nature and the purpose of grace derive from Pelagius. The lives lived by Wycliffe and his followers imitate ancient heretics in 'their way of life ... like the true offspring of their parents'. Like the Iconomachoi, Wycliffites have been seditious traitors, and, like the Donatists, fierce opponents of both ecclesiastical and secular authority. As in the *Dialogi Sex*, Harpsfield connects Wycliffite heresy with Jack Straw, the Lollards, Cobham, Cowbridge and Hus. Wycliffite heresy, he contends, is a diabolical concatenation of elements of previous heresies, with the inevitable result that, like all heretics, Wycliffe's thought possesses neither consensus with historical faith nor internal consistency with itself or other heretics. The Wycliffites, like all heretics, lacking any integrity or ecclesial authority, are 'divided and fragmented amongst themselves'. They represent, in other words, the mirror image of Catholics; when Harpsfield went on to turn his fire on the Puritans for their pharisaical criticism of other Protestants for not being anti-Catholic enough, he must have struck a chord with his seventeenth-century readers as much as the sixteenth-century ones he had in mind.[70]

In a fascinating final word on his Marian past, also, Harpsfield outlines the historical consistency with which English Catholics have pursued and punished heretics of all kinds, not least the Wycliffites. Wycliffe's works have been refuted by an illustrious succession of England's finest minds: Thomas Walden, William of Woodford, Fisher, Gardiner and More. His followers have been burned, rightly, according to an 'ancient and universally held law', which he traces back in England to the time of King John. Miracles have been given to England as testimony against the heresy, at the shrines of Becket and of the Virgin at Ipswich, as well as in the cross of the Glamorgan tree, 'on which, see the fourth of the dialogues of Alan Cope' (i.e. the *Dialogi Sex*). In speaking of this consistent treatment of heretics, Harpsfield reveals how, in his view, the Reformation represents the resurfacing of an ancient heresy in a new and deadly form, and the concomitant need to deal with it decisively; in England:

> The Catholic faith, also, until now had remained in perfect repair and inviolate. But recently many wicked sectaries of new and

---

70 ['vivendi ratione ... quasi genuini filii parentes' ... 'inter se distracti & dissecti sunt'] *Ibid.*, pp. 676, 680, 694, 695–8, 700–3, 707, 711, 728 ff. For the use of the notion of 'heretical succession' in Harpsfield's Marian and Elizabethan works, see above, pp. 71 ff. and 127 ff.

> diabolic doctrines have burst forth, who hold bad and wicked views about the sacraments and the Church's authority, and who arrogantly tout their own disputatious work, with human scorn rather than by divine law, and who set up wicked assemblies and filthy doctrines, which are utterly opposed, both to Catholic faith and the holy things of the Church, and who for the furtherance of their doctrines set up subversive meetings and alliances, and uphold wickednesses, and draw up books together, and, as far as they are able, excite the people to greater wickedness and sedition and great disagreements and arguments in the kingdom, and every day they create terrible new sacrileges, to the great undermining of the Catholic faith, the authority of God, all the freedom of the Church, and the inviolability of its privileges.[71]

The final chapter fires a last salvo against Foxe's reply to Harpsfield's previous pseudonymous attack on the history of Cobham and Acton. Indeed, Harpsfield finally blows his cover, lapsing into the first person in his description of the work of the *Dialogi Sex*, and challenging Foxe that, if he can prove Cobham not to have been a traitor, Harpsfield in turn will withdraw the charge of heterodoxy against the martyrologist. Foxe's comparison of Cobham with the early Christian martyrs cannot stand either, unless he can prove Henry V to have been a Diocletian, intent upon the destruction of Christians in England: as with the *Dialogi Sex*, Harpsfield exploits the shaky ground on which Foxe's narrative here stood. As with history, so with scripture, Foxe corrupts and distorts the plain truth in order to accommodate his error and arrogance:

> For he interprets the Fathers and scriptures, not according to their own meaning, whose words are well known, and whom the Catholic Church has constantly up to now followed as though directed by the Holy Spirit; but he interprets them from his own private and depraved understanding and ... he mangles and dirties the truth.[72]

71 ['communi ... & antiquo iure' ... 'Fidem quoque catholicam, hactenus sartam tectam, atque inviolata, permansisse. At nuper multos erupisse, novorum & damnotorum dogmatum improbos sectatores, qui de sacramentis & de ecclesiae auctoritate pessime & perditissime sentirent, quique spreta tam humana, quam divina lege, concionandi ipsi sibi munus arroganter vendicarent, concionandoque improbata & execranda dogmata proponerent, quae catholicae fidei atque ecclesiae sanctionibus prorsus repugnarent, quique ad disseminanda eadem dogmata illicitos conventus & foedera inirent, scelasque tenerent, libros conscriberent, & quoad possent, populum ad pernitiosus motus, seditionemque, magnasque dissidia atque contentiones in regno excitarent, quotidieque alia horrenda piacula designarent, ad extremam fidei catholicae ruinam, ad divinae maiestatis, omniumque ecclesiae libertatum, & praerogativarum immuntionem']; *Ibid.*, p. 772.

72 ['Patres enim ille & scripturas non ad eum sensum, quem & verba prae

It was Harpsfield's final word against the martyrologist whose work he so fiercely disputed, and the basis of whose thought he so doggedly refuted, and the last word also in a long fight to make plain the Catholic heritage the English should claim, in order that they might reject its heretical adversary, unmasked in its historical context and its true colours.

Catholica Ecclesia ... tenax est: Harpsfield and continuity

Alison Shell has helpfully pointed out that, in speaking of Elizabethan Catholicism, we need to speak not of a 'community', but of a number of such communities[73]; sometimes the boundaries between them are unclear and the point of departure from Catholicism hard to define. Bossy and Wooding generally mean the Catholicism of the recusants when they speak of the 'English Catholic Community': the body of men and women whose commitment to traditional religion led them to resist what they saw as the compromise of the 'church papists' and to realise their need to reject Elizabeth's royal supremacy in order to remain religiously authentic. It was to this group that Harpsfield primarily wrote; it was to this group that Allen sent his missionary priests to provide Mass and confession, channels of sacramental grace to keep Catholic character and identity alive. It was this group, therefore, who were being encouraged to trace for themselves the kind of sense of historical continuity which has been described. That the material written for them should influence wavering 'church papists' or doubtful Protestants would have been a bonus.

A further complication, as has been said, surrounds the divisions which arose within the priestly community, a division to do with authority and control, and which threatened the harmony of the English Catholics for a considerable period of time. Coupled with the enormous sociological changes, and the huge alterations to the practice of Catholicism which recusancy required, it is small wonder that English Catholicism in this period has been seen as a body disconnected from its pre-Reformation ancestor. Nor is it surprising that it has been difficult to trace continuity, in a body so constrained in its religious expression and therefore so different in behaviour from its predecessors. But sociological change, alterations to practice and inter-clerical divisions have often blinded scholars to the very real ecclesiological and theological

se ferunt, quemque quasi a Spiritu sancto dictatum, ecclesia catholica constanter hactenus sequuta est; sed a privatum & depravatum tradit, veritatemque ... commaculat & conspurcat']; *Ibid.*, pp. 728–32.

73 Shell 1999, p. 108.

continuity which underpinned the ongoing Catholicism of the English. That, at least, seems to be the witness of the published works of the late sixteenth and early seventeenth centuries. Wooding's claim that the writers of the 1560s lived and worked within 'a different intellectual world' to their martyr co-religionists of the 1580s does not reflect the views of the works examined here, still less the importance to contemporary and later Catholics of the works of Nicholas Harpsfield.

The continuity which English Catholics were encouraged to claim for themselves was essentially historical, a firm conviction of their possession of an unbroken inheritance of the faith of the Church Universal, led by the Spirit, guarded by popes and bishops, and confirmed in the lives and deaths of the saints and martyrs. Against this, Harpsfield and his successors set a 'shadow', of the similar continuity throughout the Church's history of forces of heresy and opposition, forces which rose up to afflict each succeeding generation. The tools were thus given to English Catholics to discern the features of each succession, and to have courage in their own choice, in the face of the regime's hostility towards them. As John Foxe attempted to redraw his martyrs as standard-bearers for truth, the Catholic polemical tradition begun and continued by Harpsfield tried to point to deeper, firmer and more authentic patterns of religious commitment, patterns with roots further back in time and with a more reliable pedigree than Foxe's claim, of a constantly resurfacing true faith, possessed. Harpsfield's twin Marian aims, of demonstrating the folly of separation from Rome and of using Thomas More as the figure who, in dying for that cause, stood in the line of the saints and martyrs of every age, underpinned this very Elizabethan project. Indeed, as seminary priests and others began to meet with torture and execution, such historical emphases began to seem ever more prescient and necessary. Just as Marian Catholics were encouraged to see the sacraments as holy conduits of grace, guaranteeing authenticity, so Elizabethan Catholics, largely without access to the sacramental, were offered the history in which they stood as their own, imperishable, channel of truth and life. The resources being offered and the challenge being made by Harpsfield and his successors were primarily intellectual, about assent to the papacy and rejection of the national church, an assent which English Catholics had to give whilst deprived of the sacraments and devoid of priests. But for all that, they were resources, and it was a challenge, which reflected earlier ones and which demonstrated the ongoing vitality of the Marian mindset.

It is failure properly to understand this Marian mindset, therefore, which underlies mistaken ideas about a lack of continuity within Elizabethan Catholicism. Such a failure leads, for instance, to Wooding's difficulties in having to see the works of the 1560s as *both* humanist, seeing little need for the papacy except as an 'administrative necessity', *and* increasingly scholastic, forced back towards papal supremacy by the clever manoevering of Jewel and Foxe. The Marian authorities saw themselves, rather, as reclaiming the historical continuity to which More and Fisher had pointed, and from which traditionalist supporters of the royal supremacy eventually realised they had departed. Nicholas Harpsfield attempted to articulate this understanding in his work on the Henrician and Edwardian periods, and in his celebration of More. He pursued that very understanding in his Elizabethan writings, attempting to show English Catholics their illustrious descent. His work shaped subsequent Catholic writing in ways which have rarely been acknowledged: the More tradition, taken up by Stapleton and others; the ongoing attack on Foxe, and especially Persons' *Treatise* which in many respects merely puts into English the argument of the *Dialogi Sex*; the renewal of the martyrological tradition in English Catholicism; and the importance attached to the eventual publication of the *Historia*, which seemed to Jacobean Catholics to trace the very historical authenticity of their faith that they sought to elucidate.

In all these respects, Harpsfield's legacy was a welcome one to the generations after his death. The use of it by them still points to a greater degree of indebtedness and similarity between early and late Elizabethan Catholicism than has been allowed in much recent scholarship. Their use of medieval themes and concerns shows not a caricature but a real understanding of what the Reformation had swept away; their claims to continuity with the past were not a matter of mere false rhetoric, but rooted in demonstrable fact. The sense of historical inheritance and loyalty which recusants were consistently encouraged to find in these late Elizabethan writings pointed to a very practical purpose, of lives rooted in the sacraments and aimed at holiness, following the example of past generations, despite English Catholic hardship and limitation. Elizabethan Catholics were reminded that, even in a minority and under pressure from the regime, they were, like Thomas More, still linked to a far greater number of the faithful in previous generations whose witness was the same as their own. 1570 and the years following it marked therefore not so much a 'discontinuity in the historical sequence', but a deliberate attempt to forge and cherish a continuity of belief with the past. In that process, far from being a period which Catholics would rather forget, the hard-won convictions and basic assumptions of the Marian period proved important. A fresh understanding of the importance of traditional patterns of devotion, a new sense of connection with the past and of the witness of the saints and martyrs, an appreciation of the events which led to national decay and of the resources for renewal, and a return to the fundamental principles of Catholic faith:

all these were rediscovered in the Marian period and transmitted to the recusant age. Nicholas Harpsfield, from a prison cell, and even after death, remained a key voice, and a vital figure in giving shape to the convictions which underpinned recusant Catholicism and continued to fight tirelessly against its opponents.

APPENDIX I

Harpsfield's *Life of Christ*

Only one material trace of evidence remains of Harpsfield's early Elizabethan writing, a manuscript in a secretary's hand at Lambeth Palace Library called *The Life of our Lord Jesus Christ written in Latin by Nicolas Harpsfield Doctor of Civil Law faythfully translated*. The work dates itself to 1559, in detailing a miracle at Canterbury of that year which occurred 'in the selfe time we have this treatise in hande',[1] and speaking with the customary caution of the *Dialogi Sex* about the Queen herself. It is a short work, of eighty-four folios.

The work is not really a life of Christ at all. Harpsfield takes the events of the gospel accounts of Christ's life, passion and death and uses them as the initiators of longer discussions on Catholic practice, and especially for a defence of a belief in the miraculous. It is therefore, rather like the *Dialogi Sex*, a book inclined to wander widely in its discussion, as even the author admits. The work was never published, and has barely survived, but to the reader already familiar with the *Dialogi Sex* its purpose, as in some sense Harpsfield's first run at some of the themes and issues of that book, is immediately clear. There is barely any material in the *Life* which is not repeated in the later, much larger, book. In particular, the *Life* stresses the same themes: the importance of miracle, the authority of the Church's traditional practice, and the importance of connection to Catholicism for England to remain authentically Christian, and authentically English.

A few examples of the book's thrust make the similarity obvious. A brief mention of Christ's baptism leads into a discussion about baptism and confirmation, the assertion that 'the holy ghoste is given in both twaine', and an attack on Protestants who arrogantly reduce the Church's traditional teaching: 'Would to God their prophane innovations had kept themselves within the bounds of ceremonies.'[2]

Similarly, after Harpsfield has recounted that Christ performed miracles, he goes on to describe and celebrate the greatest of them,

---

1 Harpsfield, c.1559, fol. 79.
2 Ibid., fols. 12–13.

the eucharist, offering scriptural commands, patristic interpretations, accounts of associated miracles and testimonies of those transformed by it. The language is strong, reminiscent of the sacramental writings of bishops under Mary and transmitted through the works of the 1560s to a recusant age. It evokes therefore the *Dialogi Sex*, in claiming that 'for us to be turned into that flesh in very deed, and only by love, that, I say, is done by that meat, which he hath given us ... let no man therefore foolishly flatter himself with the name of a Catholic Christian man if ... in this article of the Sacrament he perceive himself to swerve from the Catholic belief'.[3]

The impetus of the stories told about miracles associated with the Eucharist is the same as that in the *Dialogi Sex* also; they are offered not least as cumulative evidence of the unassailable authority given to the Church's traditional practice:

> If to any man they should seem not certain, and of sure credit enough, let him consider with himself what absurdity will follow, of this, if God sometime uphold and set forth the true and right doctrine of the Church with these examples, as with an extraordinary probation. But if the old ancient custom of the whole Church from the beginning hitherto seem nought worth to any man, let him despise and set at naught these wonderful miracles we have recited.[4]

A prominent feature of this long section too is an attack on sacrilege, and the telling of stories of those miraculously cut down after dishonouring the host, or defiling altars or attempting to celebrate when unfit to do so.[5] England's own recent involvement in such acts and similar behaviour has drawn down a spate of miracles and punishments, sure indication, Harpsfield urges his readers, of divine displeasure and also hope for the future, if England will return to Rome. God will not, he says, 'leave his Churche (though now being sore troubled for a time) destitute of all such miracles and aid when it shall please him to appoint the time, albeit in the sight of men things seem never so desperate and unrecuperable'.[6]

The final section of the book deals, with almost medieval vividness, with the passion of Christ, and leads in turn into a passionate defence of the sign of the cross, the crucifix, images and relics. Here, the English tone of the work is most prominent, as Harpsfield cites English events and portents as indications of the divine displeasure England

3 *Ibid.*, fols. 22, 26–7.
4 *Ibid.*, fol. 37; see above, p. 96.
5 *Ibid.*, fols. 40–50.
6 *Ibid.*, fol. 50.

has incurred. Helena makes a predicable appearance, with Constantine; Augustine of Canterbury is praised as the bringer of genuine sacraments to England; the account ends with a series of briefly sketched English miracles, and the comment that 'our country of England is very fertile of such things'.[7] Most fulsomely treated, perhaps, is the account of the miraculous appearance of the cross in a fallen Welsh tree, of which Harpsfield was later to make much in the *Dialogi Sex*.[8] All these signs, then, despite Harpsfield's cautious treatment of the queen herself, demonstrate divine disapproval of the 'casting out of the churches the monuments of the holy saints and honourable Crosse of Christ' and of the 'cankered stomachs and malitious minds' which have been responsible: another thinly veiled attack on Harpsfield's *bête noire*, Thomas Cranmer, and his episcopal successors.[9]

The *Life* is therefore an interesting indication of the way in which Harpsfield had been working, from the beginning of his confinement and even before it, on the transmission of Marian themes and emphases to isolated Catholics under Elizabeth. It concentrates on English material, and centres its appeal in the continuity of tradition and in the very vivid language of the miraculous which feature so prominently in the later *Dialogi Sex*. It is, however, very much a fragment of what was to follow in 1566, its arguments less assured and its material more compressed than in Harpsfield's *magnum opus*. Its style is difficult to assess, being in an English translation of the original Latin, but certainly it should be viewed only as a sort of maquette of the work he eventually produced. Its arguments and themes and even material were reproduced in the *Dialogi Sex*, but immeasurably broadened, polished and expanded. It stands at the beginning of the work he had described in the *Life*, a work which he continued with apparent zeal in the 1560s, gathering together stories, 'whereunto not only the consideration of our time, and matter we have in hand hath induced me: but also for that it never happed to me to read any heretofore, which had thoroughly travelled herein. Wherefore such histories of this kind as now lie abroad dispersed in divers authors I will assay to collect and gather together. Then will I so distribute and place them that every one shall seem to be uttered in his own room. Last of all, having respect to brevity, I will compact them all in one body together'.[10]

---

7 *Ibid.*, fols. 66–7, 73, 78, 79.
8 See above, pp. 152; 233.
9 *Life of Christ*, fol. 81.
10 *Ibid.*, fol. 27.

APPENDIX II

The *Dialogi Sex*

OUTLINE OF CONTENTS BY CHAPTER

DIALOGUE ONE
THE PAPACY

- 1   Outline of the issues to be discussed
- 2–4   The calumny of the Centuriators against various Catholic historians described
- 5   The primacy of the pope: its historical authority
- 6   The role of pope and council
- 7   Africa and the Council of Nicaea: a sideline
- 8   Pope Liberius; biblical misuse by the *Apology* corrected
- 9   More on Nicaea and papal authority
- 10–11   The Centuriators on the popes: criticism and correction
- 12   The first councils of the Church: popes and rulers
- 13–14   The Centuriators' errors concerning Augustine
- 15–16   Protestant views of Peter, his successors, and the papal primacy
- 17–19   Cyprian on the pope
- 20–1   Various authorities and sources on the papal primacy
- 22–3   Response to Protestant claims about Catholic barbarity and error
- 24   Celibacy: not against the word of God or apostolic teaching

DIALOGUE TWO
MONASTICISM AND THE SACRAMENTS

- 1–2   Arguments by which Protestants undermine monasticism
- 3–4   The Catholic response to them: monasticism's biblical and apostolic basis
- 5   The futility of the Centuriators' attack: Dionysius the Areopagite
- 6–9   Early Church evidence of monasticism

10	More on the Protestant attack on Rome; Protestant immorality discussed
11–12	Celibacy: within marriage and as an element of monasticism
13–15	More charges against monasticism countered; especially on Malchion
16	On whether the monastic life is of God
17–18	The lives of the monks: Anthony, Hilarion, Jerome, Simon Stylites
19	Centuriators' scriptural challenge against monasticism dismissed
20	More on the lives of the monks, especially Anthony: his holiness celebrated
21	Cyprian and Chrysostom
22	More famous monks: Pachomus, Martin etc.
23–5	Further attack on the Centuriators' views of monks and monasticism
26	The Centuriators' denial of transubstantiation is challenged
27	Calvin's rejection of private confession confuted
28	Private confession defended and miracles associated with it described

DIALOGUE THREE

THE SAINTS, RELICS AND MIRACLES

1	Protestant opposition to prayer to and invocation of the saints described
2	Even the Centuriators' sources show prayer to the saints has always happened
3–4	The Centuriators' calumnies against patristic teaching
5	Defence of the Emperor Theodosius and of Councils on the subject
6	More patristic authority for prayer to the saints
7	Scriptural backing for prayer to the saints
8	Particular focus on the *Apology*'s views; St Bernard
9	Centuriators' false attack on histories of martyrdom
10–11	Visions and appearances of the saints to the faithful
12	Miracles associated with the saints' relics, shrines and cults
13–17	Various mistakes in Protestant historical writing about the saints
18	No reprehensible practice in Catholic cult of the saints
19–21	More on the mistakes and slurs of the Centuriators; more sources to confute them
22–3	Calvin's attack on miracles; already refuted in the works of Augustine

The Dialogi Sex

- 24 The history of St Euphemia defended
- 25–6 More on post-mortem miracles associated with the saints
- 27–8 Patron saints; miracles in their particular areas, even up to the present
- 29 Miracles in the New World and in recent times
- 30 Conclusion and summary

DIALOGUE FOUR
IMAGES AND MIRACLES

- 1–2 Protestant objections to images; Hadrian and Theodosius
- 3–4 Constantine and the sign of the cross; the attack on Helena
- 5–6 Patristic authority for images and the sign of the cross
- 7 St Augustine on the subject
- 8 Protestant lies about the sources and authorities
- 9 Catholic Easter ceremonies; miracles of the cross, inc. the Welsh miracle
- 10–12 Protestant writing on images and the cross refuted and challenged
- 13–15 Conciliar decrees on images and the cross; miracles
- 16 Recent miracles in Europe associated with images and the cross
- 17 Miracles in the New World
- 18–19 The controversy over the *Libri Carolini*: a corrective to recent Protestant claims

DIALOGUE FIVE
PROTESTANT UNRELIABILITY AND CATHOLIC AUTHENTICITY

- 1–4 Calvin's views on images and the *Libri Carolini*; a further rebuttal
- 5 The role of images as books for the illiterate
- 6 Further defence of images against Calvin
- 7–12 Various stories of the veneration of images; various Protestants criticised, including Laurence Humphrey, Calvin and the authors of the *Apology*
- 13 Defence of the conciliar declarations and decrees on images
- 14 Further criticism of the *Apology* on the papacy
- 15–16 Further criticism of the *Apology* on the Councils and images, inc. Trent
- 17 Epiphanius: not on the Protestant side, as they have claimed
- 18 Bale's errors about Augustine of Canterbury and monasticism countered

19 More on English histories, and various Protestant errors; St Boniface
20 Back to Epiphanius and Jerome on images
21 The heresies in the *Apology*; recent Tridentine decrees on images and the cult of the saints; Queen Elizabeth's crucifix
22–3 Those recently put to death: their views on images
24 Celebrating iconoclasts as martyrs
25 Pseudomartyrs revealed: how to discern true martyrdom; the start of the attack on Foxe: the cases of Cobham, Tyndale and Cranmer

DIALOGUE SIX
MARTYRDOM AND JOHN FOXE

1 The cause, and no other criterion, makes the martyr
2 The heresy, sacrilege, treason and madness of Foxe's various pseudomartyrs
3 The history of pseudomartyrs: Foxe is not the first to celebrate them
4 Heretics cannot be martyrs
5–7 Heretics, indeed, are most to be despised; the nature of heresy
8 Cyprian not a heretic
9 The providence of God against heresy, as in the New World
10 The impudence of Protestants creating 'martyrs'; their divisions and disunity
11 The example of Augustine and the Manichees
12 The great multitude of the true martyrs oppose the pseudo-martyrs
13 On whether the prophets were martyrs; the three kinds of martyr
14–15 Recent true martyrs; more on Protestant divisions, especially on the Eucharist
16 The disparate nature of Foxe's martyrs; and the Kalendar
17 William Cowbridge
18 Lutherans not martyrs, but in the heretical succession
19 Various mistakes and lies corrected, of those claimed as Protestants
20 Scripture not on the Protestant side; more on 'heretical succession'
21 Denial of Christ coming in flesh; Protestant divisions on the Eucharist again
22–5 The lives and behaviour of the Protestants contrasted with those of the true martyrs

The Dialogi Sex

26 Foxe's false claim that Erasmus belongs in his list
27 Giovanni Pico della Mirandola
28 More on the attitude of Foxe's martyrs
29 Only Catholics enjoy miracles: the heretics have none
30 Wycliffe and Foxe's mangling of his story
31 Wycliffe, Luther and Hus
32–3 The 'visions' of Protestants, inc. Karlstadt, Zwingli and Simpson denied
34–5 The history of Sleidanus attacked: no mention of the New World
36 More on claims of visions; Foxe's assertions of the miraculous
37 Foxe's claims that his martyrs were prophetic denied
38 Further denials of Protestant claims of the miraculous
39 George Bainham, John Marbeck, and other Foxian errors
40 The iniquity and untruth of Foxe's comparison of his martyrs with those of the Church
41 Celebration of Catholic martyrs
42–3 Foxe, Calvin and the Protestants: differences over who is head of their churches; only the English acknowledge their ruler as such
44 Fisher, More and the Henrician martyrs
45 Gregory I on true martyrs; the Centuriators wrong on this too
46 St Augustine on the Church and schism; the conversion of Critobolus

ADDITIONS TO THE 1573 EDITION

Dialogue Four contains two extra chapters, the first (pp. 421–8) on images, against Bale and the Centuriators, and the second (pp. 428–34) on the Decalogue.

Dialogue Five discusses Hilarius (pp. 506–9), again, against Bale's account of him.

Dialogue Six (pp. 705–17) includes more on Foxe's inclusion of renegates in his work, especially Cranmer.

Bibliography

Manuscripts

British Library Arundel MSS 72, 73
British Library Harleian MSS 416/7
British Library Harleian MS 6253
British Library Royal MS 8.B.xx
British Library Stowe MS 105
Lambeth Palace Library MS 446

Printed Primary Sources

(*Revised Short Title Catalogue* numbers in parentheses)

Alfield, T., *A True Reporte of the death and martyrdome of M. Campion Iesuite and preiste, & M. Sherwin, & M. Bryan preistes, at Tiborne*. 1582 (4537).
Allen, W., *A Briefe Historie of the Glorious Martyrdom of XII Reverend Priests*. 1582 (369.5).
Allen, W., *A Defense and Declaration of the Catholike Churchies Doctrine, touching Purgatory, and prayers for the soules departed*. John Latius, Antwerp, 1565 (371).
Allen, W., *A Treatise made in defence of the lawful power and authoritie of Priesthod to remitte sinnes: Of the peoples duetie for confession of their sinnes to Gods ministers: And of the Churches meaning concerning Indulgences, commonlie called the Popes Pardons*. John Fowler, Louvain, 1567 (372).
Allen, W., *A True, Sincere and Modest Defence of English Catholiques that suffer for their faith both at home and abrode: against a false, seditious and slanderous Libel intituled. The Execution of Justice in England*. Rouen, 1584 (373).
Aungell, J., *The Agrement of the Holye Fathers and Doctors of the churche, upon the cheifest articles of Christian religion as appeareth on the next syde folowinge, very necessary for all curates*. London, 1555(?) (634).
Bale, J., *Acta Romanorum Pontificum, a dispersione discipulorum Christi, usque ad tempora Pauli quarti, qui nunc in Ecclesia tyrannizat*. 1558.
Bale, J., *A Declaration of Edmonde Bonners articles, concerning the cleargye of London dyocese whereby that execrable Antychriste is in his right colours reveled*. John Tysdall, London, 1554 (1289).

Bale, J., *The Image of bothe churches*. London, 1545 (1296.5).
Bale, J., *The Vocacyon of Johan Bale to the bishoprick of Ossorie in Irelande his persecutions in the same and finall delyveraunce*. Rome, 1553 (1307).
Bonner, E., *A Profitable and necessarye doctryne, with certayne homelies adioyned therunto set forth by the reverende father in God, Edmonde byshop of London, for the instruction and enformation of the people beynge within his Diocesse of London, and of his cure and charge*. London, 1555 (3281.5).
Bushe, P., *A brefe exhortation set fourthe by the unprofitable servant of Jesu christ, Paule Bushe, late bishop of Brystowe, to one Margarete Burges, wyfe to Jhon Burges, clotheare of kyngeswode in the countie of Wilshere*. John Cawood, London, 1556 (4184).
Campion, E., *Rationes Decem: quibus fretis, certamen adversariis obtulit in cause fidei, Edmundus Campianus ... allegatae ad clarissimos viros, nostrates academicos*. 1581.
Cardwell, E. (ed.), *Synodalia (vol. I)*. Oxford University Press, Oxford, 1892.
Christopherson, J., *An Exhortation to all menne to take hede and beware of rebellion*. John Cawood, London, 1554 (5207).
Churchson, J., *A brefe treatyse, declaryng what and where the churche is, that it is knowen, and whereby it is tried and knowen*. John Cawood, London, 1556 (5219).
Cochlaeus, J., *Philippicae I-VII*, ed. R. Keen, De Graaf, Nieuwkoop, 1996 (2 vols.).
Cochlaeus, J., *Responsio ad Johannem Bugenhagium Pomeranium*, ed. R. Keen, De Graaf, Nieuwkoop, 1988.
Cranmer, T., *The Work of Thomas Cranmer*, ed. G. E. Duffield, Sutton Courtenay Press, Appleford Berks., 1964.
DeAdamo, A., *An Anatomi, that is to say a perting in peeces of the Mass, which discovereth the horrible errors, and the infinit abuses unkowen to the people, aswel of the Mass as of the Mass Book, very profitable, yea most necessary for al Christian people*. Strasbourg (?), 1556 (17200).
A Dialogue or familiar talke betwene two neighbours, concernyng the chyefest ceremonyes that were, by the mighti power of Gods most holie pure worde, suppressed in Englande, and nowe for our unworthines, set up agayne by the Bishoppes, the impes of Antichrist: right learned, profitable and pleasaunt to be read, for the comfort of weake consciences in these troublous daies. Michael Wodde, Rouen, 1554 (10383).
Dorman, T., *A Proufe of Certeyne Articles in Religion, denied by M. Iuell* (Antwerp, 1564), ed. D. M. Rogers, Scholar Press, Ilkley, 1976.
Eck, J., *De non tollendis Christi et sanctorum Imaginibus contra haeresim Faelician im sub Carolo Magno damnatam, et iam sub Carolo V renascentem decisio*. Ingoldstadt, 1522.

Bibliography

Eck, J., *Enchiridion Locorum Communium adversus Lutheranos*. 1525.

Edgeworth, R., *Sermons very fruitfull, godly and learned* (London 1557), ed. J. Wilson, D. S. Brewer, Cambridge, 1993.

Evans, L., *A Brieve Admonition unto the nowe made Ministers of Englande: Wherein is shewed some of the fruicte of this theyr late framed fayth* (Antwerp, 1565), ed. D. M. Rogers, Scolar Press, Ilkley, 1971.

Fisher, J., *Assertionis Lutheranae Confutatio*. Antwerp, 1523.

Fisher, J., *Defensio Regiae Assertionis*. Cologne, 1525a.

Fisher, J., *De Veritate Corporis et Sanguinis Christi in Eucharistia*. Cologne, 1527.

Fisher, J., *English Works*, ed. J. E. B. Mayor. Early English Text Society, London, 1876.

Fisher, J., *Sacri Sacerdoti Defensio*. Cologne, 1525b.

Foxe, J., *Actes and Monuments of these latter and perillous dayes, touching matters of the Church, wherein ar comprehended and described the great persecutions and horrible troubles, that have bene wrought and practised by the Romishe Prelates, speciallye in this realme of England and Scotlande, from the yeare of our Lords a thousande, unto the tyme nowe present*. John Day, London, 1563 (11222).

Foxe, J., *The Ecclesiastical History contaynyng the Actes and Monumentes ... newly inlarged by the Author*. John Day, London, 1570 (11223).

Gardiner, S., *A detection of the devil's sophistrie, wherwith he robbeth the unlearned people, of the true bylef, in the sacrament of the aulter*. John Herforde, London, 1546 (11591).

Gardiner, S., *De Vera Obedientia*. London, 1535.

Goodman, C., *How Superior Powers oght to be obeyd of their subjects: and wherin they may lawfully by Gods Worde be disobeyed and resisted*. John Crispin, Geneva, 1558 (12020).

Gwynneth, J., *A Declaration of the state, wherin all heretikes dooe leade their lives: and also of their continuall indever, and proper fruictes*. Thomas Berthelet, London, 1554 (12558).

Hanmer, M., *The Great Bragge and Challenge of M. Campion a Iesuite, commonlye called Edmunde Campion, lately arrived in England, contayning nyne articles here severallye laide downe, directed by him to the Lordes of the Counsail*. Thomas Marsh, London, 1581 (12745).

Harding, T., *An Answere to Maister Iuelles Chalenge*. Wm Sylvius, Antwerp, 1565a (12759).

Harding, T., *A Confutation of a booke intitled An Apologie of the Church of England*. John Laet, Antwerp, 1565b (12762).

Harding, T., *A Detection of sundrie foule errours, lies, sclaunders, corruptions and other false dealings, touching Doctrine, and other matters, uttered and practized by M. Iewel, in a Booke lately by him set foorth entituled A Defence of the Apologie*. John Fowler, Louvain, 1568 (12763).

Harding, T., *A Reiondre to M. Jewels Replie*. John Fowler, Antwerp, 1566 (12760).

Harpsfield, J., *A Notable and learned Sermon or Homilie, made upon Saint Andrewes daye last past 1556, in the Cathedral churche of S. Paule in London*. Robert Caly, London, 1556 (12795).

Harpsfield, N., *Archdeacon Harpsfield's Visitation 1557, together with visitations of 1556 and 1558*, ed. L. E. Whatmore, Catholic Record Society XLV–XLVI, London, 1950–1.

Harpsfield, N. (?), *Bishop Cranmer's Recantacyons*, ed. Lord Houghton, Philobiblion Society Miscellanies, 1877–84.

Harpsfield, N., *Dialogi Sex contra summi pontificatus, monasticae vitae, Sanctorum, sacrarum imaginum oppugnatores, et pseudomartyres*. Antwerp, 1566.

Harpsfield, N., *Historia Anglicana Ecclesiastica, a primis gentis susceptae fidei incunabulis ad nostra fere tempora deducta*. Douay, 1622.

Harpsfield, N., *The Life and Death of Sir Thomas Moore, Knight, sometimes, Lord High Chancellor of England*, ed. E. V. Hitchcock, Early English Text Society, Oxford, 1932.

Harpsfield, N., *A Treatise on the Pretended Divorce between Henry VIII and Catharine of Aragon*, ed. N. Pocock, Camden Society, London, 1878.

Henry VIII, *Assertio Septem Sacramentorum*. London, 1521.

Huggard, M., *The Displaying of the Protestantes, and sondry their practises, with a description of divers their abuses of late frequented within their malignante churche*. London, 1556 (13557).

Jewel, J., *An Apology of the Church of England*, ed. J. E. Booty, University Press of Virginia, Charlottesville, 1963.

Jewel, J., *A Replie unto M. Hardinges Answeare*. Henry Wykes, London, 1565 (14606).

Jewel, J., *The copie of a Sermon pronounced by the Byshop of Salisburie at Paules Crosse the second Sondaye before Ester in the yere of our Lord 1560*. John Day, London, 1560a (14599a).

Jewel, J., *The true copies of the letters betwene the reverend father in God John Bisshop of Sarum and D. Cole, upon occasion of a Sermon that the said bishop preached before the Quenes Maiestie, and hyr most honourable Counsayle*. John Day, London, 1560b (14612).

Knox, J., *The First Blast of the Trumpet against the Monstruous Regiment of Women*. J. Poullain, Geneva, 1558 (15070).

Martiall, J., *A Treatise of the Crosse gathered out of the Scriptures, Councelles, and aunciten Fathers of the primitive church*. John Latius, Antwerp, 1564 (17496).

Menewe, G., *A Confutacion of that Popisshe and Antichristian doctryne, whiche mainteineth the ministracyon and receiving of the sacrament under one kind, made Dialogue-wise betwene the Prieste and the Prentyse*. H.

Singleton, Wesel, 1555a (?) (17821).

Menewe, G., *A Plaine subversyon, or turnyng up syde down of all the argumentes, that the Popecatholykes can make for the maintenaunce of auricular confession, with a moste wholsome doctryne touchynge the due obedience, that we owe unto civil magistates, made dialogue wyse betwene the Prentyse and the Priest*. H. Singleton, Wesel, 1555b (?) (17822).

More, T., *The workes of Sir Thomas More, Knyght, sometyme Lorde Chancellour of England, wrytten by him in the Englysh tonge*, ed. Wm Rastell. London, 1557 (18076).

More, T., *Selected Letters*, ed. E. F. Rogers, Yale University Press, New Haven and London, 1961.

More, T., *The Correspondence of Sir Thomas More*, ed. E. F. Rogers. Princeton University Press, Princeton, 1947.

More, T., *The Yale Edition of the Complete Works of St Thomas More*. Yale University Press, New Haven and London, 1963–97.
  Vol. I, *English Poems, Life of Pico, The Last Things*, ed. A. S. G. Edwards, K. G. Rodgers, C. H. Miller, 1997.
  Vol. V, *Responsio ad Lutherum*, ed. J. M. Headley (2 parts), 1969.
  Vol. VI, *A Dialogue Concerning Heresies*, ed. T. M. C. Lawler, G. Marc'hadour and R. C. Marius (2 parts), 1981.
  Vol. VIII, *The Confutation of Tyndale's Answer*, ed. R. C. Marius, J. P. Lusardi and R. J. Schoek (3 parts), 1973.
  Vol. IX, *The Apology*, ed. J. B. Trapp, 1979.

Persons, R., *A Brief Censure uppon two bookes written in answeare to M. Edmonde Campions offer of disputation*. John Lyon, Douay, 1581 (19393).

Persons, R., *A Defence of the Censure*. John Lyon, Douay, 1582 (19401).

Persons, R., *A Treatise of Three Conversions of England from Paganisme to Christian Religion*. F. Bellet, St Omer, 1603 (19416).

Pole, R., *The Correspondence of Reginald Pole: Volume I*, ed. T. F. Mayer, Ashgate, Aldershot, 2002.

Pollen, J. H. (ed.), *Miscellanea I*. Catholic Record Society, London, 1905.

The Primer in Latin and Englishe (after the use of Sarum) with many godlye and devoute prayers, as in the contentes doth appeare. John Wayland, London, 1555 (16063).

Proctor, J., *The waie home to Christ and truth leadinge from Antichrist and errour*. Robert Caly, London, 1554 (24754).

Questier, M. C. (ed.), *Newsletters from the Archpresbyterate of George Birkhead*, Cambridge University Press, Cambridge, 1998.

Rastell, J., *A confutation of a sermon, pronounced by M. Jewell, at Paules crosse, the second Sondaie before Easter*. Giles Diest, Antwerp, 1564 (20726).

Rastell, J., *The Third Booke, declaring by Examples out of Aunciet Councels, Fathers and Later writers, that it is time to Beware of M. Iewel*. John Fowler, Antwerp, 1566a (20728.5).

Rastell, J., *A Treatise Intitled, Beware of M. Iewel* (Antwerp, 1566b), ed. D. M. Rogers, Scolar Press, Ilkley, 1975.

Roper, W., *The Lyfe of Sir Thomas Moore, Knighte*, ed. E. V. Hitchcock. Early English Text Society 197. London, 1935.

Sander, N., *De Visibili Monarchia Ecclesiaem, libri octo*. John Fowler, Louvain, 1571.

Sander, N., *The Rise and Growth of the Anglican Schism*, ed. D. Lewis, Burns & Oates, London, 1877.

Sander, N., *The Rocke of the Church wherein the primacy of S. Peter and of his successours the Bishops of Rome, is proved out of Gods Worde*. Louvain, 1566 (21692).

Sander, N., *The Supper of our Lord set foorth in six bookes, according to the truth of the gospell, and the faith of the Catholike Churche*. John Fowler, Louvain, 1565 (21694).

Sander, N., *A Treatise of the images of Christ, and of his saints: and that it is unlawfull to breake them, and lawful to honour them*. John Fowler, Louvain, 1567 (21696).

Smith, R., *A bouclier of the catholike fayth of Christes Church, conteyning divers matters now of late called into controversy, by the newe gospellers*. Richard Tottell, London, 1554 (Book One) and Robert Caly, London, 1555 (Book Two) (22816–17).

Standish, J., *The triall of the supremacy, wherein is set fourth the unitie of Christes churche*. Thomas Marshe, London, 1556 (23211).

Stapleton, T. (trans), *The Apologie of Fridericus Staphylus counseller to the late Emperor Ferdinandus*. John Latius, Antwerp, 1565a (23230).

Stapleton, T., *A Counterblast to M. Hornes vayne blast against M. Feckenham*. John Fowler, Louvain, 1567 (23231).

Stapleton, T., *A Fortresse of the Faith first planted amonge us englishmen and continued hitherto in the universall Church of Christ, the faith of which time Protestants call, Papistry*. John Laet, Antwerp, 1565b (23232).

Stapleton, T., *The Life and Illustrious Martyrdom of Sir Thomas More* (part III of *Tres Thomae*). trans. P. E. Hallett, Burns Oates & Washbourne, London, 1928.

Stapleton, T., *A Returne of Untruthes upon M. Iewelles replie*. John Latius, Antwerp, 1566 (23234).

Tunstall, C., *A Sermon of Cuthbert Bysshop of Duresme, made upon Palme Sondaye laste past, before the maiestie of our soverayne lorde kynge Henry the VIII kynge of England and of France, Defensor of the fayth, lorde of Irelande, and in erth next under Christ supreme heed of the Churche of Englande*. London, 1539 (24322).

Watson, T., *Twoo notable sermons, made the thirde and fyfte Fridayes in Lent last past, before the Quenes highnes, concerninge the reall presence of Christes body and bloude in the blessed Sacrament: and also the Masse,*

which is the sacrifice of the newe Testament. John Cawood, London, 1554 (25115).
Watson, T., *Holsome and Catholyke doctryne concerninge the seven Sacramentes of Chrystes Church, expedient to be knowen of all men, set forth in maner of shorte Sermons to bee made to the people*. Robert Caly, London, 1558 (25112).
Xavier, Francis, *The Letters and Instructions of Francis Xavier*, ed. M. J. Costelloe, Institute of Jesuit Sources, St Louis, 1992.
Zurich Letters (First Series), ed. H. Robinson, Parker Society, Cambridge, 1892.

Secondary Works

Allison, A. F., and D. M. Rogers, *A Catalogue of Catholic Books in English Printed Abroad or Secretly in England, 1558–1640*. London, 1968.
Allison, A. F., and D. M. Rogers,*The Contemporary Printed Literature of the English Counter-Reformation between 1558 and 1640*. 2 vols. Scolar Press, Aldershot, 1989 and 1994.
Armstrong, C. D. C., 'English Catholicism Rethought?', *Journal of Ecclesiastical History* 54 (2003), pp. 714–28.
Aston, M., and E. Ingram, 'The Iconography of the Acts and Monuments', in Loades (ed.) 1997, pp. 66–87.
Bagchi, D. V. N., *Luther's Earliest Opponents: Catholic Controversialists, 1518–1525*. Fortress Press, Minneapolis, 1991.
Betteridge, T., *Tudor Histories of the English Reformations, 1530–1583*. Ashgate, Aldershot, 1999.
Birch, D., *Early Reformation English Polemics*. Salzburg Institute, Salzburg, 1983.
Booty, J. E., *John Jewel as Apologist of the Church of England*. SPCK, London, 1963.
Bossy, J., 'The Character of Elizabethan Catholicism', *Past and Present* 21 (1962), pp. 39–57.
Bossy, J., *Christianity in the West, 1400–1700*. Oxford University Press, Oxford, 1985.
Bossy, J., *The English Catholic Community, 1570–1850*. Darton, Longman & Todd, London, 1975.
Bradshaw, B., 'The Controversial Thomas More', *Journal of Ecclesiastical History* 36 (1985), pp. 535–69.
Bradshaw, B., and E. Duffy, *Humanism, Reform and the Reformation: The Career of Bishop John Fisher*. Cambridge University Press, Cambridge, 1989.
Brigden, S., *London and the Reformation*. Oxford University Press, Oxford, 1989.

Brooks, P. N., *Reformation Principle and Practice: Essays in Honour of Arthur Geoffrey Dickens*. Scolar Press, London, 1980.
Brooks, P. N., *Thomas Cranmer's Doctrine of the Eucharist: An Essay in Historical Development*. Macmillan, Basingstoke and London, 1992.
Cameron, E., *The European Reformation*. Clarendon Press, Oxford, 1991.
Carrafiello, M. L., *Robert Persons and English Catholicism, 1580–1610*. Susquehannah University Press, Selinsgrove, 1998.
Collinson, P., *Archbishop Grindal, 1519–1583: The Struggle for a Reformed Church*. Jonathan Cape, London, 1979.
Collinson, P., *Elizabethan Essays*. Hambledon Press, London, 1984.
Coppens, C., *Reading in Exile: The Libraries of John Ramridge, Thomas Harding and Henry Joliffe, Recusants in Louvain*. LP Publications, Cambridge, 1993.
Correia-Afonso, J., *Jesuit Letters and Indian History*. Indian Historical Research Institute, Bombay, 1955.
Cuming, G. J., and D. Baker (eds.), *Councils and Assemblies*. Cambridge University Press, Cambridge, 1971.
Curtis, C., 'More's Public Life', in Logan (ed.) 2011, pp. 69–92.
Dean, J. *God Truly Worshipped: Thomas Cranmer and his Writings*. Canterbury Press, Norwich, 2012.
Delumeau, J., *Catholicism between Luther and Voltaire*. Burns & Oates, London, 1977.
Dickens, A. G., *The English Reformation*. Collins, Glasgow, 1967.
Dickens, A. G., *The Counter-Reformation*, Harcourt, Brace and World, New York, 1969.
Dickens, A. G., *The German Nation and Martin Luther*. E. Arnold, London, 1974.
Dickens, A. G., and W. R. D. Jones, *Erasmus the Reformer*, Methuen, London, 1994.
Dillon, A. K., *The Construction of Martyrdom in the English Catholic Community, 1535–1603*. Ashgate, Aldershot, 2002.
Ditchfield, S., *Liturgy, Sanctity and History in Tridentine Italy*. Cambridge University Press, Cambridge, 1995.
Ditchfield, S. (ed.), *Christianity and Community in the West: Essays for John Bossy*. Ashgate, Aldershot, 2001.
Dixon, R. W., *History of the Church of England from the Abolition of the Roman Jurisdiction*. 6 vols., George Routledge & Sons, London, 1891.
Doran, S., and T. S. Freeman, *Mary Tudor: Old and New Perspectives*. Palgrave, New York, 2011.
Duffy, E., *The Stripping of the Altars*. Yale University Press, New Haven and London, 1992.
Duffy, E., 'William, Cardinal Allen, 1532–1594', *Recusant History* 22 (1995), pp. 265–90.

Duffy, E., *Saints and Sinners: A History of the Popes*. Yale University Press, New Haven and London, 1997.
Duffy, E., 'The Conservative Voice in the English Reformation', in Ditchfield (ed.) 2001, pp. 87–105.
Duffy, E., *The Voices of Morebath: Reformation and Rebellion in an English Village*. Yale University Press, 2003.
Duffy, E., *Fires of Faith: Catholic England Under Mary Tudor*. Yale University Press, New Haven and London, 2009.
Duffy, E., 'Cardinal Pole Preaching', in Duffy and Loades (eds.) 2016, pp. 176–200.
Duffy, E., and D. Loades, *The Church of Mary Tudor*. Routledge, London and New York, 2016.
Dures, A., *English Catholicism, 1558–1642: Continuity and Change*. Longman, Harlow, 1983.
Edwards, F., *Robert Persons*. Institute of Jesuit Sources, St Louis, 1995.
Elton, G., 'Persecution and Toleration in the English Reformation', in Sheils (ed.) 1984, pp. 163–87.
Evenden, E., and T. S. Freeman, *Religion and the Book in Early Modern England: The Making of John Foxe's 'Book of Martyrs'*. Cambridge University Press, Cambridge, 2013.
Fairfield, L. P., 'John Bale and the Development of Protestant Hagiography in England'. in *Journal of Ecclesiastical History* 24 (1973), pp. 145–60.
Fenlon, D., *Heresy and Obedience in Tridentine Italy: Cardinal Pole and the Counter-Reformation*. Cambridge University Press, Cambridge, 1972.
Foster, J. (ed.), *Alumni Oxonienses: The Members of the University of Oxford 1500–1714*. James Parker & Co., Oxford and London, 1891–2.
Fox, A., *Thomas More: History and Providence*. Blackwell, Oxford, 1982.
Fraenkel, P., 'John Eck's Enchiridion of 1525 and Luther's earliest arguments against Papal Primacy', in *Studia Theologica* 21 (1967), pp. 110–63.
Freeman, T. S., 'John Bale's Book of Martyrs? The Account of King John in *Acts and Monuments*', *Reformation* 3 (1998a), pp. 175–224.
Freeman, T. S., 'New Perspectives on an old book: the Creation and Influence of Foxe's *Book of Martyrs*', *Journal of Ecclesiastical History* 49 (1998b), pp. 317–28.
Freeman, T. S., 'Burning Zeal: Mary Tudor and the Marian Persecution', in Doran and Freeman (eds.) 2011, pp. 171–205.
Frere, W. H., and, W. M. Kennedy (eds.), *Visitation Articles and Injunctions of the Period of the Reformation*. 3 vols., Longmans, Green & Co., London, 1910.
Gogan, B., *The Common Corps of Christendom: Ecclesiological Themes in the writings of Sir Thomas More*. E. J. Brill, Leiden, 1982.

Greene, J. J., 'Utopia and Early More Biography', Moreana 31 (1971), pp. 199–206.
Gregory, B. S., Salvation at Stake: Christian Martyrdom in Early Modern Europe. Harvard University Press, Cambridge, Mass., and London, 1999.
Haigh, C. (ed.), The English Reformation Revised. Cambridge University Press, Cambridge, 1987.
Haigh, C., English Reformations. Clarendon Press, Oxford, 1993.
Harris, J. W., John Bale: A Study in the Minor Literature of the Reformation. University of Illinois Press, Urbana, 1940.
Haugaard, W., Elizabeth and the English Reformation. Cambridge University Press, Cambridge, 1968.
Headley, J., 'On More and the Papacy', Moreana 41 (1974), pp. 5–10.
Holmes, P., Resistance and Compromise: The Political Thought of the Elizabethan Catholics. Cambridge University Press, Cambridge, 1982.
Houliston, V., 'Her Majesty, who is now in heaven: Mary Tudor and the Elizabethan Catholics', in Doran and Freeman (eds.) 2011, pp. 37–48.
Hsia, R. P., The World of Catholic Renewal, 1540–1770. Cambridge University Press, Cambridge, 1998.
Hughes, P., Rome and the Counter-Reformation in England. Burns & Oates, London, 1941.
Hughes, P., The Reformation in England. Hollis & Carter, London, 1950–4.
Hunt, A., 'The Lord's Supper in Early Modern England', Past and Present 61 (1998), pp. 39–83.
Kelly, J. N. D., Jerome. Duckworth, London, 1975.
Kenny, A., Thomas More (Past Masters). Oxford University Press, Oxford, 1983.
Kenny, A. (ed.), Wyclif in his Times. Clarendon Press, Oxford, 1986.
King, J. N., 'Fiction and Fact in Foxe's Book of Martyrs', in Loades (ed.) 1997, pp. 12–19.
Kristeller, P. O., Renaissance Thought. Harper & Row, New York, 1961.
Lambert, M., Medieval Heresy. Blackwell, Oxford, 1992.
Lamberts, E., and J. Roegiers, Leuven University 1425–1985. Leuven University Press, Leuven, 1990.
Law, T. J., 'The Miraculous Cross of St Donat's, 1559–61', English Historical Review 1 (1886), pp. 513–17.
Loach, J., 'Pamphlets and Politics, 1553–8', Bulletin of the Institute of Historical Research 48 (1975), pp. 31–44.
Loach, J., 'The Marian Establishment and the Printing Press', English Historical Review 101 (1986), pp. 135–48.
Loach, J., and R. Tittler (eds.), The Mid Tudor Polity, c. 1540–1560. Macmillan, London, 1980.
Loades, D., Mary Tudor: A Life. Blackwell, Oxford, 1989.

Loades, D., *Politics, Censorship and the English Reformation*. Pinter, London and New York, 1991a.

Loades, D., *The Reign of Mary Tudor* (2nd edition). Longman, London and New York, 1991b.

Loades, D., 'The Spirituality of the Restored Catholic Church (1553–1558) in the Context of the Counter Reformation', in McCoog (ed.) 1996, pp. 3–20.

Loades, D. (ed.), *John Foxe and the English Reformation*. Scolar Press, Aldershot, 1997.

Loades, D. (ed.), *John Foxe: An Historical Perspective*. Ashgate, Aldershot, 1999.

Logan, G. M., *The Cambridge Companion to Thomas More*. Cambridge University Press, Cambridge, 2011.

Luebke, D. M. (ed.), *The Counter-Reformation: The Essential Readings*. Blackwell, Oxford, 1999.

MacCaffrey, W., *The Shaping of the Elizabethan Regime*. Jonathan Cape, London, 1969.

McConica, J. K., 'The Recusant Reputation of Thomas More', in Sylvester and Marc'hadour (eds.) 1977, pp. 136–49.

McCoog, T. M. (ed.), *The Reckoned Expense: Edmund Campion and the Early English Jesuits*. Boydell Press, Woodbridge, 1996.

McCutcheon, E., 'Thomas More to Antonio Bonvisi', *Moreana* 71 (1984), pp. 37–56.

MacCulloch, D. (ed.), *The Reign of Henry VIII: Politics, Policy and Piety*. Macmillan, Basingstoke, 1995.

MacCulloch, D., *Thomas Cranmer*. Yale University Press, New Haven/London, 1996.

MacCulloch, D., *Tudor Church Militant: Edward VI and the Protestant Reformation*. Penguin, London, 1999.

McGrath, P., *Papists and Puritans under Elizabeth I*. Blandford Press, London, 1967.

McGrath, P., 'Elizabethan Catholicism: A Reconsideration', *Journal of Ecclesiastical History* 35 (1984), pp. 414–28.

McGrath, P., and J. Rowe, 'The Marian Priests under Elizabeth I', *Recusant History* 17 (1984), pp. 103–20.

Macek, E. A., *The Loyal Opposition: Tudor Traditionalist Polemics, 1535–1558*. Peter Lang, New York, 1996.

Marc'hadour, G., 'Fisher and More: A Note', in Bradshaw and Duffy (eds.) 1989, pp. 103–8.

Marius, R., 'More the Conciliarist', *Moreana* 64 (1980), pp. 91–9.

Marius, R., *Thomas More*. Collins, Glasgow, 1984.

Marshall, P., *Heretics and Believers*, Yale University Press, New Haven and London, 2017.

Marshall, P., and A. Ryrie (eds.), *The Beginnings of English Protestantism*. Cambridge University Press, Cambridge, 2002.
Mayer, T. F., 'A Test of Wills: Cardinal Pole, Ignatius Loyola and the Jesuits in England', in McCoog (ed.) 1996, pp. 21–38.
Mayer, T. F., *Cardinal Pole in European Context: A Via Media in the Reformation*. Ashgate, Aldershot, 2000a.
Mayer, T. F., *Reginald Pole, Prince and Prophet*. Cambridge University Press, Cambridge, 2000b.
Meyer, A. O., *England and the Catholic Church under Queen Elizabeth*. Routledge and Kegan Paul, London, 1967.
Milward, P., *Religious Controversies of the Elizabethan Age: A Survey of Printed Sources*. Scolar Press, London, 1977.
Moore, M. J. (ed.), *Quincentennial Essays on St Thomas More*. Albion, Boone North Carolina, 1978.
Moorhouse, G., *The Pilgrimage of Grace*. Weidenfeld & Nicholson, London, 2002.
Morey, A., *The Catholic Subjects of Elizabeth I*. George Allen and Unwin, London, 1978.
Mozley, J. F., *John Foxe and his Book*. SPCK, London, 1940.
O'Connell, M. R., *Thomas Stapleton and the Counter-Reformation*. Yale University Press, New Haven and London, 1964.
O'Malley, J. W., *The First Jesuits*. Harvard University Press, Cambridge Mass., 1993.
Olsen, V. N., *John Foxe and the Elizabethan Church*. University of California Press, Berkeley, 1973.
Parry, G., 'John Foxe, "Father of Lyes", and the Papists', in Loades (ed.) 1997, p. 295.
Parry, G., 'Elect Church or Elect Nation? The Reception of the Acts and Monuments', in Loades (ed.) 1999, pp. 166–90.
Pollard, A. F., *Thomas Cranmer and the English Reformation 1489–1556*. Knickerbocker Press, New York and London, 1904.
Pollard, A. W., and, G. R. Redgrave, *A Short Title Catalogue of Books Printed in England, Scotland and Ireland and of English Books Printed Abroad, 1475–1640*. Bibliographical Society, London, 1926; revised and enlarged by W. A. Jackson, F. S. Ferguson and K. F. Pantzer, 3 vols.
Pullapilly, C., *Caesar Baronius: Counter-Reformation Historian*. University of Notre Dame Press, Notre Dame and London, 1975.
Questier, M., 'Catholicism, Kinship and the Public Memory of Sir Thomas More', *Journal of Ecclesiastical History* 53 (2002), pp. 476–509.
Redworth, G., *In Defence of the Church Catholic: The Life of Stephen Gardiner*. Blackwell, Oxford, 1990.
Revised Short Title Catalogue: see Pollard and Redgrave.
Rex, R., 'The English Campaign against Luther in the 1520s', *Transactions*

of the Royal Historical Society 39 (1989a), pp. 85–106. RHS, London.
Rex, R., 'The Polemical Theologian', in Bradshaw and Duffy (eds.) 1989b, pp. 109–30.
Rex, R., *The Theology of John Fisher*. Cambridge University Press, Cambridge, 1991.
Rex, R., *Henry VIII and the English Reformation*. Macmillan, Basingstoke and London, 1993.
Reynolds, E. E., *Lives of St Thomas More*. Dent, London, 1963.
Richards, J. M., 'Reassessing Mary Tudor', in Doran and Freeman (eds.) 2011, pp. 206–24.
Rubin, M., *Corpus Christi: the Eucharist in Late Medieval Culture*. Cambridge University Press, Cambridge, 1991.
Ryrie, A., 'The Unsteady Beginnings of English Protestant Martyrology', in Loades (ed.) 1999, pp. 52–66.
Scarisbrick, J., *Henry VIII*. Methuen, London, 1976.
Schenk, W., *Reginald Pole, Cardinal of England*. Longmans, London, 1950.
Schroeder, H. J. (trans), *The Canons and Decrees of the Council of Trent*. Tan, Rockford, Illinois, 1978.
Shagan, E. A., *The Rule of Moderation: Violence, Religion and the Politics of Restraint in Early Modern England*. Cambridge University Press, Cambridge 2011.
Sheils, W. J. (ed.), *Persecution and Toleration* (Studies in Church History 21). Blackwell, London, 1984.
Shell, A., *Catholicism, Controversy and the English Literary Imagination*. Cambridge University Press, Cambridge, 1999.
Southern, A. C., *Elizabethan Recusant Prose, 1559–1582*. Sands & Co., London, 1950.
Strype, J., *Historical Memorials, Ecclesiastical and Civil, of Events under the Reign of Queen Mary I*. John Wyatt, London, 1721.
Sturge, C., *Cuthbert Tunstall: Churchman, Scholar, Statesman, Administrator*. Longman, London, 1938.
Sullivan, C., '"Oppressed by the Force of Truth": Robert Persons edits John Foxe', in Loades (ed.) 1999, pp. 154–66.
Swanson, R. N. (ed.), *The Church Retrospective: Studies in Church History* 33. Boydell Press, Woodbridge, 1997.
Sylvester, R. S., and G. P. Marc'hadour, *Essential Articles for the study of Thomas More*. Archon, Hamden Connecticut, 1977.
Thomas, K., *Religion and the Decline of Magic*. Weidenfield & Nicolson, London, 1971.
Tyacke, N. (ed.), *England's Long Reformation, 1500–1800*. University College London Press, London, 1998.
Underwood, M., 'John Fisher and the Promotion of Learning', in Bradshaw and Duffy (eds.) 1989, pp. 25–46.

Walsham, A., *Church Papists: Catholicism, Conformity and Confessional Polemic in Early Modern England*. Boydell Press, Woodbridge, 1993.
Waugh, E., *Edmund Campion*. Oxford University Press, Oxford, 1980.
White, H., *Tudor Books of Saints and Martyrs*. University of Wisconsin Press, Madison, 1963.
Whitelock, A., *Mary Tudor: England's First Queen*. Bloomsbury, London, 2009.
Wizeman, W. L., *The Theology and Spirituality of Mary Tudor's Church*. Ashgate, Aldershot, 2006.
Wizeman, W., 'The Religious Policy of Mary I', in Doran and Freeman (eds.) 2011, pp. 153–70.
Wooden, W. W., *John Foxe*. Twayne Publishers, Boston, 1983.
Wooding, L. E. C., *Rethinking Catholicism in Reformation England*. Clarendon Press, Oxford, 2000.

Unpublished Doctoral Theses

Alexander, G. M. V., 'The Life and Career of Edmund Bonner, Bishop of London, until his deprivation in 1549'. London University, 1960.
Pogson, R. H., 'Cardinal Pole: Papal Legate to England in Mary Tudor's Reign'. Cambridge University, 1972.

www.ingramcontent.com/pod-product-compliance
Lightning Source LLC
Chambersburg PA
CBHW032020230426
43671CB00005B/145